Culture in Networks

Cultural Sociology series

Culture in Networks

Paul McLean

polity

First published in 2017 by Polity Press

Polity Press
65 Bridge Street
Cambridge CB2 1UR, UK

Polity Press
350 Main Street
Malden, MA 02148, USA

ISBN-13: 978-0-7456-8716-2
ISBN-13: 978-0-7456-8717-9(pb)

A catalogue record for this book is available from the British Library.

Library of Congress Cataloging in Publication data
Names: McLean, Paul Douglas, 1962– author.
Title: Culture in networks / Paul McLean.
Description: Cambridge, UK; Malden, MA : Polity Press, 2016. | Includes bibliographical references and index.
Identifiers: LCCN 2016012611| ISBN 9780745687162 (hardback: alk. paper) | ISBN 9780745687179 (paperback: alk. paper)
Subjects: LCSH: Social networks. | Culture. | Culture diffusion.
Classification: LCC HM741 .M3895 2016 | DDC 302.3--dc23 LC record available at https://lccn.loc.gov/2016012611

Typeset in 11/13 Sabon by
Servis Filmsetting Limited, Stockport, Cheshire
Printed and bound in the UK by Clays Ltd, St Ives PLC

For further information on Polity, visit our website: politybooks.com

Contents

Acknowledgments

I would first like to thank Jonathan Skerrett of Polity who guided me along the process to completion of this project with gentle yet enthusiastic support – even when I periodically blew up at him via email with my frustrations. I would also like to acknowledge the input of two anonymous reviewers for Polity – one of whom strongly encouraged me to believe that what I was doing was worthwhile, the other of whom pushed me hard to try to make this a more coherent and useful book.

Many scholars have helped me to think about networks and culture in interesting ways over the years. Rather than identify them by name, I hope their influence will be evident repeatedly in the pages of this book. However, I would like to single out my teacher and collaborator, John Padgett, for encouraging me onto this path of exploring the cultural aspects of social networks many years ago.

I appreciate the assistance of May Nguyen, Haniyyah Hopkins and Susan Jaw, who at different times provided me with a great deal of help in organizing the bibliography for this book. Leigh Mueller did a great job of copy-editing the manuscript.

Much of this book was written in a faculty study at the Alexander Library at Rutgers University, where I could utilize the library's terrific collection of materials. Although I developed no strong personal relationship with the staff of the library during my evening and weekend sojourns there, I am very grateful for the use of that space, and simply for the existence of such a welcoming

Acknowledgments

place in which to work. I am a huge fan of the open-stacks, public university library, of which Alex is a great example.

I would like to thank all of my colleagues and friends in the Sociology department at Rutgers University for providing me with a hospitable academic home for the last sixteen-plus years. In particular, I thank Debby Carr, Chip Clarke, Jeanie Danner, Judy Gerson, Lisa Iorillo, Joanna Kempner, Laurie Krivo, Diane Molnar, Julie Phillips, Pat Roos, Zakia Salime, Hana Shepherd, Randy Smith, Kristen Springer, Dianne Yarnell, and Eviatar Zerubavel for times spent talking in each other's offices or otherwise hanging out. I also greatly appreciate the intellectual stimulation I received, especially with respect to the conjoined topics of networks and culture, from two former colleagues: John Levi Martin, now at the University of Chicago, and Ann Mische, now at the University of Notre Dame. I miss them both. I very much appreciate the network ties I have formed with Marya Doerfel, Keith Hampton, and Matt Weber in the School of Communication and Information at Rutgers over the last several years. And I would also like to give a shout-out to Professor Brad Evans in Rutgers' excellent English department, for our stimulating discussions about novels, networks, and the digital humanities, and simply for his friendship.

I owe my biggest debt to many students – both graduate students and undergraduates – who, in various ways, have stimulated my interest in the diverse intersections of social networks and culture, and led me to think of those intersections more coherently. In particular, I have in mind Jeff Dowd, Gina Giacobbe, Neha Gondal, Anne Kavalerchik, Preeti Khanolkar, Eric Kushins, Vanina Leschziner, Yusheng Lin, Janet Lorenzen, Derek Ludovici, Sourabh Singh, Kathy Smith, Eunkyung Song, Charles Tong, and King-to Yeung. I would like to thank Neha in particular for the especially formative role she has played in developing my understanding of, and my approach to, networks and culture, through our collaborative research.

On a more personal note, I'd like to thank Susan Liebell for being the best co-parent anyone could hope for. I thank my two younger children, Adam and Julia Liebell-McLean, who turned me into the father of twins – a network position I never anticipated occupying – in 1999, and who have lent so much meaning to my life ever since. Finally, I thank my older son, Eli Liebell-McLean, for the ways he too has enriched my life. And I dedicate this little book to him, cognizant that he has a deeper but also more intuitive grasp of the ways culture and networks go together than I am ever likely to have.

1

Culture and Social Networks: A Conceptual Framework

This book provides an extended treatment of the various ways in which we can imagine social networks to intersect with culture. The term *social network* refers to a set of entities – actors, organizations, or locations, for example – and the ties that exist among them. *Social network analysis* refers to a set of concepts and procedures by means of which social network properties may be analyzed. The term *culture* is one of the most complex terms in the social sciences to define, but we can understand it broadly to refer to the knowledge, beliefs, expectations, values, practices, and material objects by means of which we craft meaningful experiences for ourselves and with each other. It might help a bit to think of networks as hardware (circuitry) and culture as software (rules and routines for action), although that analogy is deceptively clear. The circuitry is largely inert without rules or recipes specifying how the parts go together, how information is to be created, and how communication flow will be controlled. On the other hand, the products that may be potentially created via the software are activated only via concrete pathways and connections existing in network form. Again, the analogy is simplistic, but it has the merit of reinforcing the idea that social networks and culture go together synthetically, even necessarily. What varies is only the extent to which either network structure or cultural recipes are emphasized in order to answer specific research questions.

The amount of scholarly attention devoted to the two topics of networks and culture, taken separately, has grown tremendously in recent years. The International Network for Social Network Analysis (INSNA) hosts an annual conference of ever-growing proportions, and it is home to a highly active listserv for the discussion of all kinds of networks-related questions. Meanwhile, the Culture section of the American Sociological Association has grown into one of the very largest since the late 1990s.

More substantively speaking, on the networks side, although the roots of *social network analysis* run back to the 1930s,[1] since the turn of the new century we have witnessed the birth of the so-called "new science of networks" (Watts 1999, 2003; Barabási 2002). According to this perspective, networks are understood to be everywhere – from cellular structure to the architecture of our brains and the mechanics of information processing, from transportation systems to global trade patterns. More to the point for our purposes here, networks are ubiquitous in the social world (Christakis and Fowler 2009). For example, networks provide us with social support (Wellman and Wortley 1990; Rainie and Wellman 2012), they reputedly help us find jobs (Granovetter 1995), they affect disease transmission (Morris 1993), they knit together social and political elites (Knoke 1993; Domhoff 2010), they exist in the structure of ownership in advanced capitalist economies (Mizruchi 1992; Burris 2005), they account for the emergence of new industries and organizational forms (Powell et al. 2005; Padgett and Powell 2012), they foster and support social protest (Diani and McAdam 2003), and much, much more. Besides all of that, who among us is not familiar with Facebook and Twitter, or for that matter World of Warcraft or Second Life or Reddit, among the myriad emerging forms of media where virtual social interaction takes place on a massive scale (e.g., Lewis et al. 2008)? These relatively new venues of social behavior work fundamentally on network principles, even if they remain underexplored using formal social network analytic tools.[2] Indeed, the internet itself is a giant network of communication links. We live in a "connected" (Christakis and Fowler 2009), "networked" (Castells 1996) world. Networks are our social "operating system" (Rainie and Wellman 2012).

With respect to the culture side of the picture, for several decades

2

now we have understood the social world in the wake of the "cultural turn" in the social sciences (Bonnell and Hunt 1999; Jacobs and Spillman 2005).[3] After the cultural turn, culture can no longer be seen as something simply derived from social structure – as if, for example, the democratic structure of government and democratic nature of our society ensured that we adhere to democratic values fully, consistently, and unquestioningly. An adequate treatment of the cultural turn would take us deep into social theory and the philosophy of knowledge, topics well beyond the scope of this book. Suffice to say for present purposes that historians and social scientists in the late 1970s began to turn away from accounts of social reality that focused on concrete material relations in society, such as instances of economic exploitation, to accounts that took culture seriously – culture not only in the sense of cultural objects such as art, music, theatre, or dance, but in the form of jointly produced language, symbols, schemas, institutions, and much more. Culture became newly understood as an engine of social change, and/or as webs of significance (Geertz 1973) through which we perceive, and operate in, the material world. Stated succinctly, culture became a vital, vibrant element of social explanation. The turn to culture also entailed for many scholars a turn away from positivist[4] approaches to social explanation to more interpretive approaches. Frequently enough, too, the cultural turn was accompanied by more *critical* methods for analyzing social phenomena – methods that unpacked and historicized taken-for-granted cultural beliefs, norms, values, institutions, social classification categories, and previously unexamined practices that structure the social world and systematically privilege certain groups over others (McDonald 1996; Adams et al. 2005). By these standards – a redefinition of what culture is, a new appreciation of its various manifestations, and an awareness of its independent role in sustaining inequalities of social power – attention to culture became also a new way of *doing* sociology, indicated in part by use of the label "strong program" with respect to the practice of cultural sociology (Alexander 2003; Friedland and Mohr 2004; Reed and Alexander 2009; Alexander et al. 2012).

The amount of scholarly attention devoted to the ways network and culture combine has similarly grown since 2000. But knowledge of how they may be combined may not be widely appreciated – especially by those new to the area – in part because of the longstanding character of research on each topic. Networks and culture have sometimes seemed antithetical to each other. For one thing, it has sometimes been too easy to think of networks simply in structural terms. Recall my "hardware" analogy from the beginning of this chapter: Networks constitute the architecture of connections among objects, and so they describe spatial patterns that "determine" where we can travel or where power flows. Some early work on networks insisted on the primacy of structure over content, and the comparability of the properties of social organization across networks without attending to relational content or symbolic meanings. Actually, that is a very cool idea! We need abstract models of social structures in order to develop theoretical claims, as Georg Simmel (1971b) argued long ago in "The Problem of Sociology." But there is justified concern that such a desire for developing arguments for the autonomy or even primacy of structure can go too far. Fascination today with the structural properties of networks – small worlds, six degrees of separation, clustering coefficients, degree distributions, preferential attachment, and so on, are some of the notions eagerly studied – under the rubric of the "new science of networks" is at risk of treating cultural processes and cultural content in a rather mechanical way, or ignoring them altogether. When we think of a social network architecture or circuitry, we ought to be thinking: what exactly is it that flows through this circuitry? What sustains this flow? How does change come about in network structures? How do people interact with each other inside these networks? How are people's identities – the faces they present, the goals they pursue, and the interests they develop – shaped by network structures? Conversely, how do people's identities, their beliefs about the social world, and the kinds of messages they send affect the kinds of network structures they create and how those networks evolve? How do people's expectations shape the formation, maintenance, and dissolution of social network ties? These questions of *cultural forms, content and practices* seem especially important today and for the

4

foreseeable future as we shift our attention increasingly to social media: large-scale networks of interpersonal communication.

Not only because of the structuralist bent of some network analysis, but also because of the methodological shift toward interpretation and (more or less) away from the measurement and collection of "hard" data after the cultural turn, cultural approaches and network structural approaches would seem to make strange bedfellows.[5] Nevertheless, when starting with an interest in culture – that is, processes of meaning-making, identity formation, and communication using existing practices and symbols – thinking in network terms can help us to understand with more precision where and how new cultural ideas arise, how they are disseminated, where they collect, and why they might be unevenly distributed in society.

Throughout the rest of this book, I will adumbrate diverse analytical *intersections* of culture and networks: that is, various ways the analysis of social networks and the analysis of culture can be brought together. I do not argue for the superiority of one intersection over another. As I noted above, where the causal emphasis falls and how network analytical and cultural tools are used is largely a matter of the research questions one cares to answer. But all of these intersections are interesting because they address, head on, the fact that social life is comprised of both patterns of interactions and relations on the one hand, and communicative meaning-making processes on the other. I sort these different intersections of networks and culture into five main subtopics or themes, and I devote one chapter to each theme. As a shorthand tool, I use a different preposition to represent the nature of the culture/network linkage for each theme. These themes are as follows:

- Culture *THROUGH* networks: in chapter 4, I will discuss primarily the *diffusion* or *flow* of cultural materials – innovations, ideas, practices, frames, commitments – within networks. One of the key ways in which we can build a more culturally rich understanding of diffusion is by keeping in mind the idea that, as objects and ideas diffuse, they are frequently re-invented (Rogers 2003) or adapted to new locales. In recent times, with respect to the diffusion of memes on the internet, such re-invention is practically definitional, as people creatively adapt and/or parody visual images through the apparatus of Photoshop and similar applications. I discuss some general models put forward by sociologists of how and where culture spreads through networks, and I focus illustratively on the extensive research on social movements that stresses the spread of people, protest commitments, repertoires of action, symbols, and frames across multiple movements.

- Culture *FROM* networks: here I have in mind the *creation* of culture as a product of network structure, specifically in the form of emergent identities and roles, as well as the distinctly different idea of the *production* of culture via interaction in social networks. I treat these topics in chapter 5. I discuss some classic sociological research that used blockmodeling to argue that people occupy particular roles in a network structure, and that occupancy of these roles determines their social identities, thereby strongly shaping their opportunities and practices. However, I also discuss at length a strand of research stressing that networks may be particularly fecund spaces in which invention and innovation arise in all kinds of creative fields, from science and philosophy to music and visual arts.

- Networks *FROM* culture: in chapter 6, I pick up the idea that the shape of networks may well be based on participants' cultural preferences and practices, and the kinds of norms that exist that compel us to look to certain people for certain kinds of social support. To think in this way lends culture a more "programmatic" function than we encountered in the previous two chapters. Culture may also be thought of in part as a toolkit of practices and styles people utilize as they *manage* their networks. I also discuss how culture guides the social ties we form, and how different kinds of cultural endowments (cultural capital) empower us to take advantage of network opportunities (social capital) to different extents. Networks may be seen not so much as rigid structures, but as flexible fabrics providing opportunities for interaction.

- Networks *OF* culture (or culture *AS* networks): network ideas can be used to analyze culture and cultural phenomena as *relational "systems."* In chapter 7, I discuss how certain symbols, certain words, certain ideas, and so on, are linked, either by virtue of their co-occurrence in particular texts, or by virtue of their joint deployment by specific users. What is most at stake here is the understanding and mapping of culture as *meaning*, or, more precisely, culture as comprised of a set of meanings formed in relation to each other.

- Networks *AS* culture: in chapter 8, we explore ways in which particular cultures – both historical examples and contemporary ones – are thought to entail a kind of networking mentality. Some scholars argue, for instance, that networks in the contemporary world bear within them, inherently, certain kinds of cultural values and beliefs, so that their construction and composition assume that imprint. Culture is not merely a property of actors, nor something "out there" affecting what people think and do, but is embedded as meanings attached directly to specific kinds of network ties and forms of social interaction. In the latter part of this chapter, I discuss in an exploratory way new frontiers for thinking about intersections of social networks and culture: in internet-based activity, especially Web 2.0 sites, and in virtual gameplay. Growing literatures in communications, media studies, and game studies describe these worlds, but not very much work by sociologists has yet tried to integrate network-oriented and culture-oriented approaches to them.

Before we explore these diverse empirical intersections of networks and culture, however, I devote chapter 2 to an overview of important concepts and measures in social network analysis, though with a cultural inflection, and chapter 3 to a discussion of important concepts and arguments in cultural sociology, with a view to integrating them into the study of networks. My hope is that you can refer to these fundamental concepts and arguments recurrently as needed as you make your way through the rest of the book.

7

An integrated study of networks and culture is one vital way of carrying out a richly *relational* form of sociology (Bourdieu and Wacquant 1992; Emirbayer 1997; White 2008; DiMaggio 2011; Fuhse and Mützel 2011; see especially Crossley 2011 and Mische 2011). The basic premise of relational sociology, to put it a little too simply, is that relations, rather than fully formed individuals or fixed social structures, are the proper object and fundamental unit of analysis for sociological research. Individual preferences and actions vary in different relational situations, implying that "social structure" at the macro level and "individual preference" at the micro level are concepts too rigid to account for the variation we observe in social life on a constant and ongoing basis. Studying networks is a way of processing the relationality of the world through a structural lens. Studying culture is a way of interpreting the relational basis of the meanings by which we organize our lives. Putting the two together helps us think about how these two modes of relation also mutually influence each other.

Some Caveats

A few words may be in order here to clarify my objectives in this book. First, attempting to survey such a vast, varied, and growing landscape of research is a humbling process. I cannot possibly cover topics exhaustively, but I will discuss quite a lot of fascinating literature with as much clarity as I can. Some portion of this material is *not* easy to understand. But hopefully my account of it will be tantalizing enough, even when not as subtle as it might be, for you to be encouraged to seek out and wrestle with the original material itself.

More worrisome than the treatment of individual authors or publications is the effort to identify and follow a thread connecting them, simply because multiple different ways of lumping topics exist (Zerubavel 1991). For one example, I defer discussion of the notion of duality to chapter 7, as it is a foundational idea for several of the authors and research projects discussed in that chapter. But it also could easily be brought up in the context of my discussion of Robert Faulkner's *Music on Demand* (1983) in chapter 5. The specific significance of some of the fundamental, building-block concepts utilized in network analysis and in sociological treatments of culture may not be too clear when they are first discussed in chapters 2 and 3, but it is necessary to lay out some of those building blocks in advance, rather than pause and re-cover that ground each time they are raised in the rest of the book.

I have been guided by a couple of broad selection strategies. First, without any hope of covering the field comprehensively, I have tried to be catholic in my coverage of material, rather than focusing on a very small number of exemplars. I believe it is important for readers to get a sense of the many ways the culture/networks intersection has been explored. Even more importantly, I want to prompt readers to strike out in their own directions to see what new cases and themes they can explore. For example, the ongoing explosive growth in the use of social media and the continued proliferation of participation in massively multiplayer online games are creating ever newer, formally specifiable network structures in which culture operates. The rules and norms of engagement and interaction in these spaces, and participants' relationship to the identities they adopt there, are rich terrain for analysis, but to date the surface of these involvements has barely been scratched by sociologists. For another example, formal network tools are being adopted in increasing volume by scholars in the humanities, especially in literature and in history, and young researchers ought to be aware of the opportunities for interdisciplinary work at the networks/culture intersection.

My second selection strategy has been that, while I have tried to think expansively and creatively about what a network is, and what culture is, I have left out a considerable quantity of research that doesn't quite include *both* networks and culture. As a result, this book is not the best introduction to social networks and network analysis in general. Among the networks topics barely mentioned here is the burgeoning literature examining network aspects of health and disease. Nor do I discuss much research on economic networks, at least not insofar as it treats topics like corporate coalition-building or labor markets. Something similar could be said for the culture side of the picture. There is a wealth of great cultural sociology – even cultural sociology that explicitly analyzes the production of cultural objects like music and film – that lacks any explicit grounding in concrete applications of network ideas. To name just one such example, there is fascinating research on the way symbolic boundaries are created and maintained (Lamont and Fournier 1992), but unless that boundary work is clearly established and maintained through identifiably network-based processes, I omit it here. Extending this clarification further, there are many aspects of social life in which we can speak metaphorically of networks. Groups or "groupings" are sometimes talked about as "networks" without specifying the concrete pattern of relations that comprise them; states are said to operate through "networks" of power; the global system is sometimes talked about as a "network" of forces, institutions, and organizations (for example, Castells 1996); opinion circulates through a population conceived as a kind of "network"; and so on. For the most part, I restrict myself to cases in which formal network analytic methods have been utilized in empirical research. In some instances, I expand my reach into areas where I believe formal network analytic methods could be applied in a relatively concrete way. I don't wish to discourage more innovative applications of network ideas, and especially I don't wish to discourage culturally minded sociologists from engaging with network concepts. In fact, bringing culture into networks has been an important part of my own research agenda. That said, I would like to ensure that that engagement is carried out with some precision.

With any research topic, we can bring culture in. I strongly believe that claim, but I am not intent on developing that particular polemic in this book. I also will have little to say about networks studies that deal with notions of social "behavior" or "information" in what I consider to be a rather flat way. We could undoubtedly brainstorm at length about the cultural assumptions and cognitive classifications that continually shape what some researchers simply refer to as "behavior." For example, bullying in high school networks can be examined from a largely behavioral point of view (Faris and Felmlee 2011); and yet it is also true that bullying is guided by social norms and expectations and frequently entails distinctively encoded and richly symbolic practices (Paluck and Shepherd 2012). Or consider gang violence or other cognate forms of inter-group conflict, which are susceptible to being treated as behavior, and yet are also highly culturally encoded (Gould 2003; Papachristos 2009). Similarly, what some scholars call "information flow" could probably be cast as "communicative interaction based on shared, institutionalized protocols." To do so renders much clearer the cultural underpinnings of the objects of such research; however, it is not my goal to bring culture (or networks) into everything, but to do so within practical limits.

To sum up, this book surveys a variety of ways in which the study of social networks and the study of culture have intersected in the past, and it offers some ideas about how to broaden and deepen that cross-fertilization in future research. I hope it will demonstrate that these perspectives are not narrow, subdisciplinary perspectives, but instead offer a framework for analyzing a great diversity of social phenomena in a refreshing and insightful light.

PART I

Fundamental Concepts

2

The Nuts and Bolts of Networks, through a Cultural Lens

In this chapter, we will cover some of the most important concepts and arguments in the world of social network analysis, so that you can develop familiarity with the basic terminology and core ideas that will help you as you proceed through this book and beyond.[1] In the subsequent chapter, I perform not exactly the same exercise, but a similar one, with respect to core ideas in the sociological treatment of culture, focusing especially on those concepts and theories of most relevance to networks research. In both chapters, I aim to discuss these distinctly different sets of fundamental concepts in light of each other. Thus, in this chapter, as I introduce and discuss basic network concepts, I note at each step how cultural themes and issues arise. In a sense, one could see this as problematizing network concepts from a cultural perspective, but I prefer to focus on the positively framed goal of pursuing ideas about how culturally informed thinking can *enhance* the substantive practice of network analysis, not undermine it. In the next chapter, I pursue the companion goal of exploring how network analytic thinking can enhance the ways cultural sociology may be done, to a significant extent by emphasizing the ways culture is frequently created, transmitted, and altered through concrete instances of social interaction, traceable via social network analysis.

The Most Basic Network Concepts:
Nodes/Actors and Edges/Ties

A network is comprised of a set of entities and the connections existing among them. When thinking of social networks in particular, we frequently refer to (and conceive of) the entities as *actors*; however, nothing requires that they be individual people. They could be collectives, like families, or companies, or organizations, or states. As we will see later, they could also be things like words, or texts, or actions, or emotions, or just about anything existing in some relational nexus that comprises (or impinges upon) social life. Especially when we think of a network in graphic terms, as a set of points with lines connecting them in a web-like pattern, we may refer to the entities as *nodes*, or *vertices*, and the ties as *edges* or *arcs*. This vocabulary can be quite useful in its abstractness. It gets us away from assuming that the entities in a network are necessarily rational actors, with the specific mental equipment to make rational, self-interested decisions – as if that were the only motive behind social network formation and growth. Refraining from making such an assumption has allowed researchers to focus on structural properties or tendencies within networks, without seeking to explain them in terms of actor rationality. Equally, though, and more important for us, moving away from explaining social network behavior narrowly in terms of rational action provokes us to think about the myriad ways that culture – norms, values, local attitudes and beliefs, cognitive frames, powerful symbols, conversation, and so on – can affect how specific social networks are formed and develop. Taking that step entails adopting a healthy sensitivity to local context and meaning in networks research.

Nodes/actors can be categorized in various different ways. One key *structural* property of nodes is *centrality*, and, for the moment, especially *degree centrality*. This is a measure of the number of connections a given node has to other nodes.[2] More central nodes have more ties, and accordingly they are expected to exert a stronger influence on network formation and development. People with many friends are likely to account disproportionately for the spread of tastes and fashions, for example. And a word that appears frequently in a given text – say, the word "security" in a State of the Union address – probably contributes disproportionally to the text's meaning, and influences the meaning of the words adjacent to it.[3]

It is usually also important to consider *substantive attributes* of entities in social networks.[4] Such attributes may be relatively light on cultural content. Recording actors' physical attributes like height or body mass index or vocal pitch seems pretty devoid of cultural significance – except, say, in the context of speed dating in America (McFarland et al. 2013), where tall men are considered more desirable than short men, heavier women seem to be less choosy about dates, and rising pitch in one's voice is understood to connote engagement in a conversation. You catch my drift here, I hope: these physiological attributes frequently carry culture-specific meanings, and so connection to actors possessing them may be valued or despised accordingly. I don't mean to say these are entirely culturally constituted attributes in the way a preference for country music is, or living in Dumbo, but these meanings are important to consider when we analyze and interpret issues like who is most active or most connected in a network – indeed, who contributes the most to *making* the network.

While the notion of node is flexible, the notion of tie or edge is even more so. A tie can record almost anything: a kind of social relation (for example, marriage, friendship or admiration), or shared membership in a group, or a flow of resources (trade, gift exchange, migration, favors, advice), or communication (talking together, following on Twitter), or proximity (sharing a neighborhood, words semantically joined in a sentence). Furthermore, while we commonly think of networks as a set of things (actors) tied through connections, as if nodes were subjects and edges were actions or activities predicated of them, we may reverse that: we could think of activities as the nodes and people as the edges connecting them.[5] Being a bit imaginative like this allows us, for one thing, to avoid thinking of "physical" networks as primary, and culture, as the thing that flows through them, as secondary, or "added" afterwards. The entities – the actors – may actually be (in fact, almost always are) constituted culturally through flows of activities that generate identities (White 2008). Thus, the "hardware versus software" analogy I posed in chapter 1 can quickly break down!

There are several issues to consider concerning the general properties of ties. First, network analysts typically store information about ties by grouping them into *types of tie*, or *relations*. Any given set of nodes may be connected via different relations: for example, a set of college friends may be connected by major, and/or by classes attended together, and/or by shared dorm space, and/or by exercising together, and/or by membership in clubs, and/or, eventually, by marriage and possibly having kids together! We don't want to jumble up information on these different relations as if they all did the same work and meant the same thing. Because they *mean* different things, the network patterns we expect for each relation among one set of actors are quite likely to differ, too.

Second, there is the issue of how different relations may relate to each other. Maybe roommates do exercise together; that is an empirical question. But, often enough, not only how specific types of tie go together in actuality, but whether they *can* or *should* go together *conceptually*, is a function of cultural norms and expectations. For instance, in some societies people are *expected* to go into business with their family members; then, it is not an accidental confluence of relations. Both the roommates example and the business partners example describe overlapping types of tie, which network analysts refer to as *multiplexity*. However, although both are cases of multiplexity, it should be of special concern to us whether particular instances of multiplexity are culturally mandated (or culturally prohibited), so we can understand better the cultural norms and processes that *generate* particular network structures.

Consider also that humans are exceptionally adept at stitching different types of ties together, across different domains, to forge connections. For example, I might ask my sister to speak to her neighbor about the neighbor's boss's used car I want to buy. Vedran found a new drummer for his band by talking to a guy on my pick-up basketball team that used to work as a booking agent. Derek chatted with a guy on a train in Europe who went to school with his former girlfriend's dance instructor. And so on. Sometimes those ties are formed for utilitarian reasons; sometimes, as in the last example, they simply support everyday human sociability. Regardless, much of the way our social world works lies in how different relations are utilized skillfully in combination. Note this is not about overlapping relations, but chains of relations. Some combinations are very common. For example, a husband's brother is so commonly turned to for various things that we have a name for that compound relationship: brother-in-law. In patronage-based political systems, some people – bosses – have power precisely because they can connect people they know on one dimension with people they know on another.[6] Yet some combinations of relations might be very hard to enact. Again, cultural expectations will shape the possibility of these tie combinations.[7]

Finally, one of the most important dimensions with which social network analysts have sought to classify ties and relations is the distinction between *weak ties* and *strong ties*, famously articulated by Mark Granovetter (1973). According to Granovetter himself, as well as according to a kind of common "wisdom" among network analysts, a strong tie generally denotes some combination of time spent together, emotional intensity and/or intimacy, and reciprocity. The term "weak tie," by contrast, presumably refers to social ties that involve less time spent together, or less recurrent interaction (Uzzi 1996), as well as less intensity of feeling. Classically, we talk of family ties or business partnerships as strong ties. On the other side, "acquaintance" is the consummate example of a weak tie. However, as many networks scholars have noted (see, for example, Kadushin 2012: 31), conclusively distinguishing a weak from a strong tie in substantive terms is challenging. We may have family members we have known a long time, but never see. We may see people like our hair stylist or our local grocery store cashier more frequently than some friends, yet feel little connection to them. Further, strength and weakness may be directional: a student may feel strongly connected to and influenced by a particular professor, while as far as the professor is concerned, the student is just another face in the classroom.[8] So, in the first place, it is necessary to justify carefully our coding of network ties as weak or strong in terms of prevailing cultural understandings, including the understanding of relations from the standpoint of the participants. I shall have more to say about the value of weak ties later in this chapter.

Ego-Networks

As we begin to explore the embedding of any given node in any kind of network, we may start by considering *ego-networks*. An ego-network is a network composed of a focal actor, plus all of the others (alters) to whom he or she is tied or with whom he or she interacts, plus all of the ties among those alters. Ego-networks deliberately sample on particular actors, rather than trying to incorporate everyone's ties to each other and then analyze that overall structure. One might consider such restrictive sampling to be a shortcoming, but ego-network analysis has a different object in mind than the study of whole networks (which we will come to shortly). We may want to distinguish between actors in terms of the number of alters with whom they interact, then explore both the causes and consequences of such differences. We often want to know whether people's friends are each other's friends, or whether people divide their networks of acquaintances into non-overlapping sectors. In turn, we are interested in whether those non-overlapping sectors represent culturally distinct groups – say the distinction between my group of friends who are fanatical about Beethoven the composer and my group of friends who are fanatical about Beethoven the dog. Finally, we are interested in knowing what kinds of communications and what kinds of support are provided in these personal networks. Such communication and support depend on our understandings of what persons in particular positions *vis-à-vis* each other are expected to provide. The structure of ego-networks may also depend on broader cultural factors, such as changing perceptions of the value of being or living alone (McPherson et al. 2006), or differences in national cultures (Fischer and Shavit 1995; Dávid et al. 2016), or involvement in specific cultural activities like video game play (Shen and Chen 2015).

The Dyad

Now we move our attention beyond actors/nodes to the next higher level, specifically to the *dyad*, one of the fundamental building blocks of networks (Rivera et al. 2010). Any pair of nodes in a network, whether directly connected or not, can be considered a dyad. However, we are usually especially interested in dyads in which some tie exists between the nodes. Ties within dyads, when they exist, may be *undirected* (such as "being neighbors," or perhaps "collaborators") or *directed* (such as influence or advice ties). Some directed ties, as in the diffusion processes we visit in chapter 4, are *asymmetric* (arcs); others, like exchanging gifts, are often mutual or *reciprocal*. While we can try to sort different types of ties into these "structural" or "morphological" categories based on their inherent properties (for example, it's very hard to live next door to someone without them being able to describe themselves as living next door to you, too), often we find that whether or not particular relations are directed or undirected, and whether they are one-directional or mutual, are matters of cultural context and interpretation. For instance, nothing inherently requires us to reciprocate for Christmas gifts received, but cultural norms strongly work upon us to do so. Certain favors – helping a stranger change a tire, for example, or giving advice – often imply that the favor ought not to be directly reciprocated, but "paid forward" instead. Again, this is not structurally inherent in the tie, yet it can be definitional to the tie as it is understood in its cultural context. It is almost always useful, and frequently vital, to think carefully about the cultural understandings that constitute and animate the various social relations we analyze and visualize through social network methods.[9] When we fail to do so and focus too excitedly on discovering certain network structural properties,[10] we can easily interpret those properties in a decontextualized way that is inconsistent with what is actually taking place in the network, understood from a substantive sociological standpoint.

The Crucial Notion of Homophily

As I noted above, nodes in networks have attributes. The question then arises whether actors within dyads *share* attributes with each other. This brings us to one of the most important concepts in the study of social networks, namely *homophily*. Homophily, derived from the Greek words for "love of the same," expresses the tendency for actors to form ties with others who share some important attribute with them.[11] The tendency toward homophily has been demonstrated time and again; in fact, it is a phenomenon scholars search for routinely in virtually any project on social networks. Imagine for a moment a room full of people who speak different languages. It seems pretty self-evident that people would drift around until they found someone who spoke their own language and thereupon they would strike up a conversation. Soon enough we would find a room sorted into pockets of linguistically unified dyads (and then higher-order communities). In this example, it is easy to see how shared language (culture) establishes mutually understandable protocols for tie formation. But the tendency toward homophily is quite frequently measured using other dimensions besides shared language. Shared ascriptive qualities of actors are frequently measured – things such as age, race, and sex. For instance, children in elementary and secondary schools commonly segregate along each of these dimensions. We would say their informal pairings (and higher-level groupings, too) tend to be homophilous on sex and homophilous on race, while they are homophilous on age due to the grade structure of most schools. For another example, inter-racial marriages remain the exception rather than the rule in contemporary America. Therefore, while marriage remains mostly heterophilous on sex (men usually marry women and vice versa), it also remains mostly homophilous on race and/or ethnicity, despite an overall decline in racial discrimination. All kinds of cultural meanings typically surround these ascriptive characteristics of actors, but we often bracket those meanings, since these characteristics of actors are readily measured, and they seem to affect patterns of association so widely that it pays to attend to them, almost without further reflection. Several basic acquired attributes (such as occupation, income level, or education) have such a pervasive effect in clustering actors that they, too, can be examined for their effects without further reflection.

This idea of homophily is commonly associated with the familiar proverb, "birds of a feather flock together" (McPherson et al. 2001). The question remains, though, which feather? People (or organizations, or nodes of any kind) can be alike on some dimension, while being entirely unlike each other on a thousand other dimensions (Feld and Grofman 2009). We face some temptation to cherry-pick dimensions, making it all the more important to assess carefully and justify which dimensions are the most salient ones to consider. Widespread actor attributes such as age, race, or occupation may well be significant – but so too are cognitive and moral orientations such as religious beliefs, dietary philosophies, political positions, social attitudes, musical tastes, and artistic styles, along with their attendant practices and schemas. In the case of these "value-orientations" (Lazarsfeld and Merton 1954), the cultural element leading actors to seek each other out (thus *forming* and *sustaining* networks) is obviously much more evident and effective than in the case of ascriptive attributes. This is a fundamental place where the confluence of networks and culture clearly must be studied. Furthermore, researchers should aim to ascertain whether cultural orientations precede network formation (thereby acting as instances of homophily precipitating network ties, such as perhaps when devotees of a particular rapper or a particular video game seek and find each other online),[12] or whether shared value orientations emerge from a pre-existing connection (or even proximity) within networks. A classic context for considering this question concerns different forms of deviant behavior. Do those who engage in deviant acts or adhere to deviant beliefs find each other on the basis of that orientation? Or do such deviant acts and beliefs arise and grow primarily from actors' co-location and interaction in particular social settings (Cohen 1977; Kandel 1978)? If the latter, we should also consider whether co-location in a network itself breeds shared values and attitudes, or whether such values and attitudes spread from certain actors to others via a process of influence.

The Critical Importance of Triads

Having discussed nodes (actors) and edges (ties) as the basic elements of networks, and dyads as fundamental building blocks, we now move on to consider larger kinds of networks (networks composed of multiple dyads) and the most important structural properties of such networks. Again my goal is to emphasize how these concepts resonate with cultural themes and cultural sociological issues and goals.

From dyads, the next step is to sets of three nodes, or *triads*. Triads are where social structure begins to exist independently of individuals, and independent of the dyadic relations they work out between themselves. That is, once we have triads, the relationship between any two nodes is potentially (and frequently *actually*) affected by the existence of other nodes, and by the presence of ties flowing to and from those nodes. The most often cited example of this effect is the notion that "the friend of my friend is my friend." That is, if two persons Alex and Bob are friends, and Alex is also friends with a third, Chuck, it is likely that Bob and Chuck will become friends. Bob and Chuck's relationship is not independent of Alex and Bob's, nor of Alex and Chuck's. A related idea is the claim that "the enemy of my enemy is my friend." Thus, I might get along well with someone . . . once I observe that we share a common distaste for the same third person! At the level of international relations, governments might well seek to ally themselves with other governments hostile toward a common enemy. In cases such as these, the ties among nodes in the triad are said to be in *balance* (Heider 1946; Cartwright and Harary 1956). In the "three friends" case, we also say the triad exhibits *closure*. Balance is frequently (although, as I point out below, not pervasively) observed in real social networks. To think about it culturally, balanced patterns of social relations will be generated on the basis of the consistent application of norms of interaction concerned with goals such as solidarity or competition. More generally, to recognize the dependence of dyadic ties on each other – one important expression of the relationality of the social order (Emirbayer 1997; Mische 2011) – implies the dependence of the *meaning* of any social tie on the existence and meaning of the ties that surround it. I believe this marks an electrically important point of connection between network thinking and cultural sociology.

Friendships and alliances could be thought of as undirected ties. But triads are equally important objects of analysis when it comes to *directed* ties.[13] The main network concepts to consider here are *transitivity* and *cycles*. Many processes in the natural and social world exhibit transitivity. Ivan Chase's (1980) research on pecking order among chickens provides a classic example. One chicken attacks another; thereafter the victor typically attacks a third to establish its superiority over both losers. Out of such contests, represented as directed ties, rank orderings of chickens arise, first at the level of three participants, subsequently in longer chains of dominance and submission. Thus *hierarchies* arise out of interaction.[14] Let's consider "issues orders to" as an example of a directed tie in the human world. If Angel issues orders to Brent, and Brent issues orders to Cathy, it seems unlikely in most cases that Cathy would issue orders to Angel; instead, a chain of command would be produced and reproduced through these interactions. The standings among teams in a professional sports league may afford another illustration. As teams play each other, it is likely that if the Astros beat the Braves, and the Braves beat the Cubs, the Astros will probably beat the Cubs, creating a hierarchy. On the other hand, it is, in principle, possible for the Cubs to turn around and beat the Astros (hope springs eternal!), creating a cyclical pattern of victories. The implication we draw from such intransitive cycles, just like in the game "Rock, Paper, Scissors," is that, among the three participants, a kind of equality obtains. Jumping ahead slightly, when we get to larger networks, wherever cycles abound, we might be inclined to infer that equality prevails as a meaningful characteristic of the overall system.

Note in the foregoing paragraph that certain "elemental" triads are seen as having inherent meaning. A cycle "means" equality; a transitive triad "means" hierarchy. Similarly, a triad with ties between A and B and between A and C, but not B and C, defines a *structural hole*, a network position that forms a bridge or gateway between two or more otherwise disconnected positions (Burt 1992) – which "means" brokerage exists. That is quite a presumption! Actually, it might well be possible for these structures to "mean" different things in different settings. For example, a transitive triad might mean there is a tolerance for both direct and indirect forms of exchange in a network, rather than signifying hierarchy. A cyclical triad might be produced from feelings of altruism, or it might be bred from intense competition for status. Even if its presence signifies "equality" in both instances, the underlying motivations and the cultural context generating such structures can be substantially different.

Along these, lines, it is instructive to re-consider Simmel's treatment of triads (1950: 145–69) to see how important interpretation is to understanding them. Simmel starts with a triadic structure that resembles a structural hole: one actor (A) connected to two others (B and C), without those other actors being directly tied to each other. But he goes on to explain that that structure may have three different substantive significances. In some cases, the presence of the bridging actor mediates the relationship, as in the case of a child who draws together her parents and deepens their commitment to each other, or a mediator who helps to resolves disputes between management and labor. In other cases, the bridging actor benefits indirectly from the antagonism or competition between B and C; this is the so-called *tertius gaudens* (the third rejoices) situation. Third parties in Parliaments, which hold the decisive number of seats to allow either of the two equally strong major parties to rule, exercise influence disproportionate to their numbers. Popular people in a dating market gain favors from the competition between their suitors. The child of separated parents may gain an increased flow of treats as the parents compete for his affection. When actor A actively takes advantage of the situation, then the *divide et impera* (divide and conquer) form may arise: for example, now the child manipulates the situation to increase the flow of treats further, deliberately pitting the parents against each other. Managers may gain increased control over a department by requiring employees to compete over production goals; colonizers may increase their control of a subject population by setting tribes, towns, or ethnic groups against each other. The crucial point is that the same network structural element has quite distinct potential meanings. *There is a fundamental ambiguity here in the relationship between network structure and meaning.* Rather than regard that as trouble, though, it should sensitize us in a positive way to think about how network structures on the one hand, and mental processes and cultural schemas on the other, interact in interesting ways. Particular triadic structures may be pregnant with multiple possibilities of meaning; conversely, different cultural contexts and expectations can tilt ambiguously meaningful network structures and the social groups that comprise them in distinctly different directions.

From Triads to Larger Network Structures

Cohesive Subgroups

Already, in my discussion of dyads and triads, I found it hard not to move ahead toward larger network structures. If my friend's friend becomes my own friend, mightn't my friend's friend's friend become one, too? If Antoine and Bastien shun Carole, mightn't Carole seek the company of other people that Antoine and Bastien despise? To the extent this clustering of friends (ties) and partitioning of enemies occurs, we will observe *cohesive subgroups* within networks. These are locales where a denser volume of ties exists relative to the *density* of the overall network.[15] In the upper limiting case, we can discern groups of nodes, all of which are directly tied to each other and no one else, forming a *clique*.

Now, the idea of cohesion is vitally important to the intersection of culture and networks because, as Wasserman and Faust (1994: 249) have eloquently stated, it allows us to "formalize the intuitive and theoretical notion of social group using social network properties." That is, whereas we sometimes think of networks as different kinds of social objects than groups, the theme of cohesion allows us to use network concepts to treat groups – which we typically understand as having a sense of identity, or a shared set of norms and/or practices – as one kind of especially cohesive network structure (Fine and Kleinman 1983). Analyzing network structure in detail within cohesive subgroups (such as musical subcultures), and taking into account the homophily and multiplexity that constitute them, helps us to understand more precisely why some groups hold together, and even thrive, in the face of adversity. Furthermore, we can explore how the documented absence of ties in certain network spaces expresses hostility between subgroups – hostility which may be a defining principle of their make-up.

Speaking more culturally, awareness of particular classification schemes used by certain actors, and observation of their use of particular languages (slang, argot), would lead us to expect social network ties to "congregate" in certain places, with network structure "formalizing" our sense of the group-ish character of the actors. Cohesion is typically sustained by an ongoing sense of shared identity and/or ongoing communicative processes. Thus, we would expect that where such cultural factors are present, groups will emerge as a distinctive kind of network structure.

That said, it is hard to sustain pure cliques as groups grow larger: every new node would have to become directly tied to every previous member! Real-world networks typically include more unbalanced triads than our models would predict (Martin 2009; Moody 2009).[16] Think of those occasions when one of your friends is friends with someone you despise; it's not uncommon! Sometimes, it is a matter of jealousy. Sometimes, we just don't have the energy or desire to build fully consistent personal networks, focusing sensibly only on achieving balance in relationships that impinge on us constantly. But sometimes those situations in which we despise our friends' friends arise as a function of the fact that we are actually multiple persons (Mead 1934), so it is quite possible for us to get along with two different people in two quite disparate ways – ways of being that our friends do not share with each other. That "multiplicity" at the root of identities and social interaction dynamics is a social reality that quantitative network analysis may not be so well equipped to handle.[17]

Reachability

Loosely speaking, cohesive subgroups are relatively dense clusters within which all the member nodes can reach each other while being unreachable by most or all outsiders.[18] This idea of *reachability* is important from a cultural standpoint, since, in the world of networks, the transmission of anything occurs through concrete network ties rather than broadcast messages. Trends, fads, symbols, beliefs, and so on, can't transcend subgroup boundaries unless some members have ties that span outside the subgroup to non-member nodes.

Here we return to the strong-tie versus weak-tie distinction formulated by Granovetter (1973). As he famously noted, weak ties are paradoxically strong in one particular respect. Whereas strong ties link nodes that are otherwise already connected (almost by definition, as he presents the argument), weak ties act as bridges from one network locale to another. Because these bridges "create more and shorter paths" through the network, "the removal of the average weak tie would do more 'damage' to transmission probabilities than would that of the average strong one" (1973: 1365f.). In short, weak ties are necessary for disseminating information, protocols, practices, and/or values widely through a network. Now, we could deal with the transmission of "information" in a fairly flat way that doesn't engage much with ideas about culture. But it is instructive to think of various ways in which such transmission is laden with culture, and even emblematic of (or constitutive of) culture. Gossip probably spreads through weak ties rather than strong ones; if it didn't, the damage to people's reputations would not spread beyond their local network neighborhoods. Specific repertoires of collective protest or innovative organizational policies may spread through weak connections, with global consequences. Weak ties are conduits of specific culturally meaningful content and processes. And beyond that, one could argue that weak ties are themselves *valued* within a contemporary cultural framework that emphasizes personal autonomy and "networking" as a means of social mobility.[19] Thus, the process of accumulating weak ties may have important identity consequences, conferring on people distinctly cosmopolitan attitudes.

Cohesive subgroups and reachability come together in the concept of the small world (Watts 1999). Put simply, "small-world" network structures imply tight clustering of ties at the local level, combined with short average path lengths at the aggregate level – meaning actors located in particular clusters can reach all (or at least many) other clusters through a fairly small number of steps. Small worlds permit local interaction to produce fruitful fermentation of ideas and creative cultural output, combined with the capacity to spread those ideas to other "worlds" fairly quickly.

Hierarchy

I noted above that, at the triadic level, we sometimes see situations in which hierarchies arise out of interaction. If, in a round-robin tournament, Team A beats Team B, Team B beats Team C, and then Team A beats Team C, we have a neatly ordered hierarchy. Over the course of a season, the aggregation of dyadic contests among all teams – not just these three – results in some ranking of teams, so that out of dyadic contests we generate "the standings." These standings can be understood to express status differences among the teams – hence, we move to something cultural from something structural. Very good teams can even use their reputations to intimidate poor teams, so that reputations become a factor in maintaining the structure of the network. Admittedly, a certain amount of "noise" typically arises in the rankings as we move from triads to the larger network (the league).[20] Yet a high volume of transitive triad microstructures (good teams generally beat average teams, who generally beat bad ones) occurring over the whole season of games may be taken as a sign that the hierarchy that is expressed in the league's standings is a characteristic not only of triads, but of the whole system in which they occur.

That is an amazing inference to draw! But is it correct? It is tempting to think so, but actually, even if we accept that transitive triads and cyclical triads tend to embody distinctly different meanings or connotations, the "meaning" or character of larger network structures is not necessarily a simple function of aggregating these elemental structures. For example, in some collaborative research I conducted with Neha Gondal on networks of personal credit relations in Renaissance Florence (Gondal and McLean 2013b), we found that the circulation of credit among a fairly large number of elite Florentine individuals – a macro pattern that we take to be indicative of the elite's collective solidarity – was not built up from many "egalitarian" cyclical triads, but from just as many or more transitive triads. Cyclical triads may signify equality at the local level – but they also may isolate people from larger cycles of exchange in larger networks, obstructing the emergence of those larger cycles. Essentially, cyclical triads function in different ways, and thereby signify different meanings, depending on the level of analysis one employs. This is a very complex issue to explore, but the idea that network macrostructure replicates network microstructure in its character may well be too simplistic.

Centrality

In a vast number of real-world networks, ties are distributed very unevenly. Some nodes may be said to be more *central* than others – either because they have a lot of edges running directly to or from them (a high *degree*), or because it takes them especially few steps to reach many other nodes in the network (they are *close* to many others), or because they lie on paths *between* many nodes, or because they are connected to other powerful or high-status nodes like themselves.[21] However it is measured, centrality typically is thought to entail some notion of prestige, power, or influence. Again, we find a presumption – often reasonably well founded, but not universally so – that network structures inherently *mean* something about the groups they represent.

Centrality may result from the possession of certain attributes or resources by particular nodes; alternatively, accumulation of resources and acquisition of a reputation for possession of certain (desirable) attributes often arise, and grow, as a function of network centrality. This idea that identities, attitudes, reputations, and so on arise out of network structure has long been a core tenet in social network analysis (Wellman 1988). In recent years, more attention has been paid to the generative processes that might produce certain network structures. In the case of networks exhibiting considerable centralization,[22] we sometimes observe (or, at least, imagine) a pattern of *preferential attachment* (van de Rijt et al. 2014): nodes already enjoying many ties may attract more, while those with few get no more and may lose what they have. This is a "rich-get-richer" phenomenon.[23] If you have a lot of money, people are happy to lend you more; if you have little and need a loan, good luck to you! If you go to a party, you might well gravitate to the largish group that seems to be having fun. You certainly don't want to be stuck with the solitary, snot-nosed guy with the chili stain on his shirt standing in the corner. In artistic markets such as Hollywood, a small number of artists have a vast number of credits and a corresponding reputation for excellence; a vast number of artists have hardly any credits and are consequently low-status virtual unknowns. The correlation between actual talent and reputation in such markets is typically low and insignificant. Because we seem to find this process in so many settings, it is tempting to treat it as a kind of "natural" phenomenon, along the same lines that some materials are vastly more central in metabolic processes than others (Jeong et al. 2000). There are important ways, though, in which cultural factors may clearly affect the extent to which the preferential attachment mechanism works. In some cultural networks, high levels of uncertainty over quality combined with high costs and riskiness of projects may accentuate the tendency toward preferential attachment as project managers and participants are driven even more than usual to connect with proven quantities (Zuckerman et al. 2003). In other cases – perhaps some employment markets and some joint-venture networks (Powell et al. 2005), crowding and/or social norms may enforce a ceiling on the number of ties any given node can enjoy, and we observe a more even distribution.

Conclusion

I have introduced a number of fundamental network concepts in this chapter, building up from the micro level to the level of whole networks. At each step I strove to note the importance of cultural factors in the way these concepts can be, or even ought to be, defined and operationalized. As I hope I have indicated adequately, my goal is not to short-circuit network analyses at every step with obstructive questions about cultural content or meaning. Instead, it is to insist that we very frequently need to think carefully about cultural content and cultural processes for an intelligent and substantively meaningful application of these (very cool!) network ideas. Who or what, in this specific context or situation before us, is a meaningful and worthwhile alter for an actor to connect to? How do the kinds of relations "running through" a network affect its shape and the ways ties do or do not aggregate? What different kinds of meanings can basic network structures like Simmel's triad be given, and how do those meanings affect what kinds of larger patterns we might expect to find? If we don't seek answers to these questions in the course of doing our networks research, we are at risk of losing sight of the basic elements and dynamics constituting social processes, thereby misunderstanding them.

3

Basic Culture Concepts, with a Networks Inflection

Network analysis lends itself to an orderly exposition such as I set forth in the last chapter, working up from basic definitions and rudimentary concepts to more complex ones. It is hard to say the same for culture. Culture is an immense, rich, multifaceted thing – or actually, an immense, rich, multifaceted collection of rich, multifaceted things. Many different elements of culture may be emphasized. Values, language, symbols, expectations, beliefs, norms, meanings, stories, conversation, tastes, material culture, practices, classification schemes, contexts, institutions: all of these and more are arguably critically important elements of culture. Different scholars persuasively emphasize different component parts of this mix.

Beyond the challenge posed by the existence of such a variety of elements comprising culture, certain influential definitions of culture strongly suggest that it cannot be tackled in a linear way. Clifford Geertz's (1973) famous and evocative assertion that culture is made up of "webs of significance" (perhaps not unlike a very complex network) implies that a culture can be plunged into from different starting points, and it will look different from different vantage points. Interpretation is the process by which we carefully but imaginatively follow chains of association or meaningful connections from one part of a culture – whether it is a practice, or a myth, or a bit of language, or a belief, or a labeling scheme – to another, enriching our understanding through hermeneutical exploration.[1] This process of finding meaning (Alexander

2003; Griswold 2013) is open-ended and evocative. Bits of culture resonate with each other, and tracing these resonances sensitively produces excellent cultural analysis. Even so, different pathways through culture might well lead to quite different construals of what is going on! A culture is not as well defined and bounded an entity as a network. "Central" elements of a culture are probably less precisely defined and less easily identified than central elements in a network, for example. The qualitative approach to culture relies on, and revels in, "thick description" (Geertz 1973). Thick description treats culture as a sophisticated, complex, highly developed, and nuanced system of objects and representations – with elusive (rather than transparently measurable) structure, based on allusive resonances rather than explicit connections.

In contrast to the interpretivist approach to culture, some recent theorizing by a small number of social networks scholars gathered around Harrison White aims for a methodical, cumulative exposition of culture such as can be supplied for networks – starting first with elemental parts, and later accounting for increasingly complex features that operate on a larger scale and with broader scope (White 1995, 2008; Mohr and White 2008; Godart and White 2010; Fontdevila and White 2013). This body of writing excites many sociologists eager for an integrated theory of the social order, one that attends to both social structures, and "interpretive facets of action" (White 1995: 1058). At the same time, it has been a source of vexation for many readers who feel ill equipped to interpret White's arcane prose and fanciful imagery!

In this chapter, I have three goals relating to the conceptual landscape I have just laid out. First, I briefly describe some of the more important *elements* of culture, as culture has been conventionally understood by sociologists. I focus on those elements of culture that have intersected particularly fruitfully with networks research. I provide some definitions and background information that will help to clarify ideas and examples discussed in later chapters.

Second, I introduce some of the most important network-oriented *approaches* to culture developed over the last few decades. I discuss especially the synthetic theoretical framework of Pierre Bourdieu, and the "production of culture" approach (Becker 1982; Peterson and Anand 2004) that has proven so congenial to, and synergistic with, the adoption of network methods. I also provide an account of Harrison White's efforts to integrate culture (patterned meaning) and network structure (patterned interaction). White's framework sometimes assumes a rather "thin" understanding of culture. That stance may put off many cultural sociologists, for whom *complex* religious beliefs, or complex principles of political organization, narrative forms, or poetic symbolism, have considerable causal power (Alexander and Smith 2001). At other times, though, White's followers adopt quite "thick" ideas about culture and meaning (for example, Fuhse 2009 and 2013), a tendency which places them in greater dialogue with cultural sociologists.

Third, I briefly articulate some ways that cultural approaches in sociology might benefit from thinking more creatively and enthusiastically about social networks. So, while chapter 2 encouraged you to consider that, when culture is kept in mind, we can develop a more culturally (and thus sociologically) rich approach to social networks, the last part of this chapter encourages those doing cultural sociology to consider how their research can be productively informed by a social networks perspective. That is, it will be fruitful to think of the ways in which culture emerges and operates "necessarily" within network-like settings and/or according to network-like principles.

Important Elements of Culture for the Sociology of Networks

The concept of culture is vast, with too many different connotations, and associations with too many competing schools of thought, to permit an adequate treatment in a single chapter.[2] Also, I do not wish to adjudicate among competing views of culture. Different aspects of culture are more or less appropriate to emphasize, and more or less heuristically valuable, in different kinds of sociological inquiry. Often the part of culture to emphasize depends on the empirical puzzle or question one wants to answer. Without presuming to be comprehensive, I consider the following elements in the study of culture to be especially germane when we think about different intersections of culture and networks.

Practices and Repertoires: Culture as Toolkit

Some decades ago, sociologists tended to think of culture primarily in terms of values and beliefs. To participate in a culture was to share specific beliefs about the world and to have particular values guiding one's actions. These beliefs and values were thought to be held in a largely unexamined way, informing behavior in a consistent manner. Often these values and beliefs were considered constitutive features of a society, so acquiring them came via a kind of osmosis, or absorption from the environment, rather than via concrete, discernible chains of influence.[3] Given the consistency and immediacy of the effect of culture, people could be thought of as the vessels of their culture, rather than culture being thought of as an instrument in people's action. But Ann Swidler (1986, 2001) argued that culture is more like a toolkit that we dip into than an atmosphere we breathe. On the basis of interviews she conducted with people about love and the relationships they had gone through, Swidler suggested that people don't act like they have a single, unified set of beliefs about the world, but instead draw on a varied repertoire of practices, gestures, turns of phrase, and vocabularies of motive at different times, invoking and recombining these elements as they deem appropriate for the situation at hand. We can enact quite disparate elements of the overall repertoire at different times. This image of culture as toolkit allows for practices to float and circulate somewhat freely of the individuals or organizations who adopt them.

Treating culture as *practices* or *repertoires* is useful and instructive in conjunction with the analysis of social networks, first, because we can think of the ways in which cultural practices may diffuse or circulate in social space, perhaps becoming more salient and more frequently used as they are passed through networks of connected actors, and especially through the hands of particularly well-connected actors. For example, organizational anti-harassment policies or executive compensation practices may diffuse across organizations that are in contact with one another. Similarly, techniques and concepts utilized in research frequently diffuse to a great extent through personal connections between advisors and students, and in turn those students' own students.

Another way that practices – in the form of bits of knowledge, turns of phrase, and repertoires for giving accounts of oneself to others – are germane to networks is that such materials are often the raw material of "networking." Here I mean primarily conscious efforts by strategic actors to connect with powerful or desirable others, as in the case of the self-aggrandizing Renaissance patronage letters I have studied (McLean 2007). But if you have participated in any kind of online discussion forum (see, for example, Baym 2010), or the side chat during a multiplayer online game (for example, Ducheneaut 2010), or if you have ever considered how karma is accumulated in Reddit (Tong 2013), you may be familiar with the fact that certain language, certain turns of phrase, certain quips, and certain kinds of images attract more attention than others. Popularity in these network-like spaces is culturally achieved, often via attention-grabbing practices salient in popular culture. I pursue this idea in chapters 6 and 8.

There is yet another way in which Swidler's understanding of culture may resonate with network thinking. Adapting Swidler's argument, John Levi Martin (2010) likens culture not merely to a toolkit, but to a very large junkyard. He suggests we have an overwhelmingly large stock of cultural bits and pieces at hand, most of which we will never use. Our tendency when conjuring up experience or memory of the world is that, rather than recording it as a fully coherent story line or set of endlessly reverberating significances, we retrieve it as a barebones set of elements, which he refers to as "a network of concepts and ideas" (2010: 232). According to this view, our actions are always based on a more or less inaccurate network or *Gestalt* of mental associations involving particular objects or representations. So, then, cultural elements not only pass through a network, or can be used to build social networks; cultural elements exist *in*, and can be represented *as*, a network.

We should resist here the idea that cultural elements go together as a matter of logical coherence, or that they are assembled into simply formulated, coherent and durable "cultural worldviews" (cf. Haidt 2001; Vaisey 2009; Vaisey and Lizardo 2010),[4] or that they are ordered according to some underlying structure, such as a system of binary opposites (Alexander and Smith 1993). Efforts to identify, for example, "institutional logics" (Thornton et al. 2012) within which organizations (or social networks, for that matter) function typically operationalize culture at far too high a level of abstraction and expect far too great a degree of consistency to capture the vibrancy and hybridity of culture as it is actually deployed in interaction (Eliasoph and Lichterman 2003). In fact, it is precisely the fact that cultural things "clump," but not necessarily in logical or inevitable ways, that makes the network metaphor and network ways of thinking so useful for analyzing empirical ensembles of cultural elements. The structure of culture is relational (Mohr 2013), but not hard-wired and architectonic as some structuralist accounts would have us believe.

Culture as Norms

I use the term *norm* to designate some set of beliefs or expectations we might have concerning what would be considered appropriate action in a particular situation. A norm is like a rule of thumb or a heuristic guiding our behavior rather than something experienced and/or consciously adopted as a strong moral precept. However, it has some moral content to it, in that acting contrary to the norm can result in us being looked upon unfavorably. This is, at least in part, because norms express shared expectations (Elster 2009). For one simple example, wearing a suit to a job interview is a widespread norm. It is an expectation we use to guide (not necessarily determine) our behavior, although it does not have the character of an externally sanctioned law (in the way that driving drunk brings the risk of being fined or imprisoned, in addition to being looked down upon by our peers). Nevertheless, when violated, we may experience a certain amount of negative judgment, including negative judgment we impose on ourselves, feeling that somehow we have behaved inappropriately or abnormally.

It is instructive to think about both the ways norms can guide the formation of social networks, and the ways networks might assist in the formation and reinforcement of social norms. On the former front, norms can guide the kinds of relationships we form, and with whom we believe we ought to form them. Norms of trust are integral to the establishment of commercial networks, for example, where they otherwise might not exist. Norms about who is an appropriate alter can be crucial in guiding the formation of networks of social support (Wellman and Wortley 1990), the core groups within which we discuss important matters (Marsden 1987), and sexual partnering (Bearman et al. 2004). A norm of loyalty often defines the boundaries of a network of gang members. Devoted gamers obey certain norms concerning the appropriate targets of trash talk, modifying their behavior depending on the nature of the social networks in which they are operating (Consalvo 2007). Norms of democratic participation in processes of deliberation and decision-making, for example, may "inhabit" and continually re-animate certain kinds of political network structures (Mische 2008). And norms concerning the appropriate spatial distance to maintain between people during social interaction, and the appropriate degree of frankness of conversation to observe – norms which certainly vary cross-culturally – would clearly seem to have an impact on social network formation.

Culture as Schemas and Frames

John Levi Martin's suggestion that we interact with the world through *Gestalt* typifications that have network-like properties resonates with the idea that culture provides us with schemas through which we organize and sort experience.[5] Such a representation of culture was articulated perhaps most notably by William Sewell (1992). According to Sewell, schemas are some set of mental constructs, typically not fully conscious, that give shape to our perception and knowledge of the world, and the expectations we bring to bear on it.[6] The notion of schema encompasses things like "conventions, recipes, scenarios, principles of action, and habits of speech and gesture" (1992: 8), transposable across situations, guiding our action. They are definitely cultural constructs – not just biological features of how we perceive the world.

Schemas differ from norms in two ways. First, norms have a moral connotation to them in a way that is not necessarily true of schemas, which are fundamentally perceptual and cognitive (DiMaggio 1997; Zerubavel 1997; Vaisey 2009). Second, whereas norms can be commonly formulated about specific, individual actions or situations, the notion of schema suggests a more complex set of interrelated perceptions and rules, some – but not all – of which may have a normátive aspect. Some aspect of schemas may be more related to styles of thinking and acting than to "social facts" about how to behave. Eating spaghetti with a fork instead of your hands might be a kind of gastronomic norm; but the ritual of an Italian dinner, knowing what wine goes with what food, knowing what things are served when and knowing their names in Italian, knowing the difference between *rigatoni* and *orecchiette* and which might be better eaten with what sauce, knowing that there is no "x" in *espresso*, and so on – these things collectively constitute something like a schema of the Italian meal. These component parts need not always appear together, nor do they go together as a matter of logical inevitability. Nevertheless, they appear to form a more or less coherent constellation of practices, judgments, and expectations.

Somewhat akin to the idea of schema is the idea of frame, famously explored by Erving Goffman (1974), and later adopted by many others. Following Goffman, Jan Fuhse (2013: 191) defines frames as "abstract and general models of 'what is going on.'" More rooted in social interactional than a schema – and therefore more thoroughly impinging on ongoing action within social networks – a frame establishes (or tries to impose) a common understanding of a social situation, and therefore creates expectations within situations (and, especially, within interpersonal encounters) about what should be done, how it should be done, and with whom.

The concept of the frame can run the gamut from complex things like differing national cultures framing and filtering the interpretation of films, plays, and novels, and guiding the terms on which social interaction is undertaken (in which case it blurs into the notion of schema), to ostensibly simple (though often ambiguous) issues like: "Is this thing you are doing for me an expression of friendship, or more like a business transaction?" A frame can entail fairly non-strategic cognition (in which case, again, it is quite like a schema), but it can also be the fundamental instrument of highly strategic or emotionally charged social network activity, as in con games, favor-seeking, social movement mobilization, and representations of different groups in the media (Goffman 1969; Snow et al. 1986; Bail 2012). As Fuhse (2013: 192–3) reminds us with respect to interpersonal relationships, multiple frames might be in play at any given time: is this interaction to be understood as "friendship, casual acquaintance, flirt, love affair, love," or perhaps yet something else? Figuring out the appropriate and/or intended meaning of an interaction involves discerning cues or signals as to which frame is actually primary, and subsequently implementing a schema appropriate for the interaction. Thus, frames are fluid and contingent, in some contrast with norms and schemas, which are typically thought of as more static, prior to interaction, and not very quickly changeable (although changes in norms can diffuse, for example, through networks over time).

Schemas and frames are crucially important to the study of networks when we can articulate clearly how they guide the formation of networks in the first place – for example, who connects with whom, how strongly ties are forged, whether they can be broken, and so on. Think, for example, of the traditional Catholic notion of heterosexual marriage as a schema, with the expectations it encourages that people will form kinship networks in which they will be married forever, have many children (because birth control is discouraged), forge strong ties to extended family, and favor the entrance of eldest sons into the priesthood or the family business. And think of how different a get-together will be, and how many different people could be involved, if it is framed as a social outing instead of a date.

Important Approaches to Culture for the Sociology of Networks

While theorists like Swidler and Goffman certainly provide distinctive "approaches" to the study of culture, I have used them instead to identify elements of culture that sociologists could study when exploring the different ways that culture and networks intersect. In this section, I shift to more thoroughgoing conceptual frameworks, or schools of thought, concerning the intersection of networks and culture. I discuss Pierre Bourdieu's conceptual framework for the study of culture, the production of culture perspective of Richard Peterson, and Harrison White's efforts to re-think the entire study of networks through a cultural lens.

Culture as Generative Dispositions: Pierre Bourdieu

Undoubtedly one of the most important and provocative contributors to the study of culture in the last fifty years has been Pierre Bourdieu. This is so for several reasons, and many of these reasons are relevant to the intersection of culture and social networks. First, he articulates (1990) how actions in the world are deeply affected by what he calls *habitus*: the set of mental dispositions we bear and the principles we act upon for classifying things, derived from our occupancy of particular structural positions in the social order. Habitus resembles the notion of schema discussed in the previous section (Vaisey 2009) – except that it refracts the idea of schema through the crucial lenses of social structure and social inequality. Habitus is a concept for expressing how culture is formative to experience, specifically how it contributes to the reproduction of a social order – including patterns of social relations – characterized by inequality. Second, Bourdieu (1984) stresses that social inequality – distinction – is crucially expressed through cultural objects and practices. Furthermore, the meaning of those objects and practices is generated doubly *relationally*: they derive their meaning relative to each other, and relative to the persons and groups who possess or enact them. This idea has inspired a good deal of empirical research on cultural consumption. Third, with the concept of social capital, and the idea of the convertibility of different forms of capital, Bourdieu (1986) provides a conceptual framework for thinking about how social network patterns and cultural tastes connect and interpenetrate, potentially on an ongoing basis.

First, then, Bourdieu insists that cultural tastes are produced through the agency of habitus: sets of "durable, transposable dispositions" (1990: 53) toward the world, learned and reinforced through experience. The habitus provides the cognitive and moral framework through which one perceives objects and partakes in activities in the world. It guides practical activity and sense-making, not only with respect to familiar objects and activities, but also with respect to new objects, people, and activities as they are encountered. People from particular social classes will not have identical habituses, but there will be a resemblance of their experiences (a homology among them) – the more so to the extent they associate with each other and interact with each other to the exclusion of network ties to members of other classes.

Particular tastes are associated with distinctly different class positions, or, by extension, different positions in any social structure (Bourdieu 1984). Put too simply, a taste for classical music, nouvelle cuisine, phrases from foreign languages, black-and-white photography, designer clothing, golf, and so on, is associated with the dominant classes. A taste for country music, fast-food restaurants, mass-produced beer, family snapshots, Snuggies®, and monster trucks, on the other hand, tends to be associated with the lower classes. Frequently, specialized languages – technical languages or professional argot – are key means by which powerful sets of actors tied extensively to each other effect social network closure, thereby demarcating – both culturally and structurally speaking – the boundaries that separate them from the ordinary run of people. This practice was especially salient in the French educational system, which Bourdieu (1988) examined critically and at length, in which the transmission of valued cultural knowledge and credentials routinely happens through network ties between mentors and students, and through kinship and friendship ties within and between well-placed families.

Bourdieu stresses that his framework for understanding social life is thoroughly *relational* (Bourdieu and Wacquant 1992: 15). Superficially, this emphasis links Bourdieu to the various branches of so-called "relational sociology" (Emirbayer 1997; Crossley 2011; Mische 2011; Dépelteau and Powell 2013), of which social network analysis is one branch. More substantively, Bourdieu sees the value of cultural objects and the status position of social actors as deeply intertwined. Black-and-white photography is an esoteric art form *because* high-status people value it; "monster trucks" is a low-status cultural pastime *because* low-status people enjoy it. Overall, there is a correspondence between the hierarchy of cultural goods and the hierarchy of culture consumers, because the two hierarchies *constitute* each other. Culture provides equipment for success in achieving privileged positions, and those positions in turn provide privileged access to the cultural means of achieving distinction (Mohr 2013: 106–7). This correspondence is one of the prime reasons that patterns of social inequality typically get reproduced durably over time.[7]

The relational quality of cultural tastes runs deeper than Bourdieu himself suggested (Crossley 2011; Mohr 2013). Cultural preferences associated with particular classes are dynamic, and will shift as the cultural equipment of *other* classes changes. Network analysis might help us tackle this dynamism by incorporating evolving data on how cultural goods are actually used. For example, as middle-class consumers acquire Coach or Gucci bags, those goods become abandoned by elites, for whom such possessions are no longer prestige markers. The value of high-status goods is not inherent, but always defined relative to the value of other goods, within a relational field. Now, a field is not quite a network, because the idea of concrete connections between objects in a field is not definitional the way the mapping of concrete connections is definitional to network analysis (de Nooy 2003; Singh forthcoming). Still, we can imagine emergent, inductively observed clusters of cultural objects or practices that tend to be connected to each other by virtue of being possessed by the same person or persons (Lewis et al. 2012). We can also imagine groups whose distance from each other is precisely measurable in terms of the *lack* of overlap in the clusters or networks of cultural objects they esteem (Edelmann and Vaisey 2014).

Much literature in the sociology of culture in recent years has argued that different class positions are distinguished not so much by differentiation of tastes, but rather by the quantity and diversity of tastes expressed. High-status consumers don't consume only high-status goods, thus reflecting only highbrow tastes. Frequently, they consume a broader range of goods, thus earning the label "cultural omnivore." A considerable body of research has explored whether patterns of exclusion in society are expressed more in terms of highbrow preferences or omnivorousness (see, for example, DiMaggio 1987; Peterson 1992; Bryson 1996; Peterson and Kern 1996; Van Eijck 2001; Han 2003; Coulangeon and Lemel 2007; Tanner et al. 2009). Patterns in how cultural tastes are expressed and how they cluster can both be thought of in network terms: tastes are mapped onto, or linked to, groups differentially; and tastes may be concretely linked to each other via the people or groups who share them. A subtle attention to different social positions and their relative empowerment – think not only of class-based hierarchy, but also more complex, historically embedded class positions and subcultures such as "middle-class children of the Depression," or "impoverished graduate students" – is necessary to understand the distribution of cultural tastes today. Clusters of valued cultural objects continue to evolve, and an ever-expanding collection of cultural objects or areas of cultural activity become the raw material of expertise. Comic books, once trashy publications, become the objects of devoted fascination and detailed knowledge. Graphic novels, once indistinguishable from comic books, become venerated by young *literati*, catalyzing enthusiasts' network solidarity. In short, and without being able to explore the details here, the actual objects and activities that serve as markers of social exclusiveness change; but network thinking is a flexible method for tackling empirical changes in the ways that cultural objects cluster.

Bourdieu was mostly distrustful of network analysis, because he judged it capable of expressing only lifeless and superficial representations of social structure at its most evanescent (Bourdieu and Wacquant 1992: 114; Mohr 2013: 117). The partly accidental patterns of networks at particular moments in time could not capture adequately the qualitative differences between ties, nor evaluate the relative significance of particular groups or particular practices for characterizing deep social structure. Nevertheless, Bourdieu's (1986) treatment of the different types of capital, especially social capital and cultural capital, provides an enlightening framework for linking networks and culture. For Bourdieu, social capital refers to "a durable network of . . . relationships of mutual acquaintance and recognition" (1986: 248). It includes such notions as friends of friends, in addition to membership in high-status groups. Ideally, it results in a kind of prestige ("in-degree centrality" in network terminology), whereby one is known to more people than one knows oneself. Cultural capital refers to the cultivation of one's tastes, as well as possession of status-conveying cultural goods such as books, music, furnishings, and educational credentials. The most interesting thing is Bourdieu's idea of the convertibility of one kind of capital into another: social networks can be an instrument for the accumulation of cultural capital, while tastes and credentials offer entryways into the formation of new networks of social relations (Lizardo 2006; Lewis et al. 2008; Wimmer and Lewis 2010). On the former front, we acquire tastes and beliefs from our friends, and from those we aspire to be like. On the latter front, gifts, dinners, recognition ceremonies, and so on, all play an important symbolic role in cementing network ties.

The Production of Culture Framework

In the 1970s, Richard Peterson began to develop an approach to understanding culture by exploring the circumstances of its production and the technologies by means of which cultural materials are made. As Peterson and Anand (2004: 311) summarize, this perspective "focuses on how the symbolic elements of culture are shaped by the systems within which they are created, distributed, evaluated, taught, and preserved." So, for example, microphones facilitate certain kinds of singing styles, like crooning. Radio needs content and tends to demand formulaic, easily categorized performances. Records and radio networks were essential to the dissemination of popular songs, indeed making them popular. And synergies developed between business and music whenever music and musicians played a role in advertising (Peterson 1997). Among those "systems" that shape cultural production, one must include formal organizations, occupational structures, capitalist markets, and mass media – but also social networks, as a kind of architecture through which and in which culture may be produced and circulated. While social networks were not particularly emphasized in some of the seminal "production of culture" studies (including Diana Crane's (2000) study of fashion, Tia deNora's (1991) account of the institutional and organizational conditions underlying the birth of "serious music" in the time of Beethoven, Priscilla Ferguson's (1998) study of French gastronomy, and Peterson's (1997) entertaining account of the origins and growth of country music), several of the earliest efforts at articulating the perspective (Crane 1976; DiMaggio and Hirsch 1976; Hagstrom 1976; Kadushin 1976) did acknowledge the importance of networks, although without going into much empirical detail. Crane (1976) identified the importance of "gatekeepers," an important structural position, in fostering or suppressing creativity at different times. Gatekeepers can control the flow of persons into networks, the distribution of cultural products out of networks, and/or the flow of contacts between persons (or roles) within networks. DiMaggio and Hirsch (1976) identified the "informal social circle" as a kind of network buffer protecting cultural producers' feelings of self-worth in spite of the fact that their success is typically dependent almost completely on the approval of others, such as audiences, agents, and producers. Such circles can also help to maintain guild-like solidarity in the face of wide disparities in success that different members of a cultural industry may enjoy. DiMaggio and Hirsch (1976: 77) furthermore suggested that cultural production networks must be thought of as including not only artists, but also producers, concert hall owners, fashion house executives, gallery owners, newspaper critics, publicists, and the like, for all are linked in a complex web of dependencies.

This claim for an expansive understanding of the multifarious contributions made to cultural output is also found seminally in the artworlds perspective of Howard Becker (1982). Becker's core idea is that art is produced collaboratively, and frequently massively so. Stay to watch the credits at the end of any movie and meditate on the number of people named there; then multiply that number many times over to begin to approximate the size of the population of contributors to Hollywood movie production at any given time. These contributors may have a lot to do with the tasks perceived as core elements of the artistic product – for example, consider the camera operator on a movie set. Or they may be upstream suppliers – caterers on sets, or suppliers of undeveloped film, or special effects software developers seemingly far removed from movie-making. Not even named there will be downstream distributors – say marketers of DVDs to niche-market consumers, years after the movie was made, or film critics who help to sustain a market for Hollywood's product. Together, though, they form a complex, networked ecology of cultural production.[8] And what is true for Hollywood is equally true for jazz (Lopes 2002), or punk (Crossley 2008), or the broad field of fashion design (Pedrona and Volonté 2014), and any number of other fields.

One might also consider the ideas of "subculture" (Hebdige 1979) and "scene" (Straw 1991, 2002; Bennett and Peterson 2004) in this context. Dick Hebdige (1979) argued classically that subcultures bring together like-minded people, typically on the margins of society – people who may feel partially or wholly left out of mainstream society, and out of tune with social standards. Participation in a subculture allows them to develop a sense of identity and convey that identity through expressive symbolic equipment and gestures: styles of dress, management of the body, specific language or slang, shared activities, and so on. As Fine and Kleinman (1979) suggested long ago, though, the notion of subculture can be rather imprecise. Their view was that past usages of the term focused too much on shared values, or too simply on shared spatial location or shared positions in the social order, and not enough on interactions and practices that defined the boundaries of the group and lent it its vitality. This critique lies behind Fine's (1987, 2012) development of the notion of *idioculture* to deal with the specifics of interaction in quite local settings. Sometimes the notion of subculture leaves imprecise the problem of who is and who is not included in the group. Influence may be understood to float around throughout the subculture, rather than being exercised through particular chains of contact. On the other hand, network-based approaches to the production of culture may not be able to handle the diversity of types of participating actors, nor account for the multiple scales (interpersonal, organizational to personal, broadcast, etc.) at which action may take place, nor tap adequately into the diffuse influences shaping cultural outcomes. In fact, even more than subculture, "scene" seems well designed to capture this heterogeneous composition and flow of influences, but perhaps therefore less amenable to social network analysis techniques. "Scene" emphasizes more than subculture the spatial basis of cultural activity, over and above the active coming together of participants. Consequently, "scene" imparts a heightened sense of dynamic ebb and flow over time, rather than static membership.

Culture at the Heart of Network Theory

Since Harrison White published *Identity and Control* in 1992, but especially since the mid-1990s (White 1995; Mische and White 1998; Mohr and White 2008; White 2008; Godart and White 2010; Fontdevila and White 2013), network theorists have sought to incorporate culture directly into the core of network theory. Their fundamental claim has been that "social (read: networks) and interpretive (read: culture) remain entangled right down to basal construction" of the social order (White et al. 2007: 548).

The cultural content of network relations typically comes from the vast array of cultural materials and communicative competencies persons and organizations develop as they mature. But White's starting point is to imagine those moments of potential network building where rich cultural competencies have not yet been accumulated, or – more realistically – where we have some cultural equipment, but we are not sure what cultural framing of the situation is the most apt one (cf. Padgett 2012). Whenever we cut into real-world social networks, we should find plenty of culture there. But for exposition purposes, can we consider carefully how networks get started? And how can something like culture be present there, at the origins? Once we establish that point – that it *is* there – we can subsequently think about how more complex, detailed, rich, iterated, forms of culture arise to constitute and guide network formation.

Joel Podolny (2001) has referred to networks as the pipes and prisms of the market. While he intended the "prisms" image to signify the "cultural" part – we evaluate the quality of market participants through the lens of the types of network ties they have, and participants are constrained by the status ranks and cognitive categories into which they fit – consider instead for a moment the pipes metaphor. Imagine a bunch of pipes, possibly of different sizes, lengths, and materials. These can be assembled into a "plumbing" network. But pipes require some kind of coupling devices or other specific design features to fit together. Sometimes there is a whorl pattern etched into the pipe's end allowing it to be screwed into another piece; sometimes coupling pieces exist (elbow joints, t-joints, and so on) into which the main pipes can be inserted. We could think of these coupling devices as instruments of communication or connection between the pipes. The whorl pattern, or the joint, communicates possible and not-so-possible connections. These couplings "afford" opportunities for connecting (White 1995: 1046).

We could also think in terms of relational "protocols" (Padgett and Powell 2012: 3): some simple kind of script or routine or equipment facilitating connections within networks – say, chemical reactions within metabolic processes, or dropdown menus of potential recipients within email programs, or deposit slips used to facilitate banking. These don't sound richly cultural, but they get us thinking about the need for communication at the most basic, even primitive, genesis of social network connections (Fuhse 2015). White (1995) uses the example of pheromone chemical signaling among animals as an example of an elemental, pre-cultural communicative device. Yet grunts and gestures, as well as "talk," are *continuations* of such devices, not utterly different from them.[9] "Talk" is conceptually distinct from "discourse." "Discourse" conjures rich vocabularies, conceptual sophistica-tion, and reflexive thought – all of which develop later, but are largely absent in the preliminary instances of talk (1995: 1058). Eventually, a lot of cultural material – well-known idioms, jokes, popular cultural products, other fodder for conversation – is lying about, waiting to be activated at the point where networks are initiated. Templates also arise between non-individual actors: con-tract templates between companies, declarations of war between countries, and so on. So discourse and communicative sophistica-tion develop over time, at the collective level, and within particular social network settings, just as rudimentary instruments of com-munication exist from the outset.

Consider speed dating (McFarland, Jurafsky, and Rawlings 2013) as an illuminating example. First moves are tentative and hesitant. Talk is present, necessarily, but uncomfortably so, as it is hard to bring rich vocabularies and deep narration into play. Talk is more or less idle, halting (though sometimes suggestive) banter at this point. We are minutely attuned to gestures as signals, based on past experience; but we may hardly be able to put into words what we are thinking when we perceive those gestures. We simply couldn't participate in this formation of network ties without talk; but it would be a mistake to think all of the rich cultural meanings and significance of romantic love, for example, are fully in place or explicitly activated yet! They become so, as we deepen our tie with a particular actor (Fuhse 2013), and/or as we build up a repertoire of ties with multiple actors.[10]

Let's continue, keeping the speed dating example in mind. Participants seek a *footing* with each other (Goffman 1981): some alignment of their actions that makes rudimentary coupling possible. The amount of uncertainty in initial social encounters is great, and we generally want to reduce it.[11] We are driven by a search for what White calls "control": getting some grasp on things, or some minimal sense of "what is going on here."

Drawing on Goffman's terminology, the urge to get a grasp on "what is going on here" catalyzes the establishment of a "frame" (1974) within which the exchange of gestures or signals takes place; or perhaps we can think of the enactment of a "line" (1967), a stream of verbal and nonverbal behavior that communicates a recognizable course of action. Seeking control by establishing a "line" creates and conveys an "identity." This is a thin notion of identity, not the "thick" one adopted by many sociologists, implying self-consciousness and the embedding of actors in rich historical and cultural contexts. In empirical settings, identity can become enriched and develop into a sense of self, but that is not theoretically necessary. Establishing a line need not convey something "real" about the actor who establishes it. It is chosen, perhaps capriciously, from available communicative tools. These tools are meaningful, not in the minds of actors as richly significant subjective understandings, but between actors, as functional, recognizable coupling devices (Fuhse 2015). Swidler's notion of a toolkit applies: lines are pieced together hastily out of available bits and pieces, using successful past repertoires of action when they are handy. The quest for "control" will then involve tagging others with identities as much as establishing our own. Thus those people we encounter in initial networking sessions become to us "Ms. Diet Coke," or "the guy with the Hello Kitty backpack," or "Bad Breath," or "Toronto."

The lines and identities established through talk give some fixity to social life; but that fixity is constantly disrupted by the flow of events. The bell rings in our speed dating set-up: suddenly you are on to the next person! White (1995) and later Godart and White (2010) refer to these moments as switchings, a term that is frustratingly ill defined. As we exit one episode and enter another, that switch demarcates the first experience (White 1995: 1049). Presumably, as it ends, some period is put on it that stops the flow of action and bounds it. Boundaries impart meanings (Abbott 1995; Lamont and Molnar 2002); and, in fact, boundaries define entities – so that both the entities found in networks and the events happening in networks emerge through the flow of communication and exchange. Furthermore, Godart and White

(2010) claim that the meaning of any one episode or network tie arises in contrast with other ties. Say we get a text from a friend while finishing up dinner with the family. We are quite adept at switching between the two modes of interaction, and in some way the meaning of each interaction is made clearer by its contrast with the style and content of the other. We are also not really likely to switch into the wrong mode in either relation, suggesting we act with a clear, albeit often implicit, schema of what each specific network is about.

As we move to higher levels of aggregation, ties tend to cluster with other ties that are constituted by the same meanings. That is, some of the fixity in the meaning of network connections may be achieved by the involuted, clustered nature of many networks, wherein meaning is reinforced and repeated across ties. For example, cordial business-like forms of interaction may proliferate and become reinforced among networks of acquaintances at professional conferences. This example might suggest that networks come first, and cultural frames follow. But successful footings in one locale could well lead actors to attempt similar footings in proximate settings, which, if successful, will create new network clusters.

When particular meanings are concentrated in particular ties, a *netdom* emerges: a network structure comprised of ties recurrently formed using the same domain or constellation of "stories, symbols, and expectations" (White et al. 2007: 549). The netdom idea doesn't sound so different from the kinds of social groupings cultural sociologists frequently study: a set of actors bound to each other in some way and interacting through distinctive forms of communication. But rather than assuming the existence of a group, and a culture that circulates within the group, White et al. unpack the emergence of any group and trace its pathway to shared meanings, starting from contingencies in interaction which trigger identities. The network concept permits a more concrete tracing of the boundaries of a group, and a finer assessment of which positions enjoy disproportionate influence in catalyzing particular cultural practices.

The netdom concept splices culture and network with each

other at a semantic, and hence substantive, level. Undoubtedly, frequently, certain conversations fit better in certain networks than others. However, don't assume too "hard-wired" a view of the relationship between network on the one hand and cultural domain on the other.[12] Ostensibly similar networks may operate within different meaning domains. For instance, one network of people undertaking the task of living a more "green" lifestyle may talk about their activity in terms of simplifying life and reducing their carbon footprint, while another doing essentially the same thing may talk in terms of stewardship and joint responsibility (Lorenzen 2012). For another thing, frequently there are switchings among meaning domains within a given network. To take an extreme example, a bridge club and a swingers' club may have very different interaction styles – even if the membership of the two groups is identical, and partnering routines just as circulatory and promiscuous! Essentially, the same network can entail multiple netdoms. More pervasively, a given network of actors will change the terms of their interaction as the setting shifts, or as new situations arise. One illuminating example is how a group of employees loosen their ties and their tongues as they shift to the bar for a drink after work. Mische and White (1998: 702) define domain precisely as "the perceived array of such signals – including story sets, symbols, idioms, registers, grammatical patternings, and accompanying corporeal markers – that characterize a particular specialized field of interaction." Thus, "domain" is not an abstract, unitary thing like "the economy," or "the office," or "family life." A netdom may be quite idiosyncratic – for example, the way talk within video game play may consist of discussion of a set of exemplary/admired games, plus trash talk, plus specialized gaming vocabulary, plus reference to appropriate gaming foods, plus medieval imagery, plus elements of misogyny and homophobia, and more (Khanolkar and McLean 2012). Once domain is understood as an actual field of meaningful action and experience, Gary Alan Fine's (1987, 2012) idea of idioculture returns to the fore as a compatible framework for identifying the idiosyncratic cultural repertoires and discursive gestures of emergent networks. While in some cases we can imagine a tight coupling between network structure and cultural domain, in other cases that connection is not very tight. That is why I object to the idea that particular networks – and even particular types of networks, such as "economic networks," or "political networks" – must be constituted by particular and distinctive "logics." Humans are too "promiscuous" (Mann 1986: 17–28) and resourceful in their use of cultural materials to accept such a simplistic mapping of culture to network.

As encounters between identities persist, "stories" emerge explaining how identities are linked (White 1995: 1042). For a somewhat silly example, let's say "Diet Coke and Toronto found out they live in the same dorm, and now they're dating!" Or, more elaborately, within the netdom of the Renaissance Florentine export-oriented commercial trade, partnership contracts and consignment sales could be thought of as stock "stories" that linked businessmen together. Stories foster the durability of ties, helping episodic ties deepen into relations – which is to say, component parts of networks.

These stories are not richly evocative literary constructs at first. They begin as post hoc, on-the-fly ways of stabilizing ties. As they become richer, they string together multiple events, and multiple identities, thus becoming themselves something like mini-networks of meanings (Godart and White 2010: 572). As they become richer still, they can grow, in the context of ongoing relationships, into highly nuanced and detailed narratives of the history of that relationship (Fuhse 2013). Relationships become laden with expectations and history: memories of particular places, meals eaten together, shared laughs, and so on. Relationships are idiosyncratic in part, but they also get constructed out of existing archetypes and existing narrative elements in the "cultural system" at large (Fuhse 2013: 189) – a reservoir of representations which only at this point in the theory begins to play a major role. Henceforth, stories can also articulate links between multiple nodes in a network: "The department administrator receives the form from the Dean, passes it to her administrative assistant to fill in details on the candidate for promotion, then sends it to the Personnel Committee for drafting and editing before handing it off to the Chair for a signature." Such a mini-story narrates the pattern of relations among organizational roles – a pattern that persists regardless of who actually staffs those positions. And if the same procedure can be used by other departments, then we observe the emergence of a transposable repertoire of rules or schemas for organizational operation – which brings us to a notion of schema quite a bit like the one I introduced earlier.

Beyond this point, White and his co-authors move on to discuss larger, more complex and more codified cultural phenomena such as styles, rhetorics, and institutions, but I refrain from dealing with those here.[13] The key point is that those developed cultural constructs need to be understood as evolving phenomena, arising after much preliminary work. That is the sense behind Godart and White's claim (2010: 582) that what we conventionally think of as culture is in fact a "second order social construct," not emerging in full flower, like Athena springing from the head of Zeus, but built up hesitantly in fresh episodes of interaction.

Why Cultural Sociology Needs Networks

I conclude this chapter with some treatment of theoretical perspectives in which culture and networks work closely together. I want to stress specific benefits that cultural sociologists may obtain from incorporating a network perspective in their research. Simply put, although culture sometimes seems to float free of society as a rich set of representations and concepts, it is important that the sociological study of culture treat culture as *situated in social structures and social interaction,* and network analysis provides one of the most rigorous and flexible ways to situate, observe, and map the deployment of cultural phenomena concretely (Kirchner and Mohr 2010). Our own personal social networks today – both face-to-face networks, and social media-based networks – are places in which culture circulates in determinate ways on an everyday basis, taking on considerable specificity of shared meaning as a result. But we can think of the situated quality of culture at the macro level as well as the micro, as I will point out below.

Equally importantly, some features of culture should be understood as *emergent properties*, rather than as simply given. Networks are places in which emergent properties of culture are incubated, and cultures may develop in divergent ways depending on these different network pathways and structures. In other words, culturally oriented sociologists *must* be sensitive to the reality that culture may be constituted, reinforced, or altered via networks, with different network structures channeling culture in different directions.

Humans don't exist in general, abstractly, but always already in relations and interdependencies (Crossley 2011: 15). A "social world" is comprised of both ongoing "networks of interaction" (2011: 138) and "shared meanings, purposes, knowledge, understandings, identities (collective and individual), conventions, etc., all of which affect the way in which those within it act" (Crossley 2010b: 7; also see de Nooy 2009). The study of social interaction, and the inter-subjectivity that resides in it and results from it, has a long history, going back to W. E. B. Dubois, Charles Horton Cooley, George Herbert Mead, and Herbert Blumer. That line of theorizing is profoundly important and insightful, and symbolic interactionism provides great conceptual equipment for understanding social interaction as a culturally embedded process. One shortcoming, though, is that it has tended to focus on inter-subjectivity and the creation of meaning at the *dyadic* level. To be sure, Mead develops the idea of the Generalized Other, as well as the notion of "institution," both of which entail developing a general orientation to the world based on the attitudes and expectations that we learn *many* others have of us as we interact with them. Nevertheless, the theoretical focus stresses the individual and the constitution of each of us as a self. Arguably more complex are those cases in which many different selves (and many different takes on social reality) are simultaneously constituted through interaction. Here I have in mind studies of small group interaction, such as William Foote Whyte's (1993 [1943]) classic work on gang life, or Gary Alan Fine's (1987) brilliant ethnography of patterns of interaction among kids on Little League baseball teams,[14] or David Krackhardt's (1987) influential research on advice flows and cultural convergence among a set of managers (also see Krackhardt and Kilduff 2002), or David Gibson's (2012) detailed re-examination of decision-making during the Cuban Missile Crisis. Such studies depend implicitly or explicitly on the idea that subcultures, or youth idiocultures, or managerial cultures, or political decision-making schemas, arise in specific social settings, settings which can be conceived of concretely as networks of interaction, communication, and influence, and which therefore often can be depicted using the vocabulary of networks and network analytic tools.

While precise mappings of the flow of culture through networks become more difficult as the scale of social groups grows, different theorists have used network language to characterize large formations in network terms, in conjunction with some sense of culture. For example, Kivinen and Piiroinen (2013) use the term *niche* to identify places in which sets of cultural scripts and structures of human interaction recursively constitute each other. Culture – in the form of language, practices, or ideas – and social structure – in the form of social networks – act as contexts for each other's development. Some look to Norbert Elias' (1994 [1939]: 442) concept of "figuration" for inspiration: a relational nexus of classes, political actors, institutions, and cultural practices, solidified into an abiding historical arrangement. Of course, Elias himself defined the civilizing process in Europe over several hundred years through the development of *both* manners (cultural recipes and schemas) and early modern state institutions (structures), in conjunction with one another.

Michael Mann's (1986) work is similar, in which "networks" replace "societies" as the most important elements in the history of power: "Human beings pursuing many goals set up many networks of social interaction" (1986: 27). These networks differ by virtue of the predominant sources of social power upon which they draw – ideological, economic, military, or political – and therefore they differ in terms of their intensiveness, and their capacity to coordinate action. Ideologically based networks in particular, such as those based on religious beliefs (think of the network of early Christian churches to which Paul wrote letters, for example), tend to extend over great expanses of space, but are diffuse in their capacity to coordinate action. At certain times, the organization of the flows of resources within stable networks in contained geographic spaces has led to the "caging" of populations (1986: 38), lifting those networks and the populations in which they exist to new levels of not only economic but also cultural development. Admittedly, the language of networks here is mostly metaphorical, but Mann intends us to think about patterns of large-scale social organization in network terms, and to think about the diverse forms of coordination and communication made possible by those diverse network structures.

I will offer here just a few points on how networks can be vitally important in causing certain cultural features to emerge or spread, since much of the next two chapters is devoted to this theme. For one thing, while we might be inclined to think of certain cultures as characterized by a great deal of within-group trust – for example, Jewish diamond merchants, or immigrant businessmen participating in rotating credit associations (Portes and Sensenbrenner 1993) – it may be that trust in those groups is really a function of network structure and the ability of members of such groups to monitor each other via multiple pathways. A similar claim has been made by Greif (1989) and by Padgett and McLean (2011) about the importance of networks for monitoring the trustworthy behavior of long-distance merchants in overseas ports. Trust emerges and is reinforced only in the context of specific network structures that permit oversight.

Dense networks afford opportunities for *creativity*. Such creativity, or innovation, is not, strictly speaking, predictable from the attributes of the actors in a network themselves, but rather arises through "coordination and mutual influence" (Crossley 2011: 146) among actors in a network. Network cohesion and density also encourage *value commitments* that can result in patterns of mobilization and consolidations of identity otherwise not achievable, such as many black, Southern church congregations supplied to the American civil rights movement (McAdam 1988). Network cohesion and density may also differentiate those within a network from those outside it, thus protecting cohesive network-based deviant groups from being "contaminated" with mainstream beliefs and schemas (for example, Becker 1963). Additionally, as Krackhardt and Kilduff (2002: 281) note, part of what is communicated through social networks within organizations is information about the social network itself. Consequently, where individuals cluster densely within organizational networks, "potentially idiosyncratic understandings of many aspects of organizational culture including the structure of roles and relationships" are likely to develop.

Network centralization may support hierarchy as a value, and may reinforce status differences as important elements of cultural *content*. Centralization will also allow certain actors to influence the spread of particular ideas to a disproportionate extent. Paying inadequate attention to network structure can lead us to misconstrue the successful spread of certain ideas as a function of their excellence or their cultural resonance, rather than as a function of their network distribution. Finally, some of the spread and the hybrid mixture of cultural ideas may arise from the layering of different social network ties on top of each other, such as occurs with the multiplex ties idea introduced in the last chapter, or the notion of overlapping social circles. We might well misunderstand how culture changes, unless we attempt to trace its reception and reproduction within and across different networks of adopters.

Conclusion

In this chapter, I have identified a number of important elements of culture, and a number of approaches to the study of culture, that are especially germane to research on social networks. I have explained how Harrison White and his co-authors have imagined culture to be present at the very origins of network formation, as well as ways in which they imagine culture grows richer and more complex as social network patterns solidify within particular netdoms. Finally, I have very briefly discussed how important it is to think of culture not in some disembodied way, but as situated in particular social spaces and expressed via social interaction.

Culture in Networks

Networks provide a framework for tracing patterns of social interaction, and these patterns can have a constitutive effect on cultural development. Thus, those students intent on doing cultural analysis, especially via ethnographic methods, ought strongly to consider gathering network data alongside their cultural data, to see how meanings are concretely shaped and distributed via networks.

PART II

Linkages of Networks with Culture

4

Culture through Networks: Diffusion, Contagion, Virality, Memes

A recent calculation suggests that some 6.8 billion mobile phones are in use around the world (mobiThinking 2014). With a global population of a little over 7 billion people, it would seem we are approaching a time in which every human being on the planet has direct, or close to direct, access to a cellular phone. Of course, this is not quite true. In some countries, there are more cellphones than people. There were more mobile phone lines than landlines in the United States by 2006, and in 2010, about 30 percent of the US population had only a mobile phone (Rainie and Wellman 2012: 25). In other countries – North Korea being an extreme case in point – cellphones remain rare. A *Time* magazine report from March 2013, using UN data, suggests that more people worldwide have access to cellphones than to working toilets (Wang 2013). Within the phenomenon of cellphone growth, smartphone usage in particular has grown – a bit slowly at first, but dramatically in the last few years, now accounting for 15 to 20 percent of all phones in use. For a technology that has been with us no more than thirty years, the penetration of the cellphone into worldwide usage is amazing.

Here we have the *diffusion* of a technology, and in fact the diffusion of a particular technology (the smartphone) within a broader process of technological diffusion (cellphones more generally). Alternatively, we might say that adoption of the technology is *contagious*, and we are observing a process of *contagion*. At first blush, there seems nothing particularly cultural in the diffusion of a technology such as this – even though the cellphone is a conduit for a vast quantity of cultural material, and it is not far-fetched to regard the cellphone semiotically as a symbol of modernity, or economic success, or personal style. Before we turn to the theme of cultural diffusion more specifically, however, the cellphone example illustrates nicely some of the basic elements involved in the general process of diffusion. The percentage of adopters is low at the beginning. That percentage grows slowly at first, but then it takes off more or less dramatically, often as a certain threshold is passed (Granovetter 1978; Gladwell 2000) with the achievement of a critical mass of users (Centola 2013). Toward the end of the process, as a saturation point is reached, growth slows.[1] The process traces out an S-curve pattern over time, more or less the defining visual representation of the diffusion dynamic (Rogers 2003: 11).

How does diffusion work? Often the process is facilitated and accelerated via broadcast[2] messages. Think, for example, of ads for the iPhone we see on television, in magazines, and on billboards. But often a crucial element in diffusion is direct contact between those who have already adopted, and those about to do so, or between those already persuaded and those about to become so. Your friends with smartphones may actively encourage you to get one. For another example, infectious diseases are often passed via direct contact between those infected and those about to become infected. Here we encounter head on the importance of social network ties for understanding diffusion. In fact, a cardinal assumption of much diffusion research is that we can better understand what is going on if we understand the topology – the shape and patterns – of the social network in which that diffusion occurs, and if we know more about the positions of particular persons or organizations within that network. Certain kinds of diffusion may take off once highly central actors in the network adopt – although it is sometimes quite marginal actors who are the very first ones willing to take a chance on new gadgets and new fashions! With respect to ideas or styles, relatively early adopters are often referred to as *opinion leaders* (Katz and Lazersfeld 1955; Burt 1999; Valente and Davis 1999).[3] Many culture industries

66

have their opinion leaders who kickstart and/or accelerate processes of diffusion: for example, fashion magazines and designers (Kawamura 2004; Godart & Mears 2009; Mears 2011), movie critics (Allen and Lincoln 2004), or food writers (Ferguson 1998). Conversely, diffusion may halt in particular communities unless what is being diffused is adopted by persons or groups who occupy bridge positions, or who cultivate weak tie relations (Granovetter 1973), to other clusters within the network.

Let's ponder the mechanisms triggering diffusion processes. Perhaps you want a smartphone because your friends already own one and are pushing you to get one, too. This would be a process of *influence*, a topic of sociological research often tightly linked with studies of diffusion (for example, Kadushin 2012: ch. 9).[4] Or it might simply be rational to do what others are doing: having a telephone makes the most sense if others have one, too (Fischer 1992). Frequently, we pay special attention to *particular* others or particular *types* of high-status others who have previously displayed their preferences (DiMaggio and Garip 2011). Emulation and sensitivity to opinion leaders is probably more important as a mechanism of diffusion when it comes to sensitive topics like politics, and assuredly more so with respect to cultural objects like fashions. Picking up a fashion depends not only on whom one is connected to, but the cultural perceptions attached to those particular ones to whom one is connected! Overall, it is important (and challenging) to tease out exactly which mechanisms of diffusion are operating, the nature of the objects being diffused, the attributes and positions of the actors among whom diffusion is taking place, and the relative importance of broadcast messages and direct network interactions, if we are to understand and explain any given process of diffusion adequately (Dobbin et al. 2007).

As I have already implied, diffusion frequently concerns the transmission of cultural materials. The sharing of knowledge, the spread of particular repertoires of protest, the propagation of fads and fashions, the spread of musical tastes, the dissemination of social norms: all these and more are cultural processes involving the diffusion of cultural "things," happening wholly or in part via social networks. Similarly, while we frequently talk about contagion with respect to diseases, enthusiasms are contagious as well (Collins 2004), the way Beatlemania was, or more recently the way Bieber Fever (www.bieberfever.com) is, or was. Such an idea of emotional contagion within a social group certainly goes back as far as the notion of collective effervescence in Emile Durkheim's (1995 [1912]) *The Elementary Forms of Religious Life.*[5]

Everett Rogers, the patriarch of diffusion studies, arguably places culture at the heart of many diffusion processes. The diffusion of innovations – his special concern – takes place not through simple infection, but by means of *communication* about a new idea, practice, or object (2003: 6, 12). Because innovative ideas or practices generally must be somehow compatible with existing cultural frames and norms, the diffusion of innovations must be seen as "a social process, even more than a technical matter" (2003: 4). This framework – that diffusion involves ideas about behavior, framed within cultural schemas, rather than the spreading of rote behaviors – is also succinctly emphasized by Elihu Katz:

> Good diffusion studies can usually answer to the definition that they are addressing the spread of (1) an item, idea, or practice, (2) over time, and (3) to adopting units (individuals, groups, corporate units), embedded in (4) channels of communication, (5) social structures (networks, community, class), and (6) social values, or culture. (1999: 147)

Culture ought to be present in good diffusion studies, both in the nature of the thing being diffused, and as one element of the context in which diffusion takes place, affecting its speed and degree of success. Studies of social diffusion processes, absent an understanding of culture as content, and culture as context, are likely to be mechanical exercises.

Rogers also stresses the importance and value of *re-invention* in diffusion processes (2003: 17; Lopes 1999). Diffusion rarely involves simple replication. Common ideas about technology diffusion might give that impression, although sociologists of science have long recognized that technology changes in significant ways as it is domesticated by new users (Oudshoorn and Pinch 2003). Emphasizing that re-invention, recombination, local adaptation, and improvisation are built into diffusion processes helps us to see them more fully as culturally shaped.

How Social Networks Affect Diffusion

In this section, I discuss specific *mechanisms* by which social network structures affect the diffusion of cultural things. I begin with James Coleman, Elihu Katz, and Herbert Menzel's (1957, 1966) study of the diffusion of the use of the drug tetracycline among a number of doctors in four Illinois cities, a study widely regarded as a classic in the field of diffusion studies. They sought to discover the social processes leading from trial use of the drug by a few physicians to widespread prescription of the drug. Their fundamental findings were: (1) that doctors most oriented to the medical profession – those having a certain professional *identity* – tended to be among the earliest adopters; and (2) "the degree of a doctor's integration among his local colleagues was strongly and positively related to the date of his first use of the new drug" (Coleman et al. 1957: 257). Thus, there were both cultural and social-network effects operating in spreading adoption. Critically, diffusion happened, in their view, by direct contact between early adopters and subsequent ones. They also found that network ties were by and large more effective in promoting diffusion early on, when there was more uncertainty about the value of the drug, rather than later.[6]

Coleman et al.'s data has been reanalyzed a number of times, most notably by Ronald Burt (1987). While acknowledging that diffusion can happen when people are infected with the ideas or inclinations of those to whom they are directly connected, Burt argued that diffusion can also happen when people are attentive to the practices of those with whom they share social structural positions, regardless of direct connection. For example, two specialists might pay attention to each other's innovations and adopt them as they compete for the same pool of patients, or they might be prompted to innovate first to gain competitive advantage. The mechanism of spread is different here: competitive emulation between persons occupying the same structural position *vis-à-vis* the rest of the network.

A major theme to explore is how the pattern of ties can matter crucially to the speed and extensiveness of diffusion processes. Most simply, diffusion may happen more quickly and fully in relatively dense networks (Hedstrom 1994). Somewhat more subtly, when those with an initial commitment to a new technology or movement are *clustered* with each other within a larger network, they can affirm each other's commitment, influence those to whom they are in turn connected to join the movement, and thereby initiate a cascade of growing participation (Kim and Bearman 1997). But the early enthusiasts often must be clustered or such a critical mass for further diffusion may not arise.

Oliver and Myers (2003: 174) offer a variety of models of how network structures affect diffusion processes, to determine whether different patterns of social organization eventuate in different patterns of social protest activity. While clusters within networks can incubate ideas, they argue that random networks do better than clustered (cliquey) networks at fostering widespread diffusion and/or eliciting sufficient diffusion to spark real explosions of protest.[7] Also, they argue that although network star structures, or hubs, can be excellent for creating local pockets of potential activism, they do not propagate diffusion widely.[8] Their most sobering assessment, however, is that it is difficult to know in any empirical case just what network (or more likely, networks) is in place, and to understand adequately the complexity of how they work.

While being infected with the Ebola virus or becoming HIV-positive may only require exposure to one infected individual,[9] committing oneself to risky or momentous activities like adopting a costly untested technology, or participating in ethically oriented high-risk activism, or joining an absorptive subculture, may require persuasion from multiple sources of social contact. While not all types of cultural diffusion may require reinforcement through multiple channels (for example, maybe only one of our

70

friends need recommend a song for us to buy it and load it on our iPod), diffusion involving practices that require our commitment, or that touch on our identity, is more likely to depend heavily on such reinforcement.

Damon Centola and Michael Macy (2007) explore this issue of so-called *complex contagions* at length. They model different patterns of a generic diffusion process by varying the number of ties needed between two actors in order for one actor to adopt the cultural practice or idea of the other. Generally, we can expect the rate of diffusion to decline or even halt when such reinforcement is required. Centola and Macy remind us that in small-world networks, ties concentrate within clusters, while clusters are linked to each other only by relatively few and weak ties. While Granovetter (1973) argued that weak ties are strong in providing structurally indispensable bridges between local clusters, Centola and Macy argue that they are often not strong enough, structurally speaking, to permit complex contagions to leap outside of local clusters. Thus, again, whether risky ideas and unorthodox cultural practices will diffuse in a network depends on the topology of the network, specifically in the sense that absent patterns of non-local transitive closure, in which multiple remotely located actors are connected multiply to each other, diffusion is unlikely to happen, and certainly extremely unlikely to spread expansively through the network.

To summarize, complex contagion pertains to ideas and practices culturally coded as risky. Adoption of such objects, ideas or practices depends to some extent upon them being seen as legitimate. Chaining oneself to a tree, or participating in violent forms of protest, or for that matter, following Western medical practices in a place where traditional norms about medicine and sexuality persist (Tavory and Swidler 2009; Decoteau 2013): these are risky enough that, absent communication and a *cultural context* or *frame* making them seem reasonable, they won't happen.[10]

The importance of personal networks for the diffusion of cultural objects has been a matter of considerable interest in so-called viral marketing research. For example, Kempe et al. (2005) and Watts and Dodds (2007) have explored the importance of word-of-mouth recommendations in the spread of information concerning new products, and the spread of their appeal. Goldenberg et al. (2001) utilize Granovetter's distinction between strong and weak ties, finding (contrary to what Centola and Macy argued concerning complex contagion) that weak ties are at least as effective as strong ties in spreading product information. Remember, weak ties can help diffuse things to more remote locations in a network, thus accelerating and prolonging the process. They also argue that, while advertising (broadcast messages) is important early on, advertising is overtaken by word-of-mouth (networks) in relative efficacy as the process of product diffusion continues. Iribarren and Moro (2011) suggest that people have a tendency to pass messages along to those people they expect will be interested. Thus, intriguingly, diffusion of cultural objects is guided by expectations about the cultural tastes of one's alters, a process they refer to as "preferential forwarding" (2011: 139).

So far, there has been an implicit assumption that, depending on the structural properties of a network, and depending on where the diffusion process originates, the resulting diffusion outcome is more or less predictable. That assumption is explicitly and elegantly challenged by the fascinating work of Salganik et al. (2006). They begin with the puzzle regarding how popularity in a cultural market can be so unevenly distributed: some actors are superstars and some songs are megahits, but most are one-hit wonders – or, worse, completely unknown. Yet predicting just which products will become super-popular remains rather difficult, even by experts. For example, as they point out, several publishers rejected *Harry Potter* before one said yes; thus, rather quixotically, an international literary phenomenon was born. Salganik et al. argue that success is a function not so much of inherent quality, but of the process by which consumers influence each other in their cultural tastes/choices. They make this argument by means of an experiment involving the participation of over 14,000 young adults, solicited via a website, and a set of forty-eight songs performed by eighteen different, little-known bands.

Participants were assigned to one of two groups ("experimental conditions"). Simplifying the details somewhat, in the first group, participants could decide to listen to songs (which were presented to them on a grid-like menu) based only on information they received about the band. After hearing a song, they would rate it, and could download it if they wished – signaling, presumably, some kind of assessment of its worth. In the second experimental condition, participants were also given information in list format on how many times the song had previously been downloaded by other participants. Those in this latter condition were in turn randomly assigned to one of eight "worlds" ("networks"). Information about downloads diffused within each world, but not between them. The design of the experiment permitted the researchers: (1) to come up with some measure of objective quality or "appeal"; (2) to compare the results of social influence and quality as the basis for song rankings; and (3) to observe variability across networks in the social influence process.

The authors found, first, that disparity in the popularity of songs was always greater under conditions of social influence than conditions in which only band-related information was provided. Second, the disparity in the popularity of songs was greater when participants were shown a list of songs which either explicitly or implicitly ranked the songs by how often they had been downloaded. Popular songs attracted more listeners – an example of the preferential attachment process I mentioned in chapter 2. Third, and perhaps most importantly, they observed that the popularity of any given song varied considerably across the eight influence worlds. Thus, under conditions of social influence, whether a given song was going to become popular was rather unpredictable. They found some correlation between the quality of a song as it was evaluated by participants in the no-social-influence condition and its popularity ranking by participants in one of the eight influence worlds, but the relationship was consistently weak. As they put it, across these networks "the 'best' songs never do very badly, and the 'worst' songs never do extremely well, but almost any other result is possible" (2006: 855).

Salganik, Dodds, and Watts acknowledge that, in the real world, mass media are immensely important in channeling the diffusion of popularity in certain directions. Culture is produced, not just distributed. Also, the vastly greater number of songs in the real world probably means consumers have much more limited time to decide on their preferences, rendering signals of past popularity even more salient.[11] This might help explain how certain videos, images, links, etc., go viral on the internet. Salganik et al. also did not allow participants to share their opinions in any meaningful way. The effect of that decision for the outcome is not completely clear. Negative or perplexed feedback from other participants might diminish the disparity in the popularity of songs. Perhaps one would observe the partitioning of listeners into distinct listening communities or polarized subcultures within worlds, the way political discourse has been observed to become polarized (Baldassarri and Bearman 2007).

In one follow-up study (Salganik and Watts 2009), the authors inverted the order of popularity of songs, as they were presented to participants, after an initial wave of socially influenced downloads had taken place. The goal was to see if the group of participants as a whole reversed course in its expressed musical tastes as a function of false "rumors" about the perceived quality of songs. For the most part, this hypothesis was found to be true: "good" songs did worse than they had before when their popularity was reported as being low, and songs that had not been downloaded much became downloaded more when a signal was sent that, actually, they were popular. However, three additional effects were observed: (1) songs initially perceived to be of high quality bounced back more than middle-quality songs, as if the "noise" generated by messing around with the signals of quality would be eventually overcome; (2) listeners were attracted to listening to not only the best-ranked songs, but also the worst-ranked ones (think of the viral popularity a few years ago of Rebecca Black's "Friday" video, for example); and (3) perhaps the disjuncture between what listeners heard when they heard a "good" song and what they were told about the low popularity of the song (and vice versa) challenged listeners' enthusiasm, as the number of song downloads went down after information about song popularity was manipulated.

Let's summarize the arguments covered so far concerning how

networks matter for cultural diffusion. First, we can imagine diffusion occurring via direct network connections, or indirectly via the logic of structural equivalence. We need to consider network density and network structure: how much are actors (of a particular sort) clustered, versus how much is the network randomly structured? Further, at what different stages of the diffusion process do these different structures come into play? We also need to consider whether ideas, attitudes, values, and so on spread through simple contagion, or a more complex contagion. Finally, Salganik et al.'s results indicate that the diffusion of cultural objects, and therefore their resultant popularity, can vary dramatically when exposed to different interpersonal influences or signals – an important reminder that the better mousetrap doesn't always win out, and the best actor definitely does not always win the Oscar (Rossman et al. 2010).[12]

Networks, Culture, and Diffusion with Respect to Social Movements

Now we turn from the mechanics of diffusion to empirical applications, reviewing research in a variety of topic areas that in one way or another involve the diffusion of cultural materials – ideas, organizational practices, repertoires of action, diagnoses, norms, tastes – through networks. I devote considerable attention to social movements research, which has been one of the more vibrant areas in sociology on diffusion processes for many years. Later I will touch briefly on important studies concerning religion-related, business-related, and health diagnosis-related diffusion. I will conclude the chapter with a treatment of meme diffusion (Shifman 2014), which I see as a very promising venue for future sociological research at the intersection of networks and culture.

Social movements scholars' attention to diffusion derives from the perception that social protest comes and goes in waves, and that some of the same people, actions, symbols, values, and language show up in different places in rapid-fire succession. The Arab Spring and recent waves of pro-democracy, anti-globalization movements, such as Occupy Wall Street, provide ample illustration of this wave-like phenomenon since the early 2000s (Castells 2013). Much research on social movements has shown that personal ties are crucial for recruiting new participants (Snow et al. 1980; McAdam 1986; McAdam and Paulsen 1993; Opp and Gern 1993; Schussman and Soule 2005; Walgrave and Wouters 2014). While such personal ties might not be culturally rich – perhaps I go to a rally because my friend is going, independent of any ideological commitment to the movement itself – it is frequently the case that "networks are important *because* of the meanings they transmit" (Jasper and Poulsen 1995). The point is echoed by Kitts (2000), who distinguishes explanations of mobilization that treat networks merely as information conduits from those that treat networks as crucibles of identity formation. There is ample room in ongoing research to explore more how identities diffuse and are enacted as a key part of social movement recruitment.

Besides the diffusion of commitment or movement identities via people, we can also study the diffusion of repertoires of collective action – cultural practices – across organizations or events, and we can document the flow of social movement frames, or cultural schemas, across movements. Social movements can readily be considered "clusters of new cultural items – new cognitive frames, behavioral routines, organizational forms, tactical repertoires, and so on – subject to the same diffusion dynamics as in other fields" (McAdam and Rucht 1993: 60).

Repertoires

A diverse array of forms of social protest – rallies, marches, riots, petitions, and more – can be thought of as culturally rich practices crackling with symbolic content (Tilly 1995: 26; 2005: 217). These practical and performative elements of protest are ripe for diffusion in one way or another. There is good reason to believe repertoires and claims spread across social movements by various types of contact – certainly via broadcast media (like newspaper reporting), but also via direct contact between members of different activist organizations, and between those organizations themselves.

Charles Tilly (2005) identified a cluster of social movements' orientations and tenets that came to be articulated with a new coherence and staying power in the late eighteenth and early nineteenth centuries: what he terms "WUNC" (worthiness, unity, numbers, and commitment). Adopting this repertoire of orientations and tenets entailed the adoption of certain symbols (clothing, colors), and practices (for example, petitions, the use of the human chain, or the use of barricades).[13] In keeping with the emphasis on re-invention articulated by Everett Rogers, Tilly notes that "negotiation and adaptation . . . goes into the very process of diffusion," stressing that local culture "informs the actual operation of any transplanted performance" (2005: 223). Tracing out the exact pathways by means of which these modern protest performances and ideas diffused, and offering convincing accounts of how one event was responsible for another, despite changes in content and style across locales, remained for Tilly a major agenda item for future social movements research.

Various scholars have taken up Tilly's challenge to identify the concrete pathways through which protest repertoires diffuse. Chabot (2010) describes the history of the diffusion of "the Gandhian repertoire of nonviolent direct action" from India to the civil rights movement of the 1960s in the United States. In their work on contemporary activism, Jennifer Earl and Katrina Kimport (2011) comment on several spreading uses of the internet for mobilization purposes, one of which they categorize as "e-tactics." For example, they point to sites such as PetitionOnline, which had gathered over 50 million signatures from its inception in 1999 through the middle of 2010. Such petitions, addressing a wide variety of issues – including appeals against corporate practices, for example – are a clear illustration of an old social movement tactic being diffused (through re-invention) to a new space of activism. Bunce and Wolchik (2010) identify a set of tactics which they term the "electoral model," which diffused across a set of postcommunist states between 1996 and 2005.[14] They ground this diffusion process not simply in ideas "in the air," but in "transnational democracy promotion networks composed of local oppositions, activists from other countries in the region, and American democracy promoters" (2010: 143).[15] Finally, surveying the field as a whole, Wang and Soule (2012) concluded that collaboration within networks of social movement organizations (SMOs) was a noteworthy feature of much late-twentieth-century social protest. Such collaboration serves prominently as a means for the diffusion of protest tactics and strategies, communication about catalytic events, and ideas for framing movement goals.

Frames

The importance of cultural frames for social movement mobilization has been long documented (Snow et al. 1986). The meaning of a public event may not be self-evident, and its meaning may differ between people and/or across organizations. For example, is the beating up of one person an isolated event, or additional evidence of a pattern of police brutality? Is the extinction of a particular species a natural process, or is it the effect of environmental degradation caused by humans? One of the most important tasks of social movement leaders is to establish a frame for contextualizing events in order to motivate people to join.

In its earliest stages, research on frames focused primarily on how frames were deployed within movements. What frames and framing techniques are most effective in attracting new recruits? But recently there has been an upsurge in the study of the diffusion of frames – "interpretive frames that actors construct to define the issues, codify problems and solutions, target responsible parties, and mobilize political claims" (Givan et al. 2012: 2) – across events and across movements. For example, Roggeband (2010) documents the importation of the American notion of "sexual harassment" into European discussions of workplace gender relations. Framing those relations as potential sexual harassment is a kind of diffusion process, involving both local adaptations of the notion of sexual harassment, and linkage of local situations to commensurate (if not identical) situations elsewhere. And Compa (2010) explains how the frame of "workers' empowerment" that had been used for so long to support collective bargaining, unions, and wage increases in the United States became discredited as the

American labor movement's legitimacy declined, starting in the 1980s, only to become replaced early in this century with a frame of human rights, using the language and participation of Amnesty International and Human Rights Watch to support workers' claims. Hence, one can begin to imagine using formal network analytic tools to map relations among places or events by virtue of the diffused social movement frames they utilize.

We might well expect personal and inter-organizational networks, protest repertoires, and cultural frames all to be involved in social movement diffusion together. For example, drawing on the work of Jan Kubik (1994), Sidney Tarrow (2010: 206–7) explains that the Solidarity Movement in Poland in the 1980s emerged "through a combination of old and new networks: old ones, such as the KOR (Komitet Obrony Robotników, Workers' Defense Committee), factory councils and even party cells; and new ones like the interfactory councils." However, it also developed certain practices – for example, the so-called "round table" format as a bargaining technique – that spread throughout East-Central Europe, and its specific framing as a trade union-based movement borrowed from a particular configuration of industrial relations. Furthermore, Catholic practices and Catholic doctrines (frames) were appropriated and retained as the movement spread.

Global Social Movements and Diffusion in the Internet Age

A new landscape of globally oriented social protest has clearly emerged in this century (della Porta 2007; Juris 2008; Earl and Kimport 2010 and 2011), one that features new patterns of diffusion, and depends upon the cross-fertilization of social networks and culture in new and profound ways. Diffusion of movements' organizational forms, protest repertoires, and frames of meaning across locales is aided by the existence of informal networks of transnational organizations and activists that promote globally aware social protest. The process is facilitated and accelerated considerably not only by mass media, but by social media and the internet. As Castells (2013: 58) notes, Twitter makes it possible for multiple diverse individuals to emerge as movement leaders and trendsetters. Yet networked connections today are challenging to track and isolate, as diffusion passes across and up and down between diverse types of actors willy-nilly (persons, organizations, blogs, text messages, broadcasts, tweets, and more).[16] The explosion of this feverish type of diffusion involving both mass marches and individual actions may be what lies behind the idea of "scale shift" developed by Tarrow and McAdam (2005: 125): one can observe "a change in the number and level of coordinated contentious actions leading to broader contention involving a wider range of actors and bridging their claims and identities." We already know that diffusion is typically a nonlinear process; but scale shift implies not only the diffusion of protest techniques, but the emergence of new kinds of actors engaged in protest. For Tarrow and his collaborators, the concept of diffusion is too static, implying the spread of something through a static population of potential adopters, whereas protest actually *creates* group identities.

We can understand the contemporary spread of protest better if we seek to identify precisely the specific tactics, enthusiasms, personal participations, symbols, proclamations, language, foci of attention, and so on, that have spread via concrete connections across movements, from the WTO protests in Seattle to those in Quebec City in 2002, from protests in Spain in 2006 and Iceland in 2009 to the Arab Spring and Occupy movements thereafter (Juris 2008; Castells 2013; Rhue and Sundararajan 2014). After all, at the same time that contemporary diffusion has become more complex and chaotic, many of the connections through which protest spreads are recorded and archived in digital media (Golder and Macy 2014), making it hypothetically and/or actually possible to trace out at least some of those connections more concretely than was possible in the past. This is great news for future researchers of social movements – as long as the cultural content of protest communication is carefully examined.

We may remain too rooted in the idea that, to study networks in relation to social movements, one must study networks of people or networks of organizations. But what about networks of websites, or, in other words, hyperlinks between organizations (see, for example, Reiter et al. 2007; Rootes and Saunders 2007)? Or networks of readers of blogs? Or, somewhat more radically still, concrete, network-like patterns of diffusion of images across media sites? Or as Jayson Harsin (2010) describes, the diffusion of politically toxic rumors?[17] While the web and internet communication technologies create a whirlwind of swirling ideas and images, they also permit a more detailed and concrete tracking of the diffusion of these ideas and images using network analytic methods than was possible before, through the overwhelmingly complex but also meticulously archived system of hyperlinks, up votes, shared items, and so on, that constitute social media today.

Diffusion Elsewhere: Religion, Economy, Health, Fashion

In this section, I briefly describe some other noteworthy areas of sociology in which diffusion processes are discussed. Networks are only implicitly present in many of these studies, and cultural content and cultural context are often not very fully or explicitly developed. Nevertheless, I mention them to provoke you to develop networks and culture approaches more richly in these areas.

It is not a very large step from social movements to religious movements. Clearly, certain kinds of religious worldviews, symbols, and liturgical practices are ripe for diffusion. It has been shown that recruitment to religious organizations, especially alternative religions, is commonly accomplished through social networks (for example, Smilde 2005). It has been argued that Christianity in its earliest incarnation, as well as its recent evangelical forms, diffused through social networks (Stark 1997). The apostle Paul was instrumental in knitting together disparate Christian communities through his letters and his communication of religious "schemas," a model of pastoral communication taken up later by bishops, monks, and other luminaries in the Church

(Mullett 1997; Schor 2007). Peter Stamatov (2010) has documented that religious activists in Europe between the sixteenth and nineteenth centuries campaigned against social injustices across globe-spanning distances, by establishing long-distance advocacy networks. Some of this activity involved direct contact and influence between British abolitionists on the one hand and Dutch and French activists on the other.

In economic sociology, some attention has been paid to the diffusion of particular practices, and the diffusion of organizational forms. Gerald Davis (1991), for example, traced the diffusion of a particular corporate strategy – the so-called "poison pill" – in the second half of the 1980s among Fortune 500 companies. The poison pill was a strategy put in place by a corporation's board of directors, designed to increase the potential cost of a hostile takeover. Concern about hostile takeovers became a prominent part of American corporate culture in the 1970s and 1980s, and not only poison pills, but also golden parachutes, the lobster trap, the Jonestown defense, shark repellent, and a host of other colorfully named tactics emerged to combat them. In general, such tactics/policies, analogous to social movement repertoires, made it necessary for potential buyers to negotiate the terms of the buyout with the existing board, thereby reinforcing the board's control. Davis shows that the poison pill policy diffused across corporations linked to each other through the sharing of at least one board member in common. In another study, Palmer et al. (1993) showed that corporate interlocks affected diffusion of the adoption of the multidivisional form of organization. It can be tempting to treat organizational forms as skeletal structures, devoid of much cultural content – but, in fact, the whole institutionalist school of organizational analysis treats such forms as cognitive maps, as ensembles of role relations, and as devices for securing legitimacy – all rich with cultural significance (Powell and DiMaggio 1991; Thornton et al. 2012).[18]

Throughout this chapter, I have sought to distinguish the diffusion of cultural phenomena from the diffusion of non-cultural things. Epidemiology, in particular, studies the diffusion of disease, where it would seem cultural issues are not at stake. But that is far from true. A widely cited study by Nicholas Christakis and James Fowler (2007) informs us that obesity diffuses through a network, and specifically that obesity clusters within networks. Overeating could conceivably be construed as just a behavior; but as Christakis and Fowler acknowledge, health behaviors like this one are framed within the context of evolving social norms that stipulate acceptable amounts and types of eating. Similarly, quitting smoking has been a diffusing behavior in recent decades, one that is strongly attached to a diffusing norm about health-appropriate behaviors. Indeed, as smoking comes to cluster in certain components of a network while vehement non-smoking clusters elsewhere, the resultant polarization can "lead to the formation of identities within each group, which prevents further mixing and reinforces group behavior" (Christakis and Fowler 2009: 116f.).

In another health-related study, Liu et al. (2010) address the startling growth in the apparent incidence of autism in recent decades in the United States. What they found, however, is not so much the epidemiological spread of autism as a disease, but the cultural diffusion of an autism *diagnosis*. As they summarize, "knowledge diffuses through local social networks, enabling parents to effectively deploy resources," including finding the right doctor (2010: 1393). The diffusion process is motivated in part by parents' interest in obtaining access to those resources that will help them care better for their children.

Finally, we can turn to fashion as a social world in which diffusion processes are rampant (Simmel 1971a; Crane 1999). As Aspers and Godart (2013: 186) note, for something to be in fashion it must be adopted by a large number of actors – which implies that this inherently cultural phenomenon is an inherently contagious process. The problem is that diffusion processes in the world of fashion are extremely complicated and multidirectional (Crane 1999). How much do new styles diffuse downward from privileged classes, or upward from iconoclasts and street-level subcultures? How much fashion diffusion is accomplished through mass media, and how much via direct contact or word-of-mouth? How much of the process is so "orchestrated by large organizations selling in global markets" (Crane 1999: 23) that the diffusion process is heavily determined in advance? Aspers and Godart (2013: 187) note that diffusion may occur "through observations in public or via information that is communicated in networks" – but they do not specify when or how much of each. Celebrities, popular kids, and members of high-status organizations all enjoy a heightened capacity to influence the direction of fashion – but in what relative proportion? This is an area where the idea of diffusion is perfect for framing a study, but tracing out connections with precision is especially challenging.

One New Direction: The Diffusion of Memes

I conclude this chapter with a plea for sociologists to consider turning toward analyzing the diffusion of memes and other cultural content on the internet as a thoroughly cultural, network-based phenomenon. In no other place is the presence of network patterns and cultural agency arguably so concretely and richly apparent. As Shifman (2014: 2) notes, "meme" is a term "coined by Richard Dawkins in 1976 to describe small units of culture that spread from person to person by copying or imitation." Digital memes, Shifman writes, are such cultural entities located in digital space, diffusing from person to person (or post to post), although frequently "scaling up" (2014: 18) into a shared social phenomenon, shaping, representing, and re-constituting shared understandings and "general mindsets" (2014: 4) as they spread. In other words, cultures (in the form of identities and a sense of belonging, as well as a repertoire of practices of representation) are "continually constructed" (2014: 61) through the process of meme diffusion.

Just how small or "elemental" a meme might be is hard to say. An emoticon is a quite simple meme. Think about how the use of the simplest emoticons (for example, :-)) diffuses constantly through digital conversations every second of every hour of every day, affecting the meaning of conversation flow – and network formation – in minute ways. Yet most memes are more complex than emoticons. The Maneki cats gracing the cover of this book are a kind of diffusing meme, with multiple possible origins in Japanese folklore and Buddhist iconography, multiple forms exhibiting modest variations (different colors, different bibs, and so on), and contemporary reverberations running the gamut from convenience store windows to Super Mario (https://en.wikipedia.org/wiki/Maneki-neko). Memes like Grumpy Cat juxtapose fairly straightforward photographic images with a changeable verbal caption, introducing a kind of hybridity and playfulness. Videos like "Gangnam Style" draw together a vast number of images and messages. Such memes are themselves network-like complexes of cultural elements, spread via networks of users. Their inherent complexity invites us to distinguish between virality – the rapid spread of a single, relatively unchanging cultural unit – and meme diffusion, which involves complex forms of cultural agency and ubiquitous local adaptation (Shifman 2014: 157).

As with other networks through which diffusion may take place, the topology of the meme network is uneven. Well-known Web 2.0 platforms for creating and exchanging user-generated content – platforms such as 4chan, Reddit, and Tumblr – would seem to provide excellent venues for examining the core mechanisms of meme diffusion, and linking the analysis of network structural properties like degree distribution, preferential attachment, and homophily synthetically to issues of message *content*.

However, the content of memes is complicated, as that content almost always incorporates multiple elements: different characters, different colors, different bits of text. But memes also have form: specific visual or aural manifestations, and specific means of production (as lipsynch video, as clip-art, as flashmob scenario, as animation, as advertisement, and so on). And they have something referred to by Shifman (2014: 40) as "stance": something is communicated via the meme itself about the orientation of the person behind its expression, very much like what Goffman (1974, 1981) had in mind in his notion of "footings" and in his discussion of keying with respect to frames. Notably, memes frequently present an ironic or critical commentary about something in the world: "Leave Britney Alone" gets spoofed as "Leave Justin Bieber Alone," which in turn gets spoofed as "Leave Rebecca Black

Alone." Each of the primary elements – content, form, and stance – can be picked up separately through imitation, thus initiating or continuing a process of diffusion. And they can be recombined in myriad, surprising ways that collectively demonstrate the vast intertextuality of the internet. The fecundity of that recombination makes a network analysis of meme diffusion daunting, but also fascinating.

Despite the profusion of material, Shifman argues that one can begin to trace out some of the aspects of content (and form and stance) that make for successful meme diffusion. Extending that line of interpretive analytic work could be the vocation par excellence of 21st-century sociologists of culture! The use of ordinary people, representations of flawed masculinity, humor (especially in the form of juxtaposing discordant elements), simplicity, repetitiveness, and whimsical content all seem to be hallmarks of successfully diffusing memes, as are scornful forms of imitation, somewhat coarse production values, and a pop cultural orientation, rather than, say, a political one (2014: 74, 81, 90). Furthermore, one can begin to trace the dominant genres of meme production; lipsynching, for example, or displays of rage, which might be thought of as comparable to organizational forms or repertoires. All told, content, form, and stance begin to assemble into a kind of internet cultural "toolkit" (Swidler 1986) indicative of the emergence of a bona fide "meme subculture" (Shifman 2014: 118).

In short, the process of meme diffusion involves the propagation of cultural objects by means of clearly definable, culturally rich repertoires of practices and schemas. These cultural objects are manipulated through users' explosively improvisational cultural agency, motivated by as yet unclear (but researchable) desires for social play, prestige, and/or a sense of group belonging. And it all takes place in social structures that are decisively network-like in character. Exploring this intersection of networks and culture will require a combination of quantitative, "big data" analysis, qualitative close reading of texts, and a sensitivity to cultural differences in different settings (Bail 2014; Shifman 2014: 175), but the research possibilities are exciting to contemplate.

Conclusion

The goal of this chapter has been to introduce you to the very widely studied phenomenon of diffusion, and to identify some of the important networks-related mechanisms by which cultural things – like practices, identities, frames, and symbols – do (or do not) diffuse widely. Despite the fact that scientists can study diffusion processes in quite a mechanical way, it is a fundamental claim of this chapter that diffusion is typically a culture-laden process, in various senses. Pathways of diffusion are guided by the cultural attributes and the cultural sensibilities of participants in networks. The things that diffuse are typically rich in cultural content – they have symbolic meaning, and/or they are programmatic for social action – and that content, like actors' sensibilities, can fundamentally shape the speed and the pathways of diffusion. As ensembles of cultural meanings, the things that diffuse are subject to processes of adaptation, recoding, re-appropriation, recombination, and re-keying as they move through networks. Tracing out connections may involve quite a lot of interpretive detective work on the part of the analyst.

Cultural practices or values that are relatively risky – high-risk activism, or the adoption of costly new rules and procedures, for example – may require different kinds of network structures in order to diffuse – structures that permit complex contagions – than is the case for low-cost or low-risk objects, like funny videos of sneezing pandas and such that go viral on the internet. But this means we will have to be careful to understand how the cultural content of what diffuses complicates substantially the goal of identifying the core properties of diffusion "in general."

It is likely that future sociological research on the topic of diffusion will have vastly more rich network data at hand to observe and analyze. The abundance of broadcast media sources, and the ubiquity of social media, both contribute massively to that potentially overwhelming quantity of data about the flow of symbols, messages, fashions, norms, and so much more. But because diffusion proceeds in the contemporary world across multiple scales of operation – persons, organizations, media outlets – network analysts will face some new challenges in modeling it, since modeling anything as a network is much easier when all nodes are of a particular type. The landscape is complicated, but integrating network-based quantitative approaches and culture-sensitive interpretive and conceptual work more fully and self-consciously into the study of diffusion will make for richer, more sociological, and, frankly, more realistic and compelling analyses.

5

Culture from Networks: The Network Genesis of Culture

In this chapter, I will discuss a few disparate kinds of networks research, but all address the genesis of cultural phenomena – roles, identities, norms, attitudes, objects, styles – within or via social networks.

The first strand, most popular in the 1980s and 1990s but occasionally still deployed today, has a structuralist bent. It treats norms, attitudes, reputations, identities, and especially roles, as generated from occupancy of particular *positions* within a network structure, and it uses techniques like blockmodeling and the analysis of structural holes to locate and identify such emergent roles. According to this perspective, network structures *induce* cultural constructs of particular sorts, in particular locations.

The second and third strands are both based on *interactions* within networks, rather than positions. I would say that interactionist approaches are more widely and flexibly utilized today than the structuralist approach; consequently, I will devote greater attention in this chapter to these interactionist strands. In the former of these, researchers explore how patterns of interaction can result in the coalescence of certain norms and expectations among network participants, or a *convergence* on certain beliefs or tastes. In the latter, researchers treat networks as sites of collaborative interaction where invention, innovation, and *creativity* can arise. The creative production of new ideas and new cultural objects is fundamentally a network-centered process. Researchers working in this vein argue that networks *incubate* culture, and these networks in turn are *galvanized* by culture. Furthermore, the culture that they produce is multifaceted, comprised of cultural objects (art works, films, music, ideas), cultural identities (as artist, as punk, as Beat poet, as goth, and so on), and ensembles of gestures, philosophies, beliefs, and styles (Farrell 2001). Frequently such ensembles exist in the form of subculture, but they can often exert an influence beyond the boundaries of the networked group itself.

Roles and Identities from Positions: The Structuralist Approach

One of the formative figures associated with the goal of linking the emergence of social roles to social structures was S. F. Nadel, whose 1957 book, *The Theory of Social Structures*, serves as one of the sacred texts of social network analysis. Nadel's basic notion of social structure was that it was "the ordered arrangement, system, or network of the social relationships obtaining between individuals in their capacity of playing roles relative to each other" (1957: 97). Although this statement puts roles and networks on something of an equal conceptual footing, roles – essentially, a set of norms or cultural scripts for how to act – are the product of particular social positions, rather than disembodied universal cultural ideas. For example, we might ordinarily think of a "foreman" as having a particular, well-known job description; but we can also think of "foreman" as a role growing and deepening from occupancy of a particular position in the organization of work: one having a direct (though subordinate) relationship with management, and a direct (and superior) relationship to rank-and-file workers. Similarly, while we have widespread shared understandings of the category of mother-in-law, that category may be conceived as an emergent feature of the compound set of relations a woman has with her child and with her child's spouse. More interesting are cases of informal roles – ones we may be able to intuit as existing, but for which people do not routinely get hired and for which no job description typically exists. For example,

Jeffrey Johnson and his co-authors (Johnson and Miller 1983; Johnson et al. 2003) note the importance of the clown in small groups: someone who adds levity, and someone who accepts derision and blame when things go wrong. Typically, such a person occupies a structural position on the group's margins. While there may be some character attributes associated with being a clown, from a structuralist perspective the clown emerges as a position in the flow of resources, the flow of attitudes, and the division of labor in the group as network, all of which minimally reinforce, if not generate, the occupant's tendency toward certain clownish behaviors.

The quantitative analysis of structural positions was advanced considerably in the 1970s by Harrison White and a number of colleagues (Lorrain and White 1971; Boorman and White 1976; White et al. 1976). Nodes in a network may be sorted into structurally equivalent blocks based on the similarity of their ties to all other nodes, regardless of whether they are connected internally among themselves. Given that each block of nodes may not feature much internal interaction, they may have limited awareness that they exist as a block.[1] Whether that self-consciousness exists or not, the result of identifying blocks is to reduce considerably the messiness of a social network and to see it as a linked set of a small number of positions. We then imagine that people will develop a similar cultural perspective on the world if they experience it from the same position. Simplifying network structure may also permit us to compare different networks for structural similarities. For example, one set of kids may get beaten up at one school by a small number of kids, while a different set gets beaten up at another school by a different set of kids. These differences, however, do not preclude us from identifying the role of "bully" across schools as a determinate position in multiple schools' informal organization (Faris and Felmlee 2011).

Several authors have subsequently applied the idea of structural equivalence first developed rigorously by White et al., and more generally the idea that network structure determines roles, identities, and actions. I will briefly touch on just a few highly formative applications here. The first is Peter Bearman, who has produced a career's worth of terrific and highly varied empirical research using network analysis. In early work (Bearman 1993), he examined kinship and religious patronage networks in England in the decades leading up to the English Revolution. As he put it succinctly, his research "was guided by the sociological belief that the fundamental bases for subjective identity – and hence the bases for purposive individual action – are defined by the structure of social relations in which individuals are embedded" (1993: 176). This "focus on the structural sources of subjective identity" (1993: 176) led him to discount the importance of social categories such as occupation, status, and religious affiliation as determinants of action, since the networks Bearman studied frequently involved the formation of ties *across* such categories. As local gentry increasingly sought and forged kinship and patronage ties with national-level elites, national-level identities – in particular religious identification – supplanted local identities and local criteria for social status, preparing the way for the gentry to perceive their social world in terms of religious sectarianism. Hence "relations" bred "rhetorics."

Certain similarities exist in the often-cited work of John Padgett and Chris Ansell (1993). Marriages and political and business ties in Renaissance Florence were often forged across social categories such as neighborhood and social class. Political factions did not differ in their social composition, but in the pattern of network ties upon which they were based. One can observe this pattern through a blockmodel rendering of Florentines' multiple social networks (1993: 1276f.). In particular – but to simplify somewhat – followers of the Medici family were divisible into distinct blocks, one of which included high-status Florentine families linked to the Medici by marriage, and another of which included middling-status Florentines with whom the Medici did business. The two blocks were seldom connected directly to each other, allowing the Medici to exert control over their followers in a way their opponents could not. This control was exerted through the practice of "robust action": the Medici could speak enigmatically and follow ambiguous courses of action until the opportune moment, confident their disparate followers would not conspire to discover their selfish political motives. We thus see identities – specifically, political identities and political strategies – generated out of patterns of relations.

Another great application of a network structuralist approach to the discernment of social roles and identities is Robert Faulkner's (1983) terrific book on composers and producers in Hollywood. Faulkner combines rich qualitative analysis based on interview data with a structural analysis of composers' reputations and styles, based on their pattern of collaborations (movie credits) with movie producers.[2] I will focus here on Faulkner's effort to identify categories of Hollywood composer based on the similarity of their profiles of working with particular Hollywood producers.

Hollywood (and here we could discuss actors, directors, producers, and so on, as well as music composers) exists as a network in which credits are highly unevenly distributed. Some people have many credits to their name (among actors, think of Brad Pitt, or Johnny Depp, or Scarlet Johansson); most have few or none. Beyond that skewed distribution, though, it is furthermore the case that the "best" composers work with the "best" producers and vice versa; those two groups co-constitute each other's excellence. Credits (relations) matter more than does talent (individual attributes).[3] Faulkner shows this co-constitution process via blockmodeling (1983: ch. 8, especially pp. 190–1 for the raw data). With whom does one affiliate? Faulkner finds, for example, that a small number of composers worked recurrently with producers of B-movies (horror flicks, "bikini youth sagas," and the like), thus becoming writers of "horror" music or "young love" music. Other composers might become writers of "western" music by virtue of working recurrently with the producers of western films and television shows (1983: 78). In short, composers were typecast by their profile of credits. Put differently, the perception of their musical *orientation* – and therefore their industry *identity* – was forged from their network position, understood as the preceding set of relations they had contracted.

Katherine Giuffre (1999) developed a similar argument to Faulkner's but with respect to fine art photographers. She claims that, in this field, critical success and prosperous careers are associated with a personal network structure rich in weak ties linking one to a diverse set of others, not dense cliques characterized by strong and overlapping ties. Just as composers depend on producers, photographers depend on galleries to ensure that their work is visible, and hence valued. Their own fame is a function of the fame of those to whom they are connected – even to the point of potentially outweighing their own skill as a determinant of success.[4] Thus one of photographers' primary goals is to establish ties to more and more prestigious galleries over time (1999: 818).[5]

Giuffre partitions the set of photographers into structurally equivalent blocks and finds different shapes of blocks (or in a sense, different kinds of network components) year by year, based on the array of galleries in which they exhibited their pictures. These component networks vary on a continuum from structural isolates (those with no gallery showings in a particular year), to tight, insular clique-like structures (made up of photographers who all exhibit in the same galleries as each other), to loosely linked clique structures, to more expansive network structures (1999: 824). This last type is made up of photographers who, in the course of a year, exhibited at a diverse medley of galleries. Some of those photographers in turn traversed a wide variety of galleries over the course of many years, resulting in substantially greater critical recognition than their rivals.[6]

A final important contributor in the structuralist tradition is Ron Burt, whose reanalysis of Coleman et al.'s data on drug diffusion through the lens of structural equivalence was mentioned in chapter 4. Here I will discuss Burt's (1992) notion of the "structural hole." The basic idea of a structural hole is a network position that forms a bridge or gateway between two or more otherwise disconnected positions in a network. Such *brokerage* conveys power and generates profit. But power is a highly plastic concept and not necessarily very full of cultural content. How can the structural hole notion be used culturally? For one thing, those who occupy structural holes put together information and ideas from separate locales in novel ways, meaning they are uniquely well situated to innovate; plus they develop *reputations* for innovation (Burt 2004). Innovative ideas (newly combined cultural

materials) and identities/roles (as innovators) are thus jointly produced out of social structure.[7]

Networks as Sites of Norm Enforcement and Taste Convergence

There is a long tradition in social psychology of studying the
emergence and convergence of ideas within groups. That tradition
is fairly readily adapted to examine, not the general effects of the
group on individual beliefs and attitudes, but the ways in which
networks of influence at the interpersonal level might affect the
distribution and strength of particular norms, tastes, and beliefs.
In a sense, discussing norms in networks could readily be situated
alongside research on diffusion, and sometimes the language of
diffusion is explicitly used with respect to norms (for example,
Horne 2001) – especially by political scientists and politically or
organizationally oriented sociologists dealing with international
issues and processes.[8] But let's think of norms and tastes here as
cultural "forms" that arise, infect, and come to characterize the
operations of a relatively fixed set of actors within a relatively
fixed space. Thus, while "spread" is sometimes an appropriate
concern with respect to norms, what I focus on here is the emergent *coordination* and mutual *adjustment* of behavior, by means
of normatively laden judgments passed among interacting individual participants within a group.

One highly developed and mathematically sophisticated line
of research here revolves around the concept of social influence, as discussed most notably by Noah Friedkin (1998, 2001;
Friedkin and Johnsen 2011).[9] In one study, Friedkin (2001) uses
the famous Bank Wiring Observation Room social network data
of Roethlisberger and Dickson to examine how the norm of a fair
"day's work" – a norm stipulating that workers should neither
work too energetically, nor slack off excessively, nor should they
"squeal" on their under-working or over-working co-workers –
could hold for an entire network of employees, despite the fact
the network was internally divided into two cliques. Members of

the two cliques took part in different group activities, bespeaking their distinct "subcultures" (2001: 180): clique A were gamblers, while clique B members horsed around together, and the groups pooled their money separately to buy different kinds of treats. Yet the work output norm held throughout the network. Friedkin uses the original data and written reports to identify patterns of interaction among the thirteen workers, and to calculate influence scores (or, conversely, measures of susceptibility to influence) for each of them. He finds that members of the B clique took on this norm of a proper "day's work" due to the disproportionate influence upon them of one specific worker from clique A. That worker was well liked, he was regarded as exceptionally skilled at his job, and he was able to manage others' behaviors and tempers in the workplace. Not coincidentally his co-workers accepted his personal standard of output as a good approximation of the group's normative standard of output. He led by example. Note, then, that unlike the way that attitudes or roles are more or less hard-wired in structural equivalence-based arguments, derived rather strictly from structural positions, according to Friedkin's view "networks of interpersonal influence mediate the effects of social differentiation" (2001: 187).

Another intriguing approach to the network bases of norm enforcement has been developed by Damon Centola, Robb Willer, and Michael Macy (2005). They explore the mechanics of situations of "pluralistic ignorance: situations where a majority of group members privately reject a norm, but assume (incorrectly) that most others subscribe to it" (2005: 1010). Think of witch-hunts, conspiracies of silence, group crazes like drinking binges, or adoration of talentless stars – regrettably these happen in the real world more than we might like to think. The famous social conformity experiments of Solomon Asch (1951) long ago suggested that people will tend to go along with a consensus judgment, even one that violates their own sense perception, rather than risk being labeled or punished as a deviant. Centola et al. cleverly point out that enforcement of a norm, even a false one, can be seen as a norm itself, and sometimes it is precisely the newest recruits who vehemently enforce a norm in order to demonstrate their commitment to the group (2005: 1013). The key question they pursue then is: how many true believers are required to trigger a cascade of norm enforcement that pulls in the disbelievers as well? And how does the network structure of contacts among true believers and the as-yet-uncommitted affect how quickly the insidious norm spreads or dissipates?

We might wish to believe that one or two committed John Proctors or naïve children[10] or concerned citizens could stop cascades of silent acceptance of questionable beliefs. But Centola et al.'s simulation results indicate that, under some circumstances, not only are disbelievers reluctant to challenge true believers, but in fact "*no* true believers are needed" to initiate a cascade of pluralistic ignorance. Widespread silence in the face of a belief that "Most others must be taking seriously this thing that I do not believe" need not be the outcome; but as they say, "cascades of false enforcement can be triggered 'spontaneously' by the random waverings of uncommitted disbelievers" (2005: 1025).

Parallel to the study of the reinforcement of norms, we could explore the formation and/or convergence of tastes via network-based patterns of influence. Clayton Childress' research with Noah Friedkin (2012) explores the social construction of meaning within cultural groups by examining data from eighteen book clubs and showing how interpretations of a particular novel are formed (at least in part) via interpersonal influence exerted through face-to-face contact. And, using data on student social networks, Danielle Kane (2004) has explored how people's embeddedness in social networks with different structural properties might affect the types of cultural engagements they pursue. She hypothesizes (2004: 105) that dense networks are associated with, and arguably induce, participation in solidarity-producing activities, while embeddedness in heterogeneous social networks induces increased participation in more high-culture activities. In fact, she finds that students with tight, clique-like friendship networks were "three times more likely than those from sparse networks to have attended a sports event in the past year"; conversely, they were "only a third as likely as students from sparse networks to have visited a museum in the past twelve months" (2004: 119).

Networks as Incubators of Culture: Conceptual Foundations

Whereas the structuralist, blockmodeling approach generally treats culture – identities, ideas, reputations – as an outcome of structural position, and influence models seek to explain attitude convergence, more recent research takes a less deterministic view of how social networks produce cultural output. This less deterministic view has somewhat diverse intellectual roots. One important foundation stone was certainly the production of culture and artworlds approaches that I introduced in chapter 3. However, there was also the emergence of interest in the 1980s in network-like organizations – flatter and more fluid organizations rather than rigid, hierarchical ones – within economic sociology and organizational studies. Fascination with team production and network-style organizations and inter-organizational fields (Powell 1990), and the development of organizational cultures (Morrill 1991; Kunda 1992) within firms, was motivated in part by the hope of creating network-based organizational structures capable of fostering unanticipated, creative, team-based innovation.

Also important was Charles Kadushin's development of the idea of the "social circle." Kadushin argued that both formal roles and informal relations within social circles, and especially within networks of idea producers, can be empirically traced using social network analysis. Under the umbrella concept of "social circle," Kadushin (1976: 111) suggests the following typology: those that emphasize values, aesthetics, ideology, and religion generally have the form of "intellectual circles"; literature, art, and music are produced in "movement circles"; and scientific knowledge producers operate in "invisible colleges" (Crane 1972). While what circulates differs in these different circles, and scientific knowledge tends to be more cumulative than other types of cultural production, their formal properties remain similar. Among the commonly observed features of such circles/networks, success in the circle is strongly a function of peer evaluation and job market dynamics (Kadushin 1976: 116) – so *judgments*, *tastes*, and *styles* flow within these networks, in addition to the cultural "products" themselves. Furthermore, although there may be evidence of diffusion of new ideas in intellectual networks (an idea I touched on last chapter with respect to the concept of "opinion leaders"), the fact that most producers of ideas and opinions are also consumers implies that ideas *circulate* and are modified through discussion and debate, rather than simply diffusing (Kadushin 1976: 108). Even more strikingly, new ideas are *created* through within-network interactions. Kadushin's effort at developing general ideas about social circles grew from his own landmark study *The American Intellectual Elite* (1974), in which he developed social network maps depicting the connections "who you talk with," and "who was mentioned as important," among the leading pundits in American public opinion formation. Since this formative work, network measures have been increasingly explicitly applied to examine networks of innovative cultural production.

Networks as Germinators of Culture: Empirical Applications

In the rest of this chapter, I will introduce various empirical applications of network ideas, and specifically network-based interaction, in the creative production of culture, with culture being understood rather broadly to mean ideas, cultural objects, and/or associated practices and symbols that are markers of a particular style or group. I will highlight as well how specific structural properties of networks may contribute to this creative production of culture.

Science as Networked Knowledge Production

Scientific advancements can be seen as the product of collaborative work within a networked "community" of scholars intent on producing new knowledge. This is the basic idea behind the notion of the invisible college, first described by Price and Beaver (1966). Scientists discuss their research with each other – at conferences, workshops, national foundations, think tanks, and more. They collaborate with each other to publish papers, operate labs, seek grants, and more. They train each other, leading to networks of mentorship and influence. They sometimes work at the same institutions, enjoying indirect ties through institutional affiliation. They spread word of each other's research to third parties. They identify problems of note for each other, with star participants playing a leading role in setting the research agenda for others. Crucially, and easily measurably, they recognize the importance of each other's work through citation of each other's publications. Discussion, collaboration, mentorship, co-affiliation, gossip, and more add up to multiple, sometimes overlapping, sometimes distinct, networks of connections – connections which can be mapped using network analytic techniques (Crane 1972: 42; Moody 2004; Gondal 2011).

Crane reports that more than two-thirds of researchers in the 1970s participating in different fields were members of a single component within their disciplinary networks; that is, they could "reach" each other via some chain of concrete links of informal discussion connections between participants in the production of scientific knowledge within their discipline. Upwards of three-quarters could do so when multiple types of tie (like those listed in the previous paragraph) were counted simultaneously (Crane 1972: 44–5).[11] Rather similar results were found by James Moody (2004) in his more recent and much more methodologically sophisticated effort to map the network space of productive collaborations among sociologists over a 35–year time period. There is, he claims, "a direct linkage between social interaction patterns and the structure of ideas" (2004: 213). With that claim in mind, he offers an elegant assessment of the extent to which local clustering, preferential attachment (the presence of a small number of stars in the network), and cohesion mechanisms account for the macrostructure of a network of over 100,000 authors who have collaborated on sociological articles. He finds, somewhat contrary to expectations, that rather than the sociological field being fractured into a number of non-overlapping, non-communicating clusters (centered on, for example, criminology, comparative-historical sociology, work and occupations, and more), actually the network forms a fairly cohesive whole, and increasingly so over time. The implication is a more even distribution of key concepts, ideas, frames, schemas, and scientific practices (especially quantification) than we might imagine were true. We could hypothetically examine how the structure of collaboration within a discipline evolves over time, and how that structural evolution is correlated (or not) with either the increasing consistency or increasing differentiation of the space of scientific ideas.

It is important to keep in mind, though, that the network structure of scientific collaboration varies by discipline. Collaborative projects in physics are generally huge (Hagstrom 1976; Knorr-Cetina 1999); collaborative projects in chemistry and psychology are ubiquitous, but generally small in size; collaborative projects in English literature are rather rare. The intellectual content of the discipline, the spatial location in which the research is carried out, the experimental demands (or lack of demands) imposed, the extent of the division of intellectual labor required to produce new knowledge: all of these factors affect the shape, size, and connectedness of the networks that produce scientific knowledge of determinate sorts.

How can we understand the production of scientific knowledge in a more specifically cultural light? As Hagstrom (1976: 97) noted long ago, participants in these scientific networks not only collaborate in knowledge-making work, they "share commitments to values, metaphysical paradigms, heuristic models and exemplars." That is, they tend to share particular ethical orientations, and they most assuredly share cognitive predispositions and linguistic practices specific to their discipline.[12] Knowledge networks do not produce merely information; they produce and reinforce shared attitudes toward the world. Shared understandings in a scientific field are achieved jointly by relationships among scientists, such as are revealed in citation data, and emergent, crystallizing relationships among concepts used increasingly in conjunction with each other (Hill and Carley 1999). As is true of any kind of social group, clusters of researchers within cohesive scientific networks "operate to socialize individual members, to reward conformity, and to punish deviance" (Hagstrom 1976: 97–8). Furthermore, although Knorr-Cetina (1999; see also Knorr-Cetina and Bruegger 2002) does not especially use the language of networks, nor the tools of formal network analysis, to describe the interactions she observes in highly technical environments, such as screen-mediated monetary markets and high-energy physics collaborations, she is evidently describing a situation in which arcane language and/or cryptic signals are used by participants co-located in an environment of empathetic coordination and symbolic communication. One could also speak of distributed cognition (Hutchins 1995) here:[13] the knowledge necessary for problem-solving or task-processing is distributed across multiple persons and/or locales linked to each other. Hence, knowledge does not just pass through the network; it is *in* the network and *of* the network.

Outside of the world of science, strictly speaking, different authors have utilized the idea of networks and/or social circles to describe intellectual interaction and attempt to address the mechanisms of intellectual influence. For example, Randall Collins (1998) tried to map a network of influences across centuries of philosophers and philosophical texts. Just as there are relationships of mentoring in contemporary science, the history of philosophical discourse includes "chains of eminent teachers and pupils" (1998: 5–6). Furthermore, authors read each other, appreciatively and/or critically, and respond to each other's work. In some cases, they don't read each other, or deny that they read each other (think of contemporary rivals), and yet their influence upon each other may be great! Collins claims (1998: vxiii), "if one can understand the principles that determine intellectual networks, one has a causal explanation of ideas and their changes."[14]

A less macrohistorical but equally intriguing effort at mapping networks of intellectual contact and influence is the historian Edward Timms' (1986) treatment of intellectual circles in 1920s Vienna.[15] This was, so to speak, a "scene" (Straw 2002; Bennett 2004), well before the arrival of goths and punks. Timms (1986: 108) describes and illustrates a landscape of overlapping circles, organized within a field of contending political ideologies. However, while the circles were basically internally consistent in their political orientation, they varied in their "disciplinary" coherence. Schoenberg, Berg, Webern, Adorno, and Krenek hung out together in a music-oriented circle, but Karl Kraus presided over a group that included architects, musicians, a publisher, a lawyer, an art historian, and an engineer. This is a reminder that identifying such intellectual circles should happen from the ground up, not on the basis of preconceived notions of who should go together categorically.

Music and Art

The network-based production of visual arts and music has been studied perhaps more widely than the network-based production of knowledge. The conceptual foundations put in place by Richard Peterson, Howard Becker, and Robert Faulkner powerfully animate this work.[16] Here I describe some more recent studies, with an eye to getting you to think about a multitude of promising venues for contemporary research.

First, we could consider Brian Uzzi and Jarrett Spiro's (2005) fascinating and methodologically complex account of the creative collaborations behind the production of Broadway musicals in Broadway's heyday, from 1945 to 1989. They seek to show that on Broadway as elsewhere, "the creativity of many key figures . . . all abided by the same pattern of being embedded in a network of artists or scientists who shared ideas and acted as both critics and fans for each other" (2005: 448). But what *kind* of network precisely facilitates artistic creativity? What is the most advantageous network *architecture* or *topology* of creativity? They argue that it is the small-world network structure (described in chapter 2) that accomplishes this goal. Small-world networks facilitate dense local interaction to produce fruitful fermentation of ideas and creative cultural output, but also incorporate the capacity to spread those ideas to other locales of production fairly quickly. In the Broadway case in particular, each show's production team was made up of a core group of specialists: a composer, a lyricist, a librettist (who writes the plot and dialogue), a choreographer, a director, and a producer who arranges the financial backing of the show (2005: 456). Once a given group of people had worked together on a particular show, they could collaborate again as a whole; but, more often, each one, or two or three in tandem, went on to new projects with a new set of collaborators. Conceptually, each new collaboration is "welded" to the first one through the activity of the specialist or specialists the two productions have in common.

Uzzi and Spiro then infer that the more an artistic network has small-world features, the more its participants are either directly connected to each other, currently or via past collaborations, or indirectly connected via persons they have worked with in the past: "These conditions enable the creative material in separate clusters to circulate to other clusters as well as to gain the kind of credibility that unfamiliar material needs to be regarded as valuable in new contexts, thereby increasing the prospect that the novel material from one cluster can be productively used by other members of other clusters" (2005: 449).[17] Innovation is produced through the fruitful recombination (Stark 1996) of old elements carried forward by skilled practitioners. Uzzi and Spiro then use this conceptual framework to show that small-world network structure is significantly associated with the success, both financial and artistic, of musicals.

Another particularly noteworthy examination of the network foundations of a musical form is Nick Crossley's (2008) fascinating work on the emergence of the punk music scene in Manchester in the late 1970s, for he seeks, via this case study, to render the insights of Becker (1982) and others more precise, by insisting that "a properly sociological understanding of culture must focus upon its production by concrete social actors linked and embedded in social networks" (2008: 90). At root, Crossley argues, the Manchester music scene took off by virtue of the formation of a network between a critical mass of key actors.[18] Within this network – a quite dense and cohesive network as it turns out (2008: 102ff.) – cross-fertilization of ideas through interaction was crucial. For example, individuals from one punk band, once dissolved, would recombine with new players in new combinations to form new bands – rather like the fundamental tie-formation dynamic identified by Uzzi and Spiro for an entirely different set of artists. Furthermore, different kinds of participants were important: not only performers, but also those who controlled performance spaces and rehearsal spaces (as well as other gathering spaces), those who booked acts, those who wrote about or otherwise promoted particular performers, and those who acted as audience members (a category not readily distinguishable from all the other categories, including performers, actually). A small number of producers were particularly central to the punk network; they held it together, but they were also sometimes resented for the power they wielded. Overall, Crossley's research is instructive and exemplary not only for his use of formal network analytic tools, but for his use of historical records to document the cultural *content* of the social interactions that jointly produced punk music. Such research has to be sensitive to the types of ties being formed – members of a common band, promoter–performer ties, audience–performer ties, and so on – yet also sensitive to the way network participants spill across those types of ties promiscuously. The main point, in any event, is the emphasis on the importance of interactions within artistic networks to catalyze creativity.[19]

Research continues to emerge in the same vein. Císař and Koubek (2012) discuss the emergence of a hardcore music scene in the Czech Republic. Although they do not employ formal network analysis as did Crossley, they describe how the scene started as a network of personal friends, then later diversified. They also describe how the production of cultural products within networks mingled with the expression of political values, blurring the line between cultural scene and social movement. Hollands and Vail (2012) make a similar argument concerning the network mechanics behind the Amber Collective independent filmmaking initiative. And Harkness (2013) adopts an intensely qualitative, interview-based method to examine the production of gangsta rap in Chicago. His main conceptual lens is the "scene," where scene is defined (following Císař and Koubek) as spaces located in particular venues, formed via social networks of interacting individuals and groups who, through their interaction, express multiple overlapping identities.

Somewhat distinct from this interactionist line of reasoning, Damon Phillips suggests that in fact it may be structural *discon-nectedness* that is the appropriate element to examine in the "social structure of creativity" (2011: 421). For Phillips, it is not so much the generative structure of *producers'* collaboration *within* networks that produces innovation, but audiences' perceptions of structural outsiders – those on the margins of artistic networks – as "off the beaten path," that leads to them being characterized as exotic, and therefore interesting. Whereas the term "structural isolate" tends to suggest impotence or irrelevance in many network studies, Phillips argues that the term "disconnectedness" is sometimes more apt, as it connotes aesthetic appeal. (This is somewhat reminiscent of Uzzi and Spiro's idea that when creative networks become too cohesive, cultural production is likely to become too homogeneous.) Phillips illustrates his argument using evidence concerning the appeal of early jazz recordings.[20] While cities like New York and Chicago undoubtedly were hubs of jazz production, and output from those places made it smoothly into the jazz canon, songs from "off the beaten path" cities could make it into the canon and become frequently re-recorded if they were quirky in one way or another. Phillips' argument is nuanced in a conceptually challenging way. He uses and meticulously measures network structure as a substrate out of which cultural products arise; but he also insists on the importance of cultural *classifi-cations* of musical output by listeners as a filter through which network positions are or are not translated into artistic success.[21]

As with music, so too with art. One of the foundational studies exploring the production of art through a network ana-lytic framework was Harrison and Cynthia White's *Canvases and Careers* (1965), published half a century ago. Much more recently, research by authors like Farrell (2001), Currid (2007), and Grams (2010) has examined the production of art, and, more broadly, artistic taste, whether at the center of everything or on the margins, through an "artworlds" and/or social circles lens – although they have typically done so without using formal network analytic techniques.[22] Of a piece with the idea that art is produced in networks is the idea that artistic *identity* is generated and reinforced in networks: being an artist, as opposed to one who dabbles in art, may depend heavily on the recognition and reinforcement of others (Lena and Lindemann 2014).

Gatekeepers as Crucial Artistic Network Participants

In a number of recent projects, researchers have focused on network gatekeepers and their preponderant influence in giving shape to different cultural fields (Wynn 2011). This work does not necessarily utilize network analytic techniques explicitly, but does make use of a structural-hole-like (brokerage) conceptual framework within a network of interactions to explain outcomes. More importantly for our purposes, these researchers stress that gatekeepers utilize not only their structural position, but also their reputations as arbiters of taste, to control fields. For example, Allen and Lincoln (2004) stress the importance of movie critics in the esteem (in-degree centrality, we might say!) generated for high-end American films. Lane (2013) highlights the importance of gastronomic guides in distributing prestige within the "fine-dining" industry. Pachucki (2012: 83) reminds us that network ties are used by museum curators to assess the quality of art, and to decide which exhibitions to sponsor. And Franssen and Kuipers (2013) analyze a world of book publishing in which informal networks of editors, scouts, and acquaintances are called upon to decide which manuscripts to publish and which books to translate.

In provocative and critical research on the fashion industry, Mears (2010, 2011) identifies bookers and clients, as well as "an historically shaped and commerce-driven network of agents, designers, and editors" (2010: 35), as cultural "gatekeepers" who filter cultural goods – specifically that most significant good known as "the look" – before they are eligible for wider dissemination. Their gatekeeping role revolves, in other words, around their taste-making hegemony. Mears furthermore describes a world in which "decisions are guided more by imitation, routine and rules of thumb than rational calculation" – a kind of self-reinforcing network-based circulation of expectations and norms that locks models into highly gendered and racialized constructions of womanhood (2010: 36; cf. Centola et al. 2005).

Using data on the agents engaged in the scheduling of bands for Boston nightclubs, Foster et al. (2011) explain the emergence of two different kinds of musical network structures depending on the nature of the cultural "material" being performed. In that segment of the market featuring bands who play their own original music, agents "maintain arm's length relations" with the bands, but participate in a dense information-sharing network among themselves. They form, as it were, the core of this creative network, aiming to overcome the risks associated with booking relatively unknown bands with relatively unpredictable audience appeal. By contrast, when one considers those bands that play familiar popular tunes ("covers"), a different sort of network develops: more or less bilateral, repeat-business ties form between certain bands and certain agents, and in turn with certain clubs. In this latter market, clubs have their favorites. As Foster and colleagues demonstrate, whereas the "original music" bands more or less roam from one club to another as they move from one gig to the next, stitching together a cohesive network structure via their perambulations, cover bands are more sedentary and thus occupy a more fragmented network structure. The interesting thing here from a "networks and culture" perspective is not only the characterization of cultural production in terms of network structure, but the claim that different *kinds* of cultural elements catalyze the development of different network topologies. This is an important idea which we will explore more in the next chapter.

Finally, Friedman (2014) has recently explored the role of comedy scouts at the massive Edinburgh Festival Fringe. Three elements are noteworthy in his ethnographic, network-oriented study. First, as Foster et al. (2011) previously indicated with respect to new, unproven talent, informal networks abound among scouts, who share information with each other but filter the information they receive very carefully, giving much more credence to the recommendations of a few trusted associates than to the information provided by casual acquaintances. Thus, information flows "unevenly" through this network. Second, scouts

routinely employ cultural schemas in their work – making infer-
ences about comedians based on the likelihood of their appeal
to audiences whose tastes are imagined rather than revealed.[23]
Thus, the network of scouts is actively *producing* the comedy
industry via qualitative judgments of what constitutes good and
bad comedy. Finally, Friedman also provides information on how
comedians' agents tried to influence scouts in their decisions about
whom to book: "One technique mentioned by several scouts,
for example, was for an agent to invite a scout to a gig and then
casually but deliberately sit next to them, proceeding to laugh
manically at their client's entire set." Here we glimpse a bit of
the active, ongoing cultural work and face-work (Goffman 1967)
actors use to construct, manipulate, and maintain networks of
cultural production.

Conclusion

The goal of this chapter has been to introduce a few different –
in fact, in some respects *distinctly* different – ways of thinking
about the creation of culture from and in networks. Decades ago,
the structuralist predilections of network analysis entailed treating culture as more or less a product, or almost a by-product, of
network structural positions. Admittedly, there was some elegance
in that effort to explain behaviors and outcomes, not to mention
values and attitudes, by means of structure. This perspective
reached its apogee in early efforts to develop blockmodeling and
illustrate its explanatory value. The best examples of that methodology, however, take culture very seriously. Faulkner's (1983)
work is an excellent case in point, in which the use of blockmodels
helps us to understand the structure of careers, the dangers of
typecasting, and the reinforcement of inequalities in the market,
while at the same time Faulkner's rich interview data presents
Hollywood cultural production as a lived experience.

More recent efforts to explore the emergence of culture out
of networks treat culture instead as an unpredictable and serendipitous product of interpersonal influence and recombination of

cultural elements through social interaction. In this viewpoint, networks channel tastes and artistry, and they provide opportunities for fruitful cross-fertilization. In my opinion, there is ample opportunity at present to apply more quantitative and formal network analytic ideas using the rich case studies of artistic collaboration already carried out by art historians, intellectual historians, scholars of literature, and historical sociologists. Furthermore, there continue to be newly emerging genres of music and art – grunge, reggae, metal, hip hop, you name it – whose provenance could fruitfully be analyzed using social network tools. As more research in this vein develops, researchers should attend to recent studies which stress that the shape of cultural networks will differ depending on the kinds of cultural goods flowing through them. As we shift toward thinking of culture as having a determinative effect on network structure, we begin to think not only of "culture from networks," but "networks from culture," which is the theme to which we turn in the next chapter.

6

Networks from Culture: How Norms and Tastes Shape Networks

Whether it concerns children in a playground, or a cluster of high school friends, or co-workers in an office, or a collection of Mediterranean villagers, or a set of firms engaged in joint production, sociologists typically recognize that what happens in social groups is fundamentally shaped by cultural meanings and cultural processes. That statement hardly seems remotely objectionable. In fact, such a taken-for-granted belief in the importance of culture typically is articulated among the earliest chapters in any introductory sociology textbook.

Nevertheless, for a long time social network analysis displayed a predilection for either ignoring the constitutive importance of culture in shaping networks, or treating culture largely as a product of network structure.[1] For example, as is stated in one heading within Barry Wellman's (1988: 33) oft-cited overview and manifesto of the social network perspective, "Norms emerge from location in structured systems of social relationships." Minimally, one could say there was some desire to see just how far we could go toward understanding the world in purely structural terms, without reference to cultural content.[2] Thinking structurally seemed to be a defensible and thought-provoking form of analytical abstraction which would permit us to draw comparisons across societies and across organizations of all sizes, without dwelling on distracting and nonessential cultural differences. That viewpoint remains appealing, though restrictive: network analysis does provide a vocabulary for insightfully comparing different instances of social organization in terms of the extent of their cohesiveness, the relative centrality of key actors, the extent of reciprocity, the degree of multiplexity, and the presence of hierarchy in exchange relations.[3] And these structural differences do have determinate consequences.

Yet there are important ways in which we can't really understand network relationships and network structures in sociology without attending to the cultural factors at the root of their development (Fuhse 2009, 2015). In this chapter we consider three different primary ways in which culture *constitutes* networks. More precisely, we will explore: (1) ways in which cultural *tastes* and worldviews affect the composition and topology (shape) of personal social networks (for example, Lizardo 2006; Vaisey and Lizardo 2010); (2) ways in which cultural competencies and communicative *skills* affect network tie formation (DiMaggio 1987; Erickson 1996; Mische 2003; McLean 2007; Pachucki and Breiger 2010; Kane 2011); and (3) ways in which people's cultural *norms* and *schemas* produce patterns in the organization of social networks (for example, Wellman and Wortley 1990; Bearman et al. 2004; Gondal 2012; Gondal and McLean 2013a). Concerning the last point, we could also say that different types of tie, and in particular the ways those ties are cognitively "coded" or construed, "steer" networks to aggregate in different ways.[4] That moves us toward thinking more about the dynamics of network growth.

To explore each of these claims requires that they be contextualized in light of some important prior theories, concepts, and ideas that have explored the relationship between culture and social structure.[5] Such prior theories, concepts, and ideas can act as foils, as it were, for more recent theorizing. In a general sense, treating culture as constitutive of networks cuts against the grain of a certain structural determinism in network analysis. That view – that culture arises from structure – lurks as a foil in the background throughout. More specifically, treating tastes as determinants of behaviors and patterns of social organization resonates to a considerable extent with Pierre Bourdieu's account of habitus and his concept of cultural capital – yet it may afford more explanatory autonomy to tastes than Bourdieu seemed inclined to accept. Treating culture as a crucial instrument for forging social connections resonates with the vast literature in the social sciences on social capital; but the viewpoint I articulate here encourages opening up the black box of social capital to explore cultural mechanisms of social tie formation, rather than treating it as the equivalent of a Rolodex of business contacts, or (for readers whose adulthood began in 2004 or later) a gaggle of frequently inert and largely vacuous "Facebook friend" ties. Identifying the norms that pattern social relationships to some extent requires that we turn a venerable body of research on social support and core discussion networks on its head. Thus, I will end up discussing each of these background perspectives to some extent in this chapter as well.

Tastes and their Manifestation in Network Structure

A long tradition in sociology deals with the social significance of cultural tastes and preferences. Georg Simmel (1971d), for example, explored the ways in which individuals can achieve a cultivation of tastes through self-development. Furthermore, Simmel (1971a) discussed the social significance of fashion, in its capacity to express individuality, but also in its capacity to mask individuality, to control us (as in the phrase "being a slave to fashion"), and to express status distinctions. Thorstein Veblen (1998 [1899]) linked the expression of particular tastes to social class – in particular, membership in the so-called "leisure class" – and saw in conspicuous forms of consumption an expression of claims to social status. Max Weber argued that social status is typically expressed in a particular "style of life" (1946: 187, 193) associated with the consumption (or avoidance) of particular goods.[6] Frequently, the pursuit of those cultural ends entails seeking connections to people in certain esteemed social groups while eschewing direct connections to persons in pariah groups, creating patterns of group solidarity and closure that can be mapped and understood in social network terms. Indeed, both historically and today, the use of arcane languages, nicknames, insider references, and status symbols has been used to create and police boundaries around exclusive social networks (Tilly 1998; Gambetta 2009). At the same time, in the contemporary world, the internet and various social media make it increasingly possible for adherents of particular tastes – tastes in musical groups, in video games, in fashion, or in political protest – to find each other more readily, forming geographically dispersed but culturally focused networks.

In chapter 3, I discussed the most substantial and influential work of the last thirty years in the sociology of culture that has analyzed the relationship between cultural tastes and social structure or social organization, specifically the phenomenal work of Pierre Bourdieu. I also mentioned there the debate about whether the people and groups that occupy privileged positions in society express rarefied tastes and adopt exclusionary practices and aesthetic judgments, or whether instead they are, as Richard Peterson (1992) and Paul DiMaggio (1987) and others have suggested, cultural omnivores characterized by the breadth and variety of their knowledge and appreciation of culture. You might refer back to that material now if you need a refresher.

The main thing to consider from the perspective of this book is that little to none of that foundational research – including the work of Bourdieu – focused specifically and explicitly on the relationship between tastes and social *networks* as a specific form of social organization and/or a precise way of conceiving of social organization. Similarly, only since around 2000 or so has the question of omnivorousness come to be examined in social network terms. This is where we pick up the story.

Research by Noah Mark (1998, 2003) provided special impetus toward the use of a social networks framework for analyzing tastes. Mark invites us to think of musical forms or genres – country, gospel, folk, rock, metal, classical, R&B, etc. – as being in competition with each other for listeners. Any musical genre secures a foothold in the market to the extent it can find a stable pool of listeners who will support it. But how is that pool of listeners found? Mark (1998) argues that musical preferences are transmitted through homophilous social network ties. The time and energy we have available for exploring various types of music (or anything else) is scarce; thus, we will tend to heed the advice of those closest to us (strong ties), who tend to be people like ourselves. Ongoing interaction within social network clusters defined by sociodemographic homophily (age groups, or racial groups, for example) creates a bandwagon effect that reinforces the differentiation among musical forms. Simply imagine college-age friends exchanging information about the latest garage bands. Then contrast that with the likelihood of taking the musical advice of the high school dropout garage station attendant you barely speak with every couple of weeks when you need gasoline!

Mark (2003) develops his analysis further by comparing the homophily-based argument for the acquisition of tastes with a Bourdieu-inspired argument that the creation and reinforcement of tastes is driven by an urge to distance ourselves aesthetically from groups or classes we despise. Both approaches can incorporate the idea that we develop new tastes from network ties – in the former case through close ties like current friends, in the latter case through close ties within, say, our families. The distancing argument suggests further that people with dissimilar tastes are relatively unlikely ever to encounter each other within networks, and when they do, there is an additional likelihood that they will exert a negative influence on each other, spurning each other's taste preferences.

Notice here that Mark remains largely within a framework in which structure influences tastes, not the other way around.[7] More recently, however, Omar Lizardo has investigated the other side of that relationship: how different kinds of cultural tastes – or, as he puts it at one point, different "profiles of cultural tastes" (2006: 779) – affect the formation of personal social networks. In fact, Lizardo offers three important observations. First he shows that those who enjoy a larger number of cultural tastes form larger personal networks (2006: 789–90). Simply the volume of one's cultural tastes is highly correlated with the size of one's personal network. As a result, he suggests, it would seem that cultural omnivores have a network-building advantage because they have the widest range of cultural knowledge and skills to connect with more different kinds of people (2006: 801). Having a wider variety of tastes makes us more cosmopolitan, and the social relations we form tend to be, accordingly, more cosmopolitan as well.

The second important issue addressed by Lizardo (2006), and by Stephen Vaisey with Lizardo (2010) in a separate article, is about determining the direction of the causal arrow linking culture and networks. This is a complex question to resolve, requiring more empirical research and very careful specification of arguments and models for those who wish to explore it. Lizardo and Vaisey argue that a plausible case can be made for cultural tastes and worldviews *preceding* the formation of social network ties. For one thing, certain key cultural tastes are formed early in life inside households (think back on Bourdieu and his notion of *habitus*), though such views go on to affect the number and kind of friendships we form later on in the larger world. Secondly, some empirical evidence suggests that cultural preferences or orientations come first, before networks are formed. For example, there may be a lot of turnover in personal networks over time (Wellman et al. 1997), while cultural worldviews are more obdurate and long-lasting. The durability of culture may be especially great in the form of hot cognitive–affective complexes – essentially, deeply held, largely unconscious value orientations that we form early in life, which act as filters in more day-to-day decisions we make and preferences we form (Lizardo and Vaisey 2010). Thirdly, social networks research from the 1970s on the world of young adolescents (Cohen 1977; Kandel 1978) indicated that, rather than social networks breeding conformity in attitudes and beliefs, a great deal of initial homogeneity of attitudes and beliefs – for example, in the orientation toward illegal drug use – preceded the formation of network ties. Lizardo (2006: 785) cites the research of Elizabeth Long (2003), too, on book groups in Houston, Texas, in which the author found that specific tastes in reading, plus a belief in the value of discussing literature, were sufficient catalysts to join these groups, in contrast to having pre-existing network ties with group members. In all likelihood, the relationship between cultural tastes and networks is typically a two-way street, with influence and reinforcement flowing in both directions. Nevertheless, we might be able to determine that the causal influence of one or the other is greater in particular circumstances. For example, previous predilections for delinquent behavior may lead youths into cliques together (i.e., cultural norms or practices come first), whereas evangelical religious movement networks (Smilde 2005) may, via their cohesive, exclusionary structure, provide the right structural circumstances for converting novices to new religious tenets.[8]

Finally, and most notably, Lizardo (2006) argues that highbrow cultural tastes, due to the restrictive, exclusionary form such tastes often take, are likely to lead to the formation of strong-tie networks with a considerable amount of local density. Think, for example, of how jokes whose comedic effect depends on a great familiarity with Chaucer's poetry, or the music of Arnold Schoenberg (or of a band like Meshuggah or Stam1na, for that matter), or the internal politics of the Qing dynasty, have a more or less inherently limited audience. It is likely that only a select number of people who have had experiences similar to those of the narrator will understand such jokes (or tolerate them!). Furthermore, and crucially, those who will laugh at such jokes probably know each other as well as you. Conversely, while graduates of elite private colleges or members of high-status social clubs might talk about the latest issue of *People* magazine or the score of last night's football game, or, most mundanely, the weather, the scope or range of people with whom one could discuss such topics is broader, and likely many of those potential alters are people one knows only weakly. In that case, the expression of popular cultural tastes is likely to lead to the formation of less dense, weak-tie-based networks. The bottom line is that different types of tastes translate into different kinds of strong versus weak and/or closed versus open personal social network structures.

Recent empirical work, especially in economic sociology, confirms the importance of cultural tastes in network formation. In a detailed ethnographic and interview-based treatment of hiring practices adopted in elite white-collar businesses, such as corporate law firms and consulting agencies, Lauren Rivera (2012) documents how much those who recruit new personnel seek applicants with similar taste profiles, experiences, and self-presentation styles as their own, to the point that one could readily say that hiring in these firms is a process of "cultural matching." Effectively, this process becomes a matter of network formation, as one's co-workers in such time-intensive occupations become one's primary social network (2012: 1007). One could treat this process in a somewhat flat way, as a matter of straightforward homophily: for example, athletic young white men recruit more athletic young white men. But similarities go beyond demographics to the detailed level of favorite sports played in college, and personal idiosyncrasies such as an enthusiasm for rock-climbing, an appreciation of Tarantino films, or a love of sushi.[9] Moreover, the matching unfolds as a process. Participants in that process read considerable symbolic meaning into the leisure-time preferences and personal characteristics of those they interview, as signs of their cultural fit with existing employees and with the organization as a whole, as indicators of the candidates' merit and/or moral fiber, and as catalysts triggering interviewers' arousal or excitement at the prospect of working together (2012: 1006).

Somewhat similarly, Catherine Turco (2010) describes how cultural filters strongly shape the experience of under-represented groups – women, and men of color – as they attempt to form relationships and build careers in the white-male-dominated bastion of the leveraged buyout industry (LBO). Male African-American informants complained that "the network nature of LBO hiring often made it feel like an exclusive country club" (2010: 900). And while women in LBO might scheme to "find ways to align yourself better [with sports-oriented male employees] because it's relationship-oriented in terms of who gets assigned deals" (2010: 901), the challenge remains substantial to acquire and maintain a convincing interest in the cultural tastes (for example, football) that predominate among men in their line of work.

Cultural Skill in Discourse

Rather closely related to the importance of tastes as formative of different kinds of networks is the theme of culturally informed skills people can utilize to form network ties. The difference may be subtle, and some of the literature on these topics does not make an explicit distinction, but whereas with tastes we are dealing with the way culture more or less automatically or unself-consciously leads to certain forms of network structure, with skill we are dealing with a more agentic use of cultural knowledge and communicative competencies with the aim of making social relations. The deployment of such skill will typically involve the use of certain kinds of cultural knowledge as the *content* of interaction; but it also crucially involves the adoption of *forms* (or etiquettes or protocols) of interaction – ways of communicating with others somewhat independent of the content of what is being communicated. Of course, such forms are themselves cultural. The use of culturally shaped skills can happen both at the level of individuals forming ties with each other, and at a more macro level, such as in the formation of coalitions between, for example, social movement organizations.

A useful starting point here is Simmel's (1950) work on the notion of sociability. He distinguishes between interactional situations in which people's talk serves the function of communicating a message or accomplishing a goal, and instances of pure sociability, where talking is an end in itself. While the analytical distinction is clear here, in fact sociability and conventions for social interaction are frequently interwoven into all kinds of functional conversations, and satisfactory performance of the gestures of sociability may be integral to the accomplishment of functional goals. One example might be flirting, discussed rather brilliantly (although also in a rather dated and sexist way) by Peter Blau (1986 [1964]) in his classic book *Exchange and Power in Social Life*. Flirting often has a quite definite purpose! – and yet many people engaging in it would regard it as offering intrinsic pleasure as well, with distinct forms of action that ought to be maintained.

As Paul DiMaggio (1987: 443) expressed it in a seminal article on the significance of culture for classifying and differentiating social groups, "conversation is a negotiated ritual in the course of which participants must find topics that reflect their level of intimacy and to which each partner can legitimately contribute."

Through conversation, we skillfully "establish co-membership" in groups, whether those groups be nations, religious organizations, fraternities, or more inchoate groups like "fans of Nick Drake."[10] In short, people typically draw upon or invoke cultural content when they try to connect with others, and they utilize accepted forms and gestures in interaction, both when they seek particular goals and when the goal of talk is the pleasure of interaction itself.[11]

This idea that talk – including both the cultural content it contains and the cultural forms it enacts – can create social networks resonates strongly with Bourdieu's (1986) formulation of the different types of capital and their mutual convertibility, which I introduced in chapter 3. Bourdieu himself stressed that social capital cannot be easily disentangled from economic or cultural capital, because creating and maintaining social ties must involve an investment of resources (for example, buying gifts, or rendering costly services), and an effort at sociability that draws on a kind of embedded knowledge – knowledge of group norms, knowledge of other people's tastes and preferences, knowledge of the etiquette appropriate for specific exchanges, and so on. We could therefore more or less "translate" our goal in this part of this chapter as exploring the potential for converting cultural capital – cultural knowledge, tastes, credentials, and so on, into social capital – the accomplishment of network connections to others, and the achievement of respected social positions. This, I believe, is very much in the spirit of what interests Bourdieu – even though he did not explore the direct convertibility of cultural into social capital in his 1986 article.

Jennifer Schultz and Ronald Breiger (2010) pick up on the importance of sociability for networks, arguing that some cultural materials serve very well as ice-breaking materials in the early stages of sociable interaction: talk of the weather, for example, or sports, as Bonnie Erickson (1996) found was skillfully deployed by managers to establish a connection with their subordinates, with whom they otherwise might share little in common. Distinct from conversational content in itself, Schultz and Breiger also offer the example of lighting up a cigarette as a culturally shaped practice which can initiate conversation, and typically conversations of a particular kind.[12] This is "weak culture," because it is not laden with deep commitments or strong value judgments; yet it is strong in its function of maintaining cordial ties with others, and, indirectly, for sustaining genial public spaces in which people can interact. Erving Goffman's superb writings on social interaction (1967, 1969), the frames of meaning deployed in interaction (1974), and forms of talk useful for entering and exiting relations (1981), all deal with the cultural material appropriate to, and necessary for, entering and sustaining social relations, including those we can think of in social network terms.

Breiger extends his examination of the value of culture in forging and maintaining social network connections in his essay with Mark Pachucki exploring the idea of "cultural holes" (Pachucki and Breiger 2010). We came across the idea of structural holes in chapter 5. Pachucki and Breiger adapt that notion to conjure up a few different ideas,[13] but here I use it mainly in the sense they give to it of signifying "contingencies of meaning, practice, and discourse that enable social structure" (2010: 215). Just as structural holes signify gaps in network structure – gaps that provide opportunities for actors to exercise brokerage, reap profits, and establish reputations for innovation (Burt 1992, 2004)[14] – cultural holes suggest places or occasions where gaps exist in cultural knowledge or skills, presumably with similar individual and/or collective benefits to reap. Those who can provide information that is lacking, or who can adopt appropriate practices for maintaining social relations, or transpose into a present situation relevant stocks of knowledge from a different domain, or, perhaps, add levity to a social situation – all such actors "occupy" cultural holes. Thus, for example, nongovernmental organizations may provide information that is vital to maintaining international treaty networks. Think tanks may supply knowledge critical to maintaining policy networks. Diplomats may supply skills of decorum and etiquette that are vital for international relations. Chatty dinner guests may help to maintain the cohesion of a network of dinner party invitees. And, following upon the research of Ostrower (1998), philanthropists may provide crucial fundraising and sociability skills that keep arts organizations afloat, rather than participating simply as an expression of their rarefied highbrow tastes.[15]

Nor need we only consider actors as the bearers of skills and culturally valuable resources. Spaces in which sociability can take place – referred to by some scholars as "publics" (Mische and White 1998; Ikegami 2005; Mische 2008) – can be "repositories" of cultural-hole-like resources. Meet-and-greet events provide locations of sociability where people can mingle within organizations across ranks – or, for that matter, across organizations. Cocktail parties are vital spaces for schmoozing, even in internet-related industries where one might think personal face-to-face contact would be of diminishing importance (Neff 2005). Job fairs provide venues for employers and prospective employees to meet up. Offices of diversity on university campuses can supply information that translates the experience of different populations on campus into mutually understandable terms, allowing them to forge connections. Universities, understood both as actors and as venues, can provide equipment, space, expertise, and a buffer against the pressures of the market, bridging between disparate actors to facilitate the growth of scientific networks of innovation (Powell et al. 2005). Protest rallies are places in which diverse communities have an opportunity to come together on a level playing field, forging network-like coalitions for coordinated social action.

One fascinating empirical example of cultural holes thinking at work in exactly such a setting of social protest comes from Ann Mische's (2003) theoretically rich work on Brazilian youth activist networks. She describes a set of techniques, strategies, or skills that are utilized in the spaces of what she calls "cross-talk" between member organizations in a complex, pluralistic social movement. She calls these "culturally constituted network-building mechanisms" (2003: 269) and identifies four of them: identity qualifying, temporal cuing, generality shifting, and multiple targeting.

Identity qualifying involves "cues as to which aspect of an actor's multiple identities and involvements are active 'right now,' in a particular set of utterances" (2003: 269). She cites the case of a student union leader who actively bracketed his identity as a socialist (and network ties to socialists) in order to appeal to a more mainstream audience of students. A similar example from a workplace setting might be a female manager who says to a female staff member, "As a woman, I know there are more important things in life than this job; but as your boss, I have to send you out of town on this project team, because you are the best-qualified person, and you can keep Bob and Doug in line." Musical theatre collaborations such as I mentioned in the last chapter (Uzzi and Spiro 2005) might be forged through such assertions as "It's true that Irving is my friend, but you're the better composer," thereby foregrounding musical skill as the more important criterion for network collaboration than friendship. Such skilled talk can be at the core of friendship formation, corporate mergers, scholarly citation, and a host of other networks, directing how those networks evolve.

Temporal cuing refers to manipulations of temporal frameworks in talk to achieve collective outcomes. For example, politicians can often build alliances with their enemies, talking "across the aisle," to obtain short-term gains while holding aside their long-term animosities. Potentially, such manipulation of temporal frameworks could be traceable through analysis of the episodes of talk between group members, and visible in graphical representations of dynamic networks over time.

The terms "generality shifting" and "multiple targeting" are used by Mische to describe words or groups or identities that can have a range of meanings, stretching from quite specific ones to highly general ones. A "student" movement can refer to the young radicals leading it, or to the broad constituency of young people for whom everyone wants a brighter future. In Renaissance Florence, the term *amicizia* (friendship) could be used to label a dyadic spiritual relationship, a tight, strong-tie-based network of political partisanship, a broader network of cordially related, mutually supportive persons, or a network of allied states. Network structures could be manipulated accordingly. Academics use the term "colleague" all the time when addressing each other to connote co-membership in an invisible college (Crane 1972) and shared commitment to its goals, even (and especially) when they are writing letters of recommendation on behalf of their students to people they have never met at other universities, hoping to insert those students in other researchers' local networks.

In reality, these discursive, network-building skills that Mische adumbrates only scratch the surface of the cultural toolkit those in networks may use to maintain old ties and to forge new ones. I took a stab at highlighting a few more of these skills, techniques, and practices in my earlier research into patronage letters in Renaissance Florence (McLean 1998, 2007). The time and place may seem remote, but a lot of what the Florentines did isn't so different from how people seek jobs and other favors from each other today. They had to provide accounts of themselves to create ties to (and secure favors from) powerful people. Often this goal of establishing network ties involved letter-writers communicating seemingly nonessential information about themselves; nevertheless, in this setting and in others,[16] nonessential information contributes mightily to painting a credible picture of oneself to others. Letter-writers cast patrons in a flattering light to curry favor – what Harvey Sacks (1992) has referred to as a strategy of "recipient design." Writers sought through letters to frame their own goals as being in alignment with the goals of those persons to whom they wrote (Goffman 1974; Snow et al. 1986) by claiming they wanted the same things, or that serving the client was in the strategic interest of the patron. And Florentines seeking favors could be surprisingly bossy, or combine bossiness with flattery in a "You're so great – surely you can do this for me!" kind of way. This rhetorical approach to favor-seeking can be seen recurrently across hundreds and hundreds of letters. It was the political culture of Florentine letter-writing – but, therefore, also the culture of network-making.

Florentines did not treat social networks or social space as givens. They *projected* a view of their networks and a picture of who was loyal to whom by contextualizing their requests in light of others' actions and attitudes (Gumperz 1992), and by switching between different possible motivations and different representations of reality (Mische and White 1998; Godart and White 2010). In short, these networks existed, at least in part, in and through the representations of them that Florentines offered in discourse.

I conclude this section with a little research by Danielle Kane

(2011) on cultural involvements and friendship formation patterns among undergraduates at an elite American university. Based on a study of approximately 300 students and their personal networks at two points in time, Kane argues that what she calls "network know-how" (2011: 268) is a critical factor that helps students acculturate themselves into college life, principally by facilitating their integration into new and diverse groupings of friends and acquaintances. Know-how includes a number of elements, such as communication skills, the ability to disclose one's feelings in an appropriate way, and the ability to provide and elicit emotional support. However, going beyond identifying a number of person-based cultural skills such as these, Kane argues that institutional norms and gender norms also contribute to steering male and female college students' friendship networks in different directions. Male gender norms denigrate the expression of feelings and the achievement of intimacy, making new tie formation more difficult. Thus, at least some significant subset of men at college experience difficulty in expanding beyond the friendships they formed in childhood or high school, often because of cultural incompetencies. Women, on the other hand, tend to be better endowed with that network know-how that permits new tie formation. As a result, they end up creating larger and more cosmopolitan personal networks, which are precisely the kind of networks favored and encouraged by elite educational institutions (2011: 270). More effective cultural endowments, along with gender and institutional norms, set women up for network success.

Given that Kane's study effectively argues for treating cultural and communicative skills in the context of (and in interaction with) norms, let's turn more fully now to the theme of norms and examine various instances in which norms can be said to guide network formation.

Norms and Schemas

I provided a brief account of the terms "norm" and "schema" in chapter 3. Here I restate those definitions for convenience. I use the term "norm" to designate some set of beliefs or expectations we might have concerning what would be considered appropriate behavior in a particular situation. And I use the term "schemas," following upon William Sewell's (1992) use of the term, to signify mental constructs, typically not fully conscious, that give shape to our perception and knowledge of the world. The notion of schema encompasses things like "conventions, recipes, scenarios, principles of action, and habits of speech and gesture" (1992: 8), transposable across situations, guiding our action.

One kind of topic that several important network analysts have explored at length is the topic of social support – or, more specifically, what different kinds of social support flow through personal ego-networks. It is instructive to consider this topic of social support in light of norms and schemas. On surveys, we ask people, "With whom do you talk regularly?", "To whom do you go for advice?", "Whom would you ask first for a large sum of money if you needed it?", and so on. We expect that certain kinds of support (Wellman and Wortley 1990; McPherson et al., 2001) and certain kinds of conversations (Marsden 1987; Bearman and Parigi 2004) will flow through certain kinds of networks, whether of kinship, friendship, or neighborhood. That certainly was one of the main findings of Barry Wellman's pioneering work on social networks in the borough of East York in Toronto. Wellman and Wortley (1990) found that most relationships provide specialized forms of support. For example, friends provide emotional support, small services, and companionship – but not, typically, financial aid. Parents and children provide financial aid to each other, but not so much companionship (1990: 567). Siblings are not commonly called upon for financial assistance; but if you have a couch to move, there's no one better. People you know at work, or from other organizations to which you belong, can be great sources of companionship, but when it comes to emptying your garage, forget about it!

It is easy to think only of the instrumentality of these networks: that is, we can imagine first that they exist, and subsequently we consider that they do certain things for us – as if the parent–child structural tie comes first, and then (subsequently) *entails* a certain set of cultural expectations or role relations. The networks are merely "functionally differentiated." However, the relationship between network tie and appropriate activation of it is actually more bi-directional than that: having a particular mental schema of what children can legitimately ask of their parents, or what siblings can ask of each other, or what is an appropriate level of favor-asking with a colleague, recurrently guides how and for what our personal networks may be activated. The vitality, and sometimes even the very structure, of those personal networks is affected by participants' adherence to specific norms and shared understandings about who generally provides what to whom. Just ask the "wrong" person for a certain kind of help and see what that does to your networks of support. That is a widespread mode in which cultural schemas affect networks.

We can get a better sense of this idea when we consider people situated in different kinds of personal network structures – for example, those who lack siblings entirely. In the absence of siblings, but with cultural understandings intact of what siblings are supposed to do for each other, to whom does the only child turn for services typically provided most often by siblings? Or, say it is culturally appropriate to turn to parents for financial support but not companionship (as has often been found): would those with fewer siblings *refrain* from turning to their parents for companionship, in compliance with a social norm, even though they had no other alternative sources? These questions animate Neha Gondal's (2012) exploration of how social support is distributed and/or re-distributed under conditions of declining family size. She shows that when people have fewer siblings, they do divert their networks toward other role relations, but they do so in ways consistent with particular cultural schemas. Parents and close friends "are viewed as appropriate 'substitutes' for siblings with respect to social support" (2012: 751); but children and spouses are not so regarded. Partners and spouses are, so to speak, *cognitively* more unlike siblings than are parents and close friends. Furthermore, those without siblings are more likely to report they have "no one to turn to" (2012: 751), implying that cultural norms concerning where social support should flow may be inhibiting them from establishing network ties. Overall, Gondal explains, "network structural effects do not operate stably across ties of different types; rather, the cultural content of ties significantly shapes structural outcomes, which, in turn, reproduce institutionalized relational content" (2012: 752).

One of the most intriguing arguments linking norms to network structure may be found in the research of Peter Bearman, Katherine Stovel, and James Moody (2004) analyzing the structure of sexual contact in an essentially complete romantic network in an American high school.[17] They discovered in that setting a so-called "spanning tree" structure: a long chain of connections that only loops back on itself after many links, and which also features a handful of long branches running off the main "trunk." Such a network structure is quite different from one in which disease (or information) is passed among members of a densely connected core, and then transmitted outwards from there. It also differs from the structure of contagion in a random mixing model – for instance, think of how you can catch a cold from someone you happen to be seated next to on an airplane, then in turn spread the cold to family members, casual acquaintances, and chance encounters when you arrive back home. The spanning tree they observed was characterized by certain unusual network properties – at least unusual relative to a population of simulated networks of the same size and overall density of ties. For example, the average shortest path distance between nodes in their observed network was much longer, and the number of cycles much smaller, than in the simulated networks. Put more simply, these ties of sexual contact did not cluster the way that, say, friendship ties would, nor the way sexual contacts cluster in other kinds of venues.

What micro-mechanisms, they ask, produce such a tree-like network structure?[18] Here is where the culture part comes in. We don't observe cycles of sexual contact involving three actors because that would frequently involve two men and a woman, or two women and a man; but homosexual contact is frequently proscribed in our culture, so such micro-level "networks" should be quite infrequent. Furthermore, Bearman et al. argue that there is an informal norm in place against dating your ex-partner's new partner's ex. Confusing as that may sound, it makes a lot of sense: most people would want to avoid dating the abandoned partner of the person their own ex-boyfriend or ex-girlfriend is now dating. It smacks of a kind of yucky incestuousness. Or one may frame it in terms of status: we often look down on those who replace us in our past partner's affections, and much more might we look down on the person whom our "replacement" jilted! Why, then, would we consider the jilted person a worthy candidate for our own affections? Taking into consideration the informal prohibition on dating your ex's new partner's ex, we now can generate a network of the sort Bearman et al. actually observed. Note carefully: they started from an observation of a network, then worked backwards to find the cultural assumptions or norms that explained the resultant pattern. But that means the norms are there at the genesis of the network, not just flowing through some pre-existing network architecture.

Delia Baldassarri and Mario Diani (2007) carried out a somewhat similar analysis of inter-organizational networks of civic organizations in Glasgow, Scotland, and Bristol, England. They observe what they call a polycentric network structure, which sounds a lot like a small-world structure as described by Watts (1999). However, going beyond an assessment of the structure of the network alone, they attempt to discern how the distribution of two different types of ties – instrumental ties on the one hand, and more affective, close, cooperative ties among organizations on the other – create that structure. They find that the affective ties act as bonds within local clusters, while instrumental ties are more commonly bridges between local clusters. That idea strongly resembles Granovetter's (1973) distinction between strong and weak ties, and, in turn, his argument about the distinct functions such ties serve. It also brings to mind Robert Putnam's (2000) distinction between bonding and bridging forms of social capital (also see Small 2009). Given sizable differences between the two cities, Baldassarri and Diani speculate that the network structures they observe might occur "largely independent of local conditions and mostly driven by the properties of the relations in which actors are embedded" (2007: 776). While that assertion taken in a certain light seems to abstract away from cultural content and context, they nevertheless argue that their goal has been to pay "simultaneous attention to both the formal properties and the content of network ties" (2007: 771).

A rather richer tradition for explaining how particular cultural norms affect network structure lies in the enormously fascinating literature on the social organization of interpersonal violence. A great example here is Roger Gould's (2003) research on the social organization of vendetta. Briefly stated, according to Gould, vendetta occurs between people and/or groups between whom there is some ambiguity or contestation over status ranking. That in itself is not particularly a network idea, and perhaps not even a very culturally rich idea;[19] but once an act of violence has occurred, the target of retribution will be highly predictable, based on the target's network ties to the original perpetrator. There is a formidable logic to vengeance killing: you kill my brother, I kill your brother. His cousin may then come after me, and I may enlist the help of my cousins in defending myself. Sometimes, who exactly may be the target of a vengeance killing is bureaucratically spelled out (Kuehn 1991), and controlling the spread of revenge through networks must sometimes be tightly regulated (Ikegami 1995; Villarreal 2002; see also Christakis and Fowler 2009: 4–5 for a brief discussion).

Fast-forward to today. Gang slayings exhibit a similar structure, as for example in Andrew Papachristos' (2009) research on the social structure of homicide. The basic idea here is that the pattern of murder he observes is highly structured by normative prescriptions as to appropriate targets, which are determined by norms of honor and of retribution, as well as the norm of in-group cohesion.[20] Murderous interactions, he notes, create networks (2009: 81). We could also imagine how Elijah Anderson's (1999) distinction between "decent" and "street" codes in inner-city neighborhoods could lead to different kinds of network groupings – although Anderson complicates that mapping beautifully by noting how much "decent" kids sometimes need to pretend to be "street" within certain limits, in order to protect themselves.

One interesting pathway going forward is to explore more fully how particular, richly specified norms and schemas affect the ways in which networks get structured, and to document that process empirically. Here I mean going beyond simply saying that strong ties cluster and weak ties spread out or span structural holes, then depositing some kind of cultural content into those types of tie. John Levi Martin (2009) has pointed us in this direction in a general way with his effort to identify the structural tendencies inherent within certain elemental network building blocks, an effort which pulls him toward at least considering the meaning-making tendencies inherent in those elements. Jan Fuhse (2009: 61) is even more explicit in his claim that network relations are organized around particular "cultural blueprints," and that those blueprints vary quite considerably.

Some recent research that Neha Gondal and I have conducted on a network of interpersonal credit in Renaissance Florence may illustrate what I have in mind (Gondal and McLean 2013a, 2013b; McLean and Gondal 2014). In examining this network of approximately 2,200 people offering personal credit to each other, we discovered that the whole network is made up of two rather distinct parts: in most of the network, credits (most of it is probably personal loans) radiate outwards from lenders to distinctly different borrowers; but for a subset of 301 persons in the network, credits circulated among them. Together, this group of 301 formed what network analysts call a strong component. What is it about the meaning and/or organization of interpersonal credit that could result simultaneously in these two rather different structures?[21]

Crucially, we argue that interpersonal credit wasn't one single thing. It could take on different meanings – or, more precisely, it meant different things to different sorts of people involved in different sorts of relations with each other in different sorts of contexts. In some cases, and between certain people, it might represent a dowry payment; in others, support for one's kin; in another, support for one's political clients; in another, a cash advance on a business deal; and so on. So, although we are seemingly measuring one type of tie in this network, we are actually capturing multiple types. And the multiplicity of those types or framings of loans is reflected in the hybrid structure of the network we found.

To give our argument a little more concreteness, we formulated models about three possible, historically situated cultural framings of the exchange of interpersonal credit in Florence. For each model, we identified which domains of social interaction would be involved, the kinds of micro-level network structures we would expect to find and those we would expect to be absent, and the kinds of macrostructures that would likely be produced by these cultural framings.[22] So, for example, if interpersonal credit were all about high-status patriarchal figures expressing care for their closest intimates (an idea for which there is considerable documentary evidence), we would observe: (a) loans flowing primarily within families and neighborhoods. At the micro level, we would expect to find: (b) unreciprocated ties, because borrowing signified dependence,[23] and (c) lender-centered stars, as lenders would probably lend to multiple borrowers. At the macro level of the whole network, we might expect a fragmented or weakly connected structure in which lenders were not directly tied to each other. If, by contrast, credits were understood in a commercial way, we would expect ties to involve more businessmen. Ties could be reciprocated, they could circulate in local eddies without raising status rank concerns, and they could aggregate at the macro level into a cohesive network with a relatively muted tendency toward a core–periphery pattern. The hybrid structure we found suggests that family-based norms of lending operated in the periphery, but more commercial norms, along with aspirations toward membership in the Florentine elite, operated in the strong component, where businessmen and community leaders predominated. Thus, variety in network structure was a product of different meanings Florentines placed on interpersonal credit.

Conclusion

To sum up, to make advances in the line of research outlined in this chapter, we need to devote much more attention to the cultural processes and specific meanings activated by actors as they generate networks. Attending to meaning need not limit us to studying the most micro level. Different kinds of tastes can be argued to lead to different kinds of social ties, and in turn aggregate into different kinds of network structures. The practice of skill in social interaction, both through the effective choice of topics and the use of proper forms, can be vital for network formation, perhaps leading skilled actors to be more central in networks, and/or to bridge to more distant populations. The existence of different kinds of norms or, more broadly, cultural schemas can affect the kinds of alters with whom we choose to interact, the kinds of interactions we layer on top of each other in multiplex fashion, and the kinds of network patterns that emerge at the aggregate level. All of these ways in which culture constitutes networks seem amenable to rigorous empirical analysis.

Nevertheless, we should be somewhat cautious as we proceed. For example, as Peter Bearman and Paolo Parigi (2004) document, it is not just high culture or serious topics that flow through strong ties. Strong network ties probably support and are maintained through a vast diversity of content, both profound ("Where is our relationship going?", "How can God become more present in my life?", "Why do I feel so moved by the music of Thomas Tallis?") and banal ("What was the score of last night's game?", "Did you take the trash out?"). Simmel (1971c) reminded us long ago in his discussion of the social functions of the stranger that sometimes very serious information can flow between people who are rather weakly tied to each other.[24] The lesson is that it can be perilous to map types of culture into types of networks based on their abstract properties. Banal topics and serious topics may be spread in a versatile way, promiscuously, across social settings. Nevertheless, it would be wise for us to remember at the outset of research that most social networks do not appear out of nowhere on the basis of purely "natural" forces. They are products of culturally informed action. Attending to that operational principle will be crucial for understanding what is really going on in networks, in terms of their topology, and in terms of how they develop dynamically.

7

Networks of Culture: Culture as Relational Structures

Among the most fundamental notions in contemporary social and cultural theory is the idea that meanings are *relational*. As the French structuralist thinker Ferdinand de Saussure established, the meaning of any word is a function of the meaning of other words to which it is connected, and/or from which it differs. Vladimir Propp (1968 [1928]) and Claude Lévi-Strauss (1963) built upon this fundamental idea that meaning is relational in some systemic way, but expanded beyond language at the level of words to examine the relational structure of myths and other stories, uncovering the skeletal structure of interlocking parts at the core of texts. Also recall that Pierre Bourdieu (1984) argued that the adoption of particular cultural tastes and styles is a function of their meaning in relation to other tastes, objects, and practices. Furthermore, he claimed, the adoption of particular cultural practices depends on the set of social groups of whom those different cultural practices are predicated. We shun certain things and embrace others as a function of *who* shuns (or embraces) what.

To put it most generally, meanings and the social contexts in which they arise co-exist necessarily in a relational nexus (Kirchner and Mohr 2010). Therefore, they ought to be studied using a relational approach and relational methods (Emirbayer 1997).[1] And, of course, network analysis supplies one powerful set of tools for mapping relations among entities formally. We ought to be able to tailor network analysis to study relations of meaning. In this chapter, we will examine some of the ways networks-inspired scholars have actually utilized network methods and concepts to uncover and distill meaning from relational patterns. Most of the examples we will visit come from sociology, but a small number come from emerging network approaches in literary analysis. In both sociology and literature, the identification of recurrent assemblages of cultural materials may be thought of in terms of *styles* (White 1993, 2008; Godart and White 2010) and *genres* (Frye 1957; Bakhtin 1986; Steinberg 1999; Lena and Peterson 2008) – seemingly simple terms masking rather complex ideas. Partly that complexity arises because a style is not just an assemblage of practices, but also some intangible way of being or doing things – a tone – and tone can be hard to capture as an element in a network. Genre may be a little more straightforward: for example, a collection of a specific set of cinematographic gestures and techniques might constitute, say, the film noir genre. Still, a mechanical juxtaposition of those gestures and techniques won't quite add up to a good film noir the way an artful assemblage and sequencing of them might. Literary theorists have handled style and genre more sensitively and proficiently than sociologists, having spent a lot more time thinking about them. But they have not tried to specify them nearly as concretely as network analysis would invite us to do.

Analyzing the relational basis of meaning through a networks lens is a somewhat different task from what we have explored earlier in this book. For one thing, what does it mean to say two symbols or words or cultural products are "tied" to each other, or have a relation with each other? Are two words connected to each other if they have a similar dictionary meaning? Or if they frequently appear close to each other in texts? Or if they are used by the same actors? Similarly, are two symbols connected if they signify the same thing? Or if they are used by the same organizations? Each of these operationalizations can be a sensible and illuminating one. And yet producing networks of words or symbols or other cultural things often requires us to code and manipulate our data rather differently than in other network applications. Furthermore, to focus on a relational network of symbols themselves (Mohr 1998, 2000: 58) can lead us to put to the side the actors involved temporarily, which some researchers may find problematic. They could persuasively argue that cultural "systems" really only come alive through the agency of actors.

One-mode versus Two-mode Analysis

An important analytical distinction that is especially germane to the study of networks *of* culture is the distinction between one-mode and two-mode network data. "One-mode data" refers to an examination of the relations among objects of one particular sort. Families marry into each other; individuals get together to make music; technologies and practices diffuse from person to person or organization to organization. Culture may be the thing produced or moved around by those entities, but frequently we conceive networks of ties as linking similar entities based on readily intelligible types of relations (marriage, collaboration, influence). "Type of relation" is not so intuitively clear in networks *of* culture. What is the relation that actually *links* objects in a network of cultural elements? Well, we might try to map the sequential *flow* between narrative elements across a set of stories (Bearman and Stovel 2000); or we might look at clusters of words in close *proximity* to one another in a set of speeches to find the "central" themes they evoke (Mohr et al. 2013); or we could examine how scientific concepts *cluster* within scholarly papers to define a research area (Hill and Carley 1999; Vilhena et al. 2014). One might establish connections among works of literature based on *common use* of themes (Jockers and Mimno 2013), or try to map *overlaps* among musical tastes (Sonnett 2004; Goldberg 2011). One also could see how songs "cite" each other via sampling (Lena 2004; Lena and Pachucki 2013); or one could map interactions among characters in a play to figure out something about the play's plot (Moretti 2013). Each of these efforts can produce intriguing results, but many of them require us to stretch the notion of relation imaginatively. Songs may exert an influence on other songs, and characters in plays may collaborate (or not) in particular scenes – those are fairly straightforward networks to consider. But how are words "tied" to each other in a network sense? Is it sensible to say that words constitute a network in some conventional sense if they are used in the same sentence? Are *all* words in such a sentence therefore connected to each other? These questions invite imaginative thought, some dose of skepticism, and careful attention to coding.

If all words in a sentence (or all songs on a playlist) are considered connected to each other, then we will have to measure how *strongly* they are connected to each other by how *frequently* they appear together across many sentences, or texts, or playlists, in order to produce a network in which the positions of words (songs) and the strength of the ties between them are meaningfully differentiated from each other. Also, we might reasonably ask how certain words in a document could "influence" other words in it. Perhaps we could argue that using certain words can *entail* the use of other words, a specific way in which we could construe relations of verbal "influence." That might be stretching things, but in any case, we must provide a careful argument as to why any given relation among cultural elements is a sensible and defensible one.

Distinct from one-mode networks involving connections among one kind of entity, like words, songs, or myths, "two-mode data" refers to a mapping of the relations between one kind of object and another.[2] One might examine which kinds of welfare organizations (mode one) provide which kinds of services (mode two) to whom (Mohr 1994; Mohr and Duquenne 1997), or which kinds of people participate in which kinds of relationships (Yeung 2005). One might examine the distribution of words (mode one) across documents, like letters (mode two), to see which words tend to co-occur in order to produce which kinds of letters (McLean 2007). One could examine what kinds of actors perform which kinds of tasks to understand how social class categories are naturalized (Martin 2000). We could also examine which style elements go together by virtue of being utilized jointly by different purveyors of fashion (Godart and Galunic 2014). In all of these cases, the pattern by which certain involvements or choices are predicated of different actors constitutes the primary meaningful organization of the social and cultural space.

An important concept associated with the analysis of two-mode data is *duality*. Classically articulated by Georg Simmel (1955) in his essay "The Web of Group Affiliations," and later formalized by Ronald Breiger (1974), the basic idea is that individuals' identities are constituted by the groups to which they belong. Conversely (or dually), any group's identity is constituted by the individuals who make it up. The two types of entity – individuals and groups – *mutually* constitute each other, in their relationship to each other, and specifically in the pattern of connections they have with each other, in what is called a bipartite network. So, for example, Richard Jean So and Hoyt Long (2013) identify and map ties (proximities) among early-twentieth-century American poets by virtue of the extent to which they published in the same outlets.[3] Poets create "schools" or circles through publication venues; dually, poets are constituted by the set of publication venues in which their work appears. Note that, while it remains commonsensically possible to define persons in terms of attributes they possess, and to define groups in terms of the functions they perform, or the rules by which they abide, the duality notion treats identities as radically relational and, moreover, built from the bottom up via patterns of involvements. That is key.

Once we have in mind that individuals and groups (or, more abstractly, one kind of object and another kind of object) co-constitute each other, we can "render" a two-mode network into two one-mode networks fairly easily. That is, we can map the links between the individuals alone, achieved via their co-membership in groups; and we can similarly draw a network solely of the connections among the groups – connections depicted as direct ties, but in fact achieved indirectly via the individuals. For example, the network relational mapping of groups into tastes, styles, or genres, can be transformed into one network of subcultural groups, spatially differentiated by the (non)overlap between their tastes, and another network of tastes, differentiated by the (non)overlap among their audiences or participants. Nevertheless, we can also preserve the duality notion by insisting that the two modes, analytically separable but substantively linked, tell us a story of how culture *makes* social organization and vice versa. As a matter of fact, many of the one-mode network analyses of networks of culture – connections among bits of imagery in literature, among scientific concepts in articles, among protest practices across social movements, and most generally the arrangement of words across texts – come implicitly or explicitly from two-mode data, the second mode being the sources in which those bits of culture are found. In some cases, we will want to preserve both modes in order to provide the most accurate rendering of a network cultural space. In other cases, focusing on one mode or the other will make sense. It depends on the goals of our analysis: mapping a cultural field, mapping a social space of groups, or explicitly showing their linkage.

Empirical Applications

In the remainder of this chapter, I will briefly discuss a small number of illustrative empirical studies to show how we may think of cultural things relationally by means of certain network concepts. A good starting example is Jennifer Lena's work (Lena 2004; Lena and Pachucki 2013). Musical artists may form a network based not only on their collaborations per se (although that is certainly conceivable for all kinds of musical genres, including jazz, rap, pop, country, and crossover songs), but also on their use of samples of each other's work. Sampling is a kind of musical citation. Through these "lineages of repetition" (Lena and Pachucki 2013: 258), artists pay homage to each other. Being sampled often by others, which in network terms would be coded as a high in-degree centrality, generally connotes prestige in the industry. Sampling others also provides an opportunity to make a claim to belonging in the network of esteemed artists. If sampling becomes reciprocal, or if sampling cycles abound among a group of rappers, then a symbolic boundary is erected around that group, and a new musical genre may crystallize as a result.[4] Via sampling patterns, we can begin to assess whether or not musical markets are segmented or cohesive and we can begin to map concepts like "crossover appeal" with structural evidence. Note that at the outset this is a two-mode network of artists and songs, although

Culture in Networks

it can be readily resolved into one-mode networks of either songs and samples, or artists, depending on whether we are interested in links among artists, or a space of musical references and gestures such as the samples themselves constitute.[5]

In recent years, network methods and concepts have increasingly been adopted in the humanities as well as sociology.[6] At the forefront of this development has been Franco Moretti (2007, 2013). In one project, Moretti maps the network of spoken interactions among characters in Shakespeare's *Hamlet* to represent the play as a "character-system" (2013: 215). This not only allows him to identify which characters are central – for example, without Hamlet himself, the network almost splits into two entirely separate components – but also enables us to observe the tangled (network) connections by which the death of different characters is accomplished. Furthermore, Moretti identifies different styles of language spoken in different parts of the *Hamlet* network, basically a distinction between the language and attitudes of the Court, and the more austere and sober language of the State. If this is true, then, as he suggests, style may be a function of plot; or, one might say, style, inscribed into the very structure of the play, is used by Shakespeare to represent allegorically different institutional and interactional spaces in society.

In another project, Moretti aims to study regularities in literature by looking for a set of plot devices that combine to constitute a specific literary genre (2013: 77, 87). To know what combination is adequate or optimal, one would really need to gather both successful and unsuccessful instances of that genre. Consequently, Moretti gathered all the mystery stories published in the *Strand* magazine during the first decade in which Arthur Conan Doyle published his Sherlock Holmes stories, examining them for the presence or absence of the particular narrative device of the "decodable clue" – a kind of plot building block that works in combination with other story elements to produce a good mystery! It turns out this defining element of the detective fiction genre was not widely adopted in Conan Doyle's time – not even systematically by Conan Doyle himself. Moretti's analysis does not go much beyond this, and it is not statistically sophisticated. Nevertheless, he explores quantitatively the idea that plot elements combine into some constellation yielding a genre.

Probably the most commonly researched type of "network of culture" is a network of words appearing in various kinds of text. Words have been studied quantitatively in various ways over time, starting with content analysis in the 1950s. But content analysis focused mostly on frequencies of word occurrences rather than devoting systematic attention to relations among them. In the 1980s and 1990s, Kathleen Carley formulated map analysis, which placed relational structure front and center in order to ascertain "the web of meaning contained within the text" (Carley 1993: 77–8). The point of map analysis was not simply to show that words occurred frequently in texts or that they were somehow proximate to each other via co-occurrence, but to identify and code the way words and the concepts they signified were linked to each other via grammatical statements. For example, the text "Scientists never fail to discover new things every day through experiments" will result in a quite different mapping (network) of relationships among concepts than the text "I discovered many scientists whose daily experiments failed to make them famous" – even though the raw content included in the two sentences is very similar.

Thus, map analysis builds verbal or concept networks attentive to the *semantics* of texts, and in turn uses the semantic patterns found to better understand the meaning of the larger fields within which such texts are written. For example, Hill and Carley (1999) attempted to understand the emergent meaning of the academic field of scholarly research on organizational culture by examining when new terminology arises, how terms are connected to each other over time, and how their widespread use in particular combinations signals an emerging scientific consensus. They complement the map analysis with a study of patterns in scholarly citations within this research field, concluding that authors who cite each other are significantly more likely to also say similar things – that is, construct similar kinds of semantic statements. However, in that study they analyzed a fairly small number of texts (the abstracts of management journal articles with the word "culture" in the title), and each of these texts was quite short.

"Semantic network analysis," as described by Marya Doerfel (1998; Doerfel and Barnett 1999), is a term covering two somewhat different approaches to determining relational meaning. One strand (for example, Monge and Contractor 2003) aims to map a semantic network within an organization based on the extent to which participants share (or do not share) an interpretation of key words or concepts. The raw data here are the participants' responses to researchers regarding the meaning of particular terms. The other strand follows somewhat more in the wake of Carley's research program, examining relationships among words within text. A body of text is chosen for analysis; so-called "stop words" are eliminated ("the," "and," "but," "of," and many others of this sort); the frequency of the remaining words is calculated; high-frequency terms are selected; and then they are examined for the volume of their co-occurrence within particular "windows" of text. That co-occurrence matrix becomes the basis for a multidimensional scaling plot that allows one to visualize distances among terms (Doerfel and Barnett 1999: 592). Doerfel and Connaughton (2009) illustrate the value of the approach through an analysis of the texts of presidential debates, arguing that speakers who repeatedly position themselves centrally with respect to key topics in the debate are more likely to win elections.

Another line of work on quantitative approaches to meaning via text has been developed by Roberto Franzosi (2004, 2010). Franzosi aims to discover "the distinguishable regularities behind narrative" (2010: 3). He focuses on the fundamental molecular structure at the heart of narrative, which he terms the semantic triplet: an *action*, typically (though not always) predicated of an *actor*, and often (though not always) visited upon some *object*. "The police arrested protesters" would be a clear example of such a triplet.[7] Narrative may in turn be understood as a sequence of these triplet-articulated events. Franzosi proposes that "if narrative, at the linguistic level, is about actors doing certain actions (including 'speech acts,' or actions of saying), perhaps in favor of or against other actors, then network analysis is an ideal tool of statistical analysis, focused as it is on bringing out networks of social interaction" (2010: 7). To be clear, Franzosi's end goal is not to identify the sequence of semantic triplets that together constitute a story. Instead, his empirical work on political protest and political suppression in early Fascist Italy (1997) uses these narrative elements to assemble a list of actors, a list of actions, and a list of things acted upon. From that raw material, he clusters actors according to the actions they have taken, or according to the extent they have been acted upon in the same way. Thus, we can identify changes in the targets of violence over time, or changing protagonists on the political scene, or changes in the mix of actions taken over time (2010: 112–13).

Franzosi's goal in taming narrative structure is ambitious, because he analyzes a large volume of textual data, and because of his desire to address causation. Narrative sequences, he argues, imply causal sequences (2010: 13). Yet only certain kinds of narrative render social causality transparent. Strictly delimited narrative may be constituted simply by the sequence of actions that comprise a story; but most real, naturally occurring narratives involve interspersed evaluative judgments and descriptive filler that round out the story. It is challenging to filter such material out of sequences of action. As narratives become more complex, going beyond journalistic accounts which often willfully suppress evaluative judgments, coding and analysis become considerably more challenging.

Another attempt at using network ideas to tackle narrative was developed by Peter Bearman and Katherine Stovel (2000). For them, a narrative network is not made up of semantic triplets, but is more simply conceived as a directed graph of arcs leading from one event to another. That formulation has a surface plausibility: stories seem to flow along a path, like a directed graph; stories have branching points, as can directed graphs; and we might expect multiple stories to contain common sequences, which would appear as identical components across multiple story networks. Furthermore, "narrative, historical, and network data are locally dense, often cyclic, knotted, and characterized by a redundancy of ties" (2000: 71). So there is some ostensible homology between narrative structure and network structure. Some clusters of events are narrated in detail, while others are skimmed over.

Elements, and chains of elements, may re-appear in a narrative, thereby taking on more value and weight (more degree centrality) in the construction of symbolic meaning. Also, some details in a good story may be extraneous to the main plot, the way isolates or small components in a network may be structurally marginal.

Bearman and Stovel offer an illustrative treatment of how one Nazi Party member narrated his pathway into that organization, and into his all-consuming identity as a Nazi, to identify what they see as the key structural properties of a typical conversion narrative. They attempt to code the story line without any imputation of motive to the actor, except insofar as he explicitly narrates his own thoughts, alongside the narration of significant local events and contextual events happening in the world more broadly (2000: 83). Using this one illustrative story, Bearman and Stovel argue that thoughts performed a more important linking function in the story of how the protagonist *became* a Nazi than in his account of his life *as* a Nazi. They also argue that the *structural* centrality of nodes in the narrative network corresponds to their *symbolic* centrality in the plot. Nevertheless, problems linger. Defining an event is by no means self-evident. Coming up with an exhaustive list of story elements and rendering ties among those elements accurately is a mammoth task, and runs the risk of being carried out in an excessively mechanical way (Biernacki 2012a). Events in stories regularly conjure up not only what came immediately before, but also events and thoughts remote in time and space. Moreover, important events and thoughts may not necessarily be remarked upon explicitly in the text itself, but merely evoked. Indeed, although what is *not* talked about in a story is usually not important, sometimes it is, and vitally so, for understanding the social organization of knowledge and the cultural landscape of moral judgments (Zerubavel 2006; Adut 2008). Story elements might be central in a symbolic sense without being central in a network centrality sense, or vice versa. Associations between story elements might be metaphorical or allegorical; but it is near impossible to capture such linkages definitively. In fact, one could argue that determining symbolic centrality remains fundamentally a hermeneutic task, and any text beyond the simplest one is open to constant reinterpretation. Bearman and Stovel themselves are not able to provide a satisfactory account of differences in narrative pathways without a good deal of evidence drawn from the content of particular elements. Thus, whatever is discerned by means of an account of the formal properties of the narrative network alone requires confirmation via substantive interpretation.

Topic Modeling

Today, topic modeling is one of the most eagerly adopted computerized methods that draws together network (relational) sensibilities with an interest in linguistic content (McFarland, Ramage et al. 2013; Mohr et al. 2013; Bail 2014). Topic models "provide an automated procedure for coding the content of a corpus of texts (including very large corpora) into a set of substantively meaningful coding categories" (Mohr and Bogdanov 2013: 546). In contrast to traditional content analysis, whereby the researcher picks terms to search for based on his or her expectations (and possibly biases), topic models seek out bundles of words appearing repeatedly in close proximity to each other, without filters being applied in advance. This makes it a highly inductive approach; only the number of topics is specified from the outset. The model proceeds by clustering words that frequently co-occur within some specified proximity to each other (that is, in sampled "bags of words") into topics. A topic, then, is not a unitary thing, but a constellation of words – nouns, descriptors, actions, etc. – that, ostensibly, collectively tell a particular story, or communicate a particular frame of interpretation.

Within a topic, all the constituent words are "linked" to each other; one might say they constitute a fully connected "network," although they are unlikely to always co-occur in every bag of words that is drawn from the corpus. The meaningfully "networky" aspect of topic modeling arises because individual words can appear in multiple topics, if they are found repeatedly nestled within disparate clusters of words. Because some topics will be mutually connected because of shared elements, while other topics will not have any shared elements, the set of topics can be nicely depicted as a network of nodes, some connected and others not (Song 2015). Furthermore, as DiMaggio et al. (2013: 577) point out, overlaps between topics via shared terms nicely illustrate the polysemy of language: specific words can connote different things in different contexts.

One use of topic models is to explore shifts in the dominant clusters of ideas characterizing a scholarly field, as McFarland, Ramage et al. (2013) did with respect to three decades of anthropology research, using more than a million abstracts as textual data.[8] By detecting shifts in terminology over time, they track the emergence of new areas of interest and subdisciplines. McFarland, Ramage et al. find evidence of anthropologists' collective shift away from so-called "primitive" societies to modern and contemporary ones. Further, there is evidence from the topic models that anthropological studies of social organization have given way to a focus on cultural practices and people's agency. Furthermore, the topic of identity has emerged as a galvanizing theme. "Networks" of words define boundaries around networks of participants in discursive and epistemic communities, thereby inducing "netdoms" (Godart and White 2010). However, in the anthropology case, we already knew of these changes, so the model has more value for verifying existing understandings of the field than catalyzing new ones.

Because a topic gathers together closely co-occurring words of different types – specifically, nouns, verbs, and modifiers – more or less indistinguishably, some practitioners suggest that a topic can express in a condensed or truncated way something semantic, such as the claim, "United States seeks security in Middle East while pursuing peace between Palestinians and Israelis," which Mohr et al. (2013) turned up in their study of American National Security Strategy documents across multiple presidential administrations.[9] These authors follow Kenneth Burke in hoping that the topics unearthed via computation will provide the raw material to tell a story, conveying what happened where, who did it, by what means, and to what end – capturing an image of the world "populated by various agents (friends, enemies, partners, neighbors, competitors) and their networked relations to each other" (2013: 675). However, topic models in fact produce word clusters without attending to how the words are actually syntactically or semantically connected, and without attending to the temporal ordering of terms (Bail 2014). In this way, it is a step back from map analysis: semantics are not part of the data-coding process, but are instead conjured from interpretation of how the topic elements seem to go together. That is cause for some caution.

Furthermore, as with semantic network analysis, topic models typically omit consideration of many absolutely key conjunctive words like "and," "or," "while," "but," and "not." Thus, topic modeling could discern, say, the various meanings of the term "honor" in a culture, or the meaning of a term like "freedom" in political discourse, by showing that the word appears in multiple different topics. It might also be able to show that "honor" occurs in certain topics in conjunction with other important terms like "profit" or "virtue" (McLean 2007), or that freedom can be linked to both personal liberty and discussions of national security. But it could have a hard time distinguishing the phrase "for honor and profit" from the phrase "for honor, not profit" – which signifies an entirely different stance. And it could have a hard time distinguishing between texts imbued with a medieval sense of honor and those, like *Don Quixote*, that parody a medieval sense of honor. For these reasons, I would argue that topic modeling is still limited to measuring what a text is "about" rather than capturing what it means in some rich, interpretive way.

My own venture (McLean 1998, 2007) into the challenge of understanding a large corpus of text as structured assemblages of concepts, frames, symbols, syntactical building blocks, and so on – networks of cultural elements – is not as methodologically sophisticated as the efforts I have outlined so far. What I did first was more in the vein of content analysis: observing the occurrence of a long list of keywords across hundreds of fifteenth-century Florentine patronage letters based on my interpretive assessment of which were important, using historical documents, secondary literature, and the letters themselves to guide my selection. It was less inductive, less automated, and less "comprehensive" than topic modeling. Beyond simply measuring the frequency of occurrences, though, I wanted to see how elements were put together, relationally, in many given letters. I used multidimensional scaling to assess the distance letters were from each other in terms of the vocabulary they used. This exercise in turn allowed me to create a two-dimensional space of letters, and a two-dimensional space of keywords – conceptually (if not exactly methodologically) pursuing Breiger's idea that the mapping of one mode (keywords) into another (letters) can be resolved dually into a mapping of the proximity of letters to each other, and of keywords in relation to each other. The map of keywords produced suggested the "discursive field" (Martin 2003; Fligstein and McAdam 2011; Bail 2014) within which Florentine patronage took place. However, to understand the agency involved in creating these "networks" of text, one must go further and interpret the texts themselves. We need to see how items in "bags of words" get put together, and we need especially to attend to the non-thematic elements of text – bits of etiquette, connective terms, emphasis, contrast, or, in short, *rhetoric* – that cultural agents use to create meaning.

Two-Mode Networks

Although it can be enlightening to map culture by showing the internal structure of a narrative, or the discursive space of a discipline, or the topical content of a corpus of text, the ultimate sociological goal of identifying structure in culture is not usually to dwell upon formal properties of cultural network composition, but to perceive, in the structure of practices, or classifications, or actions, a clue to underlying principles of social organization. By way of analogy, we might be less interested in what makes a poem hang together from a formal standpoint (Wimsatt and Beardsley 1946; Brooks 1947), and more interested in explaining how and why particular poems appeal to particular audiences. By "social organization," I mean both the organization of society into particular classes or groups, and the categorization of practices and perspectives on the world into relatively bounded, regularly patterned, fairly stable, historically contingent sets of routines, habits, attitudes, and legitimate spheres of activity – what sociologists often call "institutions" (Jepperson 1991; Mohr 2000) within the broader category of culture. We want the relational structure of culture to tell us something about the structure of the social world.

One of the pioneers in this effort to link cultural categories to social categories via network tools is John Mohr. One of Mohr's earliest projects was his analysis of the cognitive classification of poor relief in New York City in the late nineteenth and early twentieth centuries (Mohr 1994) – interesting on its own terms as a depiction of social policy in the Progressive Era, but more interesting for our purposes as an illustration of a dualistic approach to mapping cultural categories. Relief was distributed by a variety of agencies to a variety of recipients categorized by a plethora of classifications of moral worthiness, depending on assessment of their deservingness, their degree of innocence (for example, orphaned children), their gender (for example, working women), their achievements (for example, army veterans), and so on, as well as various kinds of hybrid and/or idiosyncratic classifications, such as "needy stage-dancers" or "chronic pauper insane" (Mohr 1994: 336). How can one sort through and understand this tangled and complex system of social redistribution? Who got what, from whom, and why? Mohr examines "the patterns of similarities and differences in the way that various status identities were treated by social welfare organizations" (1994: 331). He used printed directories of the New York City Charity Organization Society, a document in which member organizations listed their target categories of recipients, to code precisely which organizations served whom.[10] Then he looked for patterns of similarities (structural equivalence) as to who served whom. Clients can be clustered by virtue of the shared organizations that serve them by offering the same kinds of services (1994: 344); equally, as a corollary, organizations can be clustered by virtue of the similarity of social groups or categories of person they serve in common. Once the clustering of organizations and of social groups has been accomplished, we get a simplified image of the organization of relief as cultural practice and social institution. Status identities then can be seen as being attached to "occupants of particular sorts of *discursive roles* in the moral order" (1994: 335; emphasis in original). And an apt technique for getting at those roles, as discussed in chapter 5, is blockmodeling. Mohr uses this technique to reduce a welter of programs and populations to eight basic categories of service, which can be distinguished from each other by the moral worthiness of those served and the transience of their need, among other factors.[11]

Mohr subsequently explored the dual construction of poverty relief using Galois lattices, for a while one of the favored descriptive methods for graphically expressing the duality of classification systems. The Galois lattice is a graphical technique rooted in set theory, whereby the usage of categories from one system of classification is mapped onto the usage of categories in the dual system, whether that dual system be another system of cultural categories, or a set of actors. Imagine two (or more) trees growing, spreading their branches and extending their limbs toward each other. At the root of each tree is a concept that characterizes that whole tree. Along its branches are more specific concepts – nested, so to speak, under the root concept. These nested concepts are used in more specific applications, and therefore have more precise meanings or significance. Another way to put it might be that they are subsets of the all-encompassing root concept. But that subset quality is rooted in the fact that they are used in precise conjunction with a particular subset of concepts from the other classification system represented by the other tree. The trees are essentially branching network structures. The places where the two (or more) trees intersect define mappings of particular concepts from one classification system into particular concepts from the other. Mohr and Duquenne (1997) used the technique to elucidate more about the organization of poor relief in New York, finding, for example, that "if any class of the poor was identified as the recipients of asylum or of job-search services, then so too would they be designated as the recipients of shelter" (1997: 328). Putting it in the terms used above, the category of "giving shelter" was an encompassing concept covering the more precise services of providing asylum and job-search services, which were split apart in the lattice because they were actually distributed by different kinds of organizations.

Fast-forward 100 years to John Krinsky's (2010) examination of late-twentieth-century welfare programs in New York City. Krinsky traces the relationship between participants (mode one) in the network of debate over workfare, and the claims (mode two) that different participants staked out – a mapping of social network positions to discursive positions evolving over time. He shows that, amidst a welter of claims about what workfare would do, many of which were invoked by marginal groups in marginal settings within the broad field of public debate, some claims were discussed by multiple actors – especially those prominent actors like unions and the mayor's office, who were competing with each other (or occasionally collaborating with each other) to identify the main consequences of workfare policy. Actors' co-use of claims resulted in an "amplification" (Krinsky 2010: 629) of their importance in the debate. Over time, some actors abandoned certain claims – for example, labor unions abandoned the claim that workfare policy can be okay, so that in effect the meaning of that claim became more and more identified with, and shaped by, its exclusive use by Mayor Giuliani. In effect, Krinsky illustrates empirically the subtle argument that the meaning of claims is dependent on the identity of the (multiple) actors who make those claims. Even more radically, though, it is also dependent on the settings in which those claims are made (a third mode), and on the temporal unfolding in which they are made.[12]

I alluded to the concept of "style" early in this chapter. Style may be conceivable as a network-like assemblage of different elements, as in a one-mode network, but one that is also defined or animated by the association of those elements with particular individuals or groups, as in a two-mode network.[13] A project developed by Frédéric Godart and Charles Galunic (2014) tackles the complicated question of style, particularly style in the world of haute couture, from such a sophisticated network-relational standpoint. Stylish products are "vessels of meaning that consumers acquire when they consume the object" (2014: 6). Stylish garments, Godart and Galunic suggest, can be thought of as a compound of four elements: look, color, fabric, and print. Season after season, designers continually combine and recombine these elements in the search for a newly captivating style, constrained somewhat by the kinds of looks associated with their brand in the past. Godart and Galunic coded several hundred styles, then reduced them to 129 fundamental styles they saw repeated over time. They found that among these styles, some elements were more "resilient" – they were used often (they had high *degree centrality*), or they were used in conjunction with, or to mediate the connections among, many other elements (they had *high betweenness centrality*). Furthermore, though, they determined that the more a cultural element is associated with high-status organizations (Chanel, Versace, and so on) in an immediately previous time period, the greater its usage in the current period, suggesting that the value placed on particular styles is a function also of the status of those designers who have used them most recently. Finally, the more media attention is devoted to those fashion houses that adopt a particular stylistic element, the more that element is likely to replicate and prove resilient. The mix of elements, the status of designers, and media attention all contribute to the achievement of style.

To conclude, I briefly discuss John Levi Martin's (2000) brilliant analysis of the book *What Do People Do All Day?* by the massively popular children's author Richard Scarry. Martin sought to explain how children are socialized into a hierarchical understanding of the division of labor in society (who is destined for what kind of job) by means of the stories they hear, and specifically by means of the representations of cartoon animal characters they see performing jobs in Scarry's fictional world, Busytown. The basic idea, as Martin puts it, is that the book presents a "duality of species and job" (2000: 206). Certain animals are represented performing certain kinds of task, others distinctly different ones. One could speak of this as a task (mode 1) to animal (mode 2) mapping. For example, the portly nature of the pig makes him particular suitable for certain kinds of manual labor-type jobs.[14] The foxiness of the fox makes him suitable to be a (presumably sly) politician. The loyalty of the dog makes him an apt candidate for service-related jobs, like police work.[15] But the significance does not lie in this two-mode mapping per se, as if each job simply had its animal mate, but in its linkage to a one-mode mapping of animals to each other, and its generation of the companion one-mode mapping of jobs to each other (as in the notion of duality). That is, something about the *relationship* of jobs to each other, and thus status positions with respect to each other in the human world, is gleaned from an understanding of the animals' relationship to each other in the animal kingdom, via analogy.

To be more specific, Martin identifies a U-shaped distribution of species/jobs (2000: 222). On both arms of the U, as one ascends, one finds higher-status positions: more powerful managers and government employees as one ascends one arm (represented by predators), more skilled workers (represented by rabbits) as one ascends the other. At the base, one finds the low-skill jobs (represented by pigs, but also mice and forest animals who seem to be holdovers from pre-capitalist times). And on the rabbit arm, but in an inferior position to the rabbits, one finds cats, who are disproportionately female in Scarry's stories. Thus, something about the arrangement of the animals with respect to each other – based on the food chain, based on their size and stature – renders the hierarchical structure of the job market that children will encounter in the real world a "navigable and natural" phenomenon (2000: 197). That hierarchical structure strikes us as an accomplished and legitimate fact. Martin does not use network analytic methods per se. Nevertheless, his formal technique for clustering jobs is based on homology between one cultural relational system and another, and showing how they intersect.

Conclusion

Some very sophisticated thinking has gone into the formal modeling of culture structures – texts, narratives, styles, plot, topics, genres, subcultures – as relational systems. Similarly, some intriguing research maps out how specific cultural objects and practices are linked meaningfully to particular types of actors or situations, conveying something constitutive about the social order. While many of the techniques used to map the network structure of culture are enticing, they remain highly dependent on both creative and careful coding. In particular, the researcher has to think about what exactly is the type of relation that obtains between cultural objects. Some types of relations involve potentially direct connections between those objects; others entail more imaginative ways of linking cultural objects via the sources, events, or contexts in which they co-occur – in which case, the strength and cogency of their connection may be somewhat more tenuous. In addition, we must practice considerable vigilance so that we do not render complex cultural objects in an overly simplistic or unidimensional way. Even the simplest meaningful cultural elements (for example, nursery rhymes) may be complex, network-like assemblages of more rudimentary elements. The polysemy of words and images may be capturable in part using network techniques (DiMaggio et al. 2013), but it may be hard to respect polysemy and the richness of metaphorical resonance of cultural objects using any existing quantitative approach to culture, such as various network approaches (Biernacki 2012a). In short, network techniques can afford new perspectives on the structure of cultural phenomena, but they are not a quick fix that obviates the need for interpretive work.

8

Networks as Culture, or Networks and Culture Fused

In this final chapter, I step back from formal analysis of network structures to inquire in a more expansive way about how social networks and cultural forms mesh. Is there an affinity between particular network structures and particular cultures? Do certain kinds of network structures *produce* or *entail* certain kinds of cultural orientations? Conversely, do certain kinds of cultural recipes or programs or schemas *propagate* or *reinforce* certain kinds of sociation? Does the horizontal, "democratic" quality of many network structures encourage or require inclusive practices, egalitarian styles, and schemas for social interaction oriented toward self-determination through relationship formation? As we live in an increasingly networked world, can or should we expect our culture – our beliefs, our ways of interacting with each other, and the values we adopt – to become more "networky" in substance? While I am skeptical of strong claims that particular social structures and particular cultures entail each other, there are many intriguing examples where they do seem to go together, to the point where we can talk about *network culture(s)*.

The examples I discuss in this chapter are lighter on quantitative network analytical techniques than those in previous chapters. Nevertheless, I hope readers will be inspired to carry out *empirically rich* research on the kinds of networks I describe here, both historical and contemporary, deploying both quantitative and qualitative methods. I describe some historical cases, then some contemporary ones, in which network structure and cultural content seem to go particularly hand in hand. For example, clientage-based political structures are inherently rooted in networks, and certain kinds of cultural practices and norms could be considered distinctly clientelistic. Renaissance Florence was one of these kinds of places, and my account of clientelism as a social form is guided by my knowledge of that case – but by no means is it the only one. For example, the practice of *guanxi* in China could also be thought of as a kind of culture of networks and networking.[1] Different efforts to describe the network structure and cultural sensibilities of the public sphere fit here as well. Eiko Ikegami's (2005) research on aesthetic associations in early modern Japan, and Ann Mische's (2008) treatment of youth activist networks in 1990s Brazil, are good cases in point.

Then in the rest of this chapter I will sketch four areas of empirical research on contemporary social life where networks and culture seem to converge. First, beginning in the 1980s, organization theorists started to pay more attention to network forms of organization (Powell 1990), as well as to ways that organizations may foster cultures of collaboration and innovation (Kunda 1992; Hill and Carley 1999). Network-oriented, team-like organizations had flatter hierarchies, and more lateral communication, at least ostensibly oriented toward a more participatory ethos in the workplace. I discuss some recent research that unpacks processes of communicative interaction within networks in formal organizational settings.

Second, research on various Occupy protests and other democratization movements emphasizes the grassroots-level sparks within and between "rhizomatic" networks (Deleuze and Guattari 1988) that trigger mobilization and help it to spread. Here participation and network-based action occurs not only on the part of leaders, but also within and among the masses (Juris 2005; Castells 2013; Song 2015). These movements, according to their advocates, sponsor democratic action through democratic participation in protest activity organized "horizontally" via social networks. Much of this mobilization has occurred through, or been reinforced via, social media, prompting increasing scientific attention to Twitter, Facebook, and similar network-based information and communication technologies (ICTs) for the rapid spread of political information and symbolically charged imagery, using computational social science approaches (for example, Lazer et al. 2009).

A third and massively important strand lies in the vast frontier of daily social media-based activity that must increasingly become the focus of sophisticated attention by both network analysts and cultural sociologists. Lee Rainie and Barry Wellman (2012) have claimed that contemporary interpersonal relations, supported and constituted via social media, are driven by a new "operating system" – *networked individualism* – or what we might call a new set of schemas and practices for social interaction. Life in Facebook and on the internet more generally has brought forth a different cultural orientation – cultural in the sense of new styles and norms of interaction, and new cognitive frames for how we gather and organize information and each other. Wellman's work is part of a broad effort in the social sciences to understand the newish, networked world we live in on a daily basis. Other scholars have labeled this world using terms like "network culture" (Terranova 2004), "network society" (Castells 1996; Barney 2004), "digital culture" (Gere 2008; Creeber and Martin 2009; Baym 2010; Doueihi 2011), "convergence culture" (Jenkins 2008), "internet culture" (Porter 1998), and so on. These scholars' use of the terms "network" and "networking" is rarely based on empirical data such as would be amenable to social network analysis specifically. Nevertheless, sociologists should have some awareness of this work to see how it can inform our thinking.

A fourth and final strand I will discuss briefly concerns specific internet-based social interaction, including gaming platforms and blogs, which provide particular spaces for network activity where particular kinds of cultural practices and norms arise. I cannot begin to cover adequately the rapidly growing literature on both social media and online "communities of play" (Pearce and Artemisia 2009), even in the restrictive sense of examining the way social media and game environments can be studied for the cultural content and cultural styles they carry. However, whereas scholarly literature on the uses of social media for protest is heavy on computation and network methods without much culture, work on game environments is heavy on culture without much detailed attention to structure. Precisely because of the unrealized potentialities for developing research on the world of social media broadly construed that is more equally attuned to both networks and culture, this seems like a good place to draw this book to a conclusion. Hopefully my discussion will inspire readers to carry out analyses of social media usage that are intelligently informed by both detailed network measurements and carefully considered cultural sociological principles.

Historical Cases of "Network Cultures"

Historians and comparative-historical sociologists have documented many cases of patron–client systems: in various Mediterranean settings (Schmidt et al. 1977; Eisenstadt and Roniger 1984), in early modern England (Hillman 2008), in early modern Poland (McLean 2011), in the Philippines (Landé 1973), in the early American Republic (Gould 1996), and in American machine politics (Shefter 1976), among countless other places. One distinctive feature of patron–client systems is that, while groups and social categories exist, they are of much less importance in organizing society than concrete interpersonal relationships. The system as a whole is built up out of these dyadic voluntary ties – networks of connected individuals – frequently in ways that create cross-cutting loyalties rather than clear demarcations between groups. A norm often exists in such societies that the loyalty one feels toward one's patron, and the obligation to serve him, does not carry over to the patron's own superior. From a network standpoint, this lack of transitivity in clientage networks results in strings of dyadic attachments, rather than cohesive groups. Such strings can potentially get quite tangled. Patrons regularly have many clients, but technically it is taboo for a client to have multiple patrons. Yet that taboo undoubtedly has commonly been violated in many clientage-based societies, especially when individuals operate in multiple social networks – their neighborhood, their business world, their kin ties, the military world, their religious organizations, and so on – within each of which they might have a different patron. Furthermore, in the core of such societies, often a group of notables possess more or less equal status, and friendships can form among them, based on the mutual exchange of favors.

Clientage tends to bear distinctive cultural markers accompanying this distinctive structure. Whatever power differentials exist between patrons and clients, there is some tendency for their relationship to be expressed in terms of love and voluntary reciprocity. Furthermore, as the relationship is understood to be entered freely by autonomous individuals, there remains some danger (especially for clients) that that autonomy could be jeopardized, so each protects his status by proclaiming his personal honor. Members of such societies often practice norms of generosity, as favors are the currency by means of which loyalty is garnered: patrons offer help and advice to support their self-presentation as capable, honorworthy leaders. Precisely because patron–client ties are framed as voluntary, there is often the threat of rupture when a patron cannot cater adequately to his client's needs. The client implores the patron to help him and desires to be always held in the minds of his patron's friends, recommending himself to them (McLean 2007). And in fact patronage-based societies work as circulatory systems of reputations (Padgett and McLean 2011), with gossip and recommendations flowing constantly. Alongside assertions of loyalty, though, are constant suspicions of betrayal, and ambiguity in the way one expresses commitments (Weissman 1989). In such a context, instrumental (what can you do for me?) and affective aspects of friendship are constantly entangled. Finally, the achievement of network centrality, or at least network embeddedness, in such social groupings requires ongoing investments of effort, of money, of support. However, in keeping with Bourdieu's (1986) notion of the convertibility of different forms of capital, such investments can pay off with success in other networks: lending to notables draws one into the elite, from which position one can become involved, for example, in diplomatic missions of the state; or one expresses loyalty to a political boss, and is rewarded with a good match for one's daughter. In short, the voluntary quality of network ties, their tendency to form into string-like structures, the ambiguity in social status rankings, the importance of dyadic ties over group bonds, and the temporary quality of horizontal alliances, are strongly associated with cultural norms regarding favors and favor-seeking, cultural schemas concerning the ambiguous meaning of friendship, and cultural frames trumpeting concern for personal honor and warning against the misplacement of trust.

One could identify many other such clientage network/cultures, although they differ in the extent to which they conform to the model I just laid out. One particularly interesting similar case is the ubiquitous exchange of gifts and favors in China according to the cultural institution of *guanxi* (Yang 1994). Some scholars have seen *guanxi* primarily in instrumental terms, as a set of techniques for obtaining what one needs under conditions of scarcity or competitive demand (Bian 1997; Lin 2001). In such a view, giving gifts to one's prospective boss is the required lubricant for finding jobs and securing promotions, for example. Pursuing personal favors was especially important under Communist rule, when basic consumer goods were scarce, and systems of distribution were poor, so that obtaining necessities under the table via social contacts was especially critical (Gold et al. 2002). As China becomes more and more a market-based economy, the argument goes, *guanxi* is destined to fade in importance (Guthrie 1998). However, other scholars have stressed the Confucianist foundations of *guanxi*: that it perpetuates a longstanding cultural schema that stresses the importance of extended kin ties and spreads feelings of obligation toward family to virtually all social settings (Yang 1994; Kipnis 1997).

Guanxi has long been recognized as a networking practice, but recent theorizing about it has taken a more explicitly networks-oriented turn. Barbalet (2014) acknowledges that *guanxi* is animated with certain social norms, the rejection of which puts the individual at risk of a loss of face (*mianzi*). Such loss of face depends crucially on the spread of gossip through social networks; so it is precisely the embedding of dyadic ties in larger network structures that works in a complementary way with cultural schemas to maintain the practice. Chang argues that *guanxi* networks should be understood "in a dynamic sense that high-lights culturally constituted, meaning-laden processes wherein network forms are shaped, selected, and legitimized over the course of actors' enactment of routines and adaptation to their environments" (2011: 317). In fact, *guanxi* is pursued differently in different organizational and social network settings, suggesting that we might think of it better as a repertoire or toolbox of strategies and schemas rather than as a single cultural form. Framing *guanxi* this way diminishes the tendency to think of it as a *sui generis* cultural phenomenon, facilitating fruitful comparisons with the way favor-seeking is pursued to secure social relations and social positions elsewhere. Indeed, issues of reciprocity, making connections, engaging in pro-social behavior to gain the respect of others, and so on, are treated as important aspects of some online behavior today, especially in advice forums like chowhound.chow.com or Yelp.com, sites for file exchange like BitTorrent (Cavanagh 2007: 118), and "display" forums like YouTube (Burgess and Green 2009).

A rather different convergence of network structures and cultural schemas occurred in early modern Japan, according to Eiko Ikegami. She describes a world of "robust and vibrant networks" (2005: 3) of professionals and amateurs from diverse social classes practicing traditional forms of Japanese art and poetry. In a statement foreshadowing my discussion of Web 2.0 networks below, she claims that individuals within these networks were both producers of and audience for cultural materials. They participated eagerly in discussions of art and aesthetics, thereby jointly constituting an "aesthetic public" (2005: 4) on the basis of a "remarkable complex of private networks," horizontally organized, beyond the control of the Tokugawa state (2005: 6, 8). Some of these networks, especially those in urban settings, became a "safe haven for voluntary associational activities" (2005: 33), effectively in opposition to the state, carrying on seemingly private activities that, in a publicly significant way, implicitly critiqued the lack of freedom in Tokugawa society. Participation in these horizontally structured networks led to a temporary suppression of social roles, flattening class and occupational distinctions and inviting participants to conceive of their personal identities in transformed ways. The structural "flatness" of this network of networks and its cultural "openness" could be seen as two sides of the same coin.

Ikegami's treatment of Japanese aesthetic networks is clearly influenced by the theoretical orientation of Harrison White. She asks (2005: 45), in the spirit of White's attention to netdoms, "Where and how do the webs of culture and social networks overlap?" And she notes that she is interested in "networks of meaning and symbols as well as the concrete social-structural networks that undergird them" (2005: 47). Using a key term White employed to discuss the emergence of identities in and between netdoms, she expresses interest in the "switches" people must engineer between different modes of interaction as they shift across and among multiple different network connections (2005: 45). And in a way not unlike what Chang (2011) said about *guanxi*, and following Ann Mische's work with White (1998) on publics, she views identity, culture, and meanings as "'emergent properties' arising from the interplay of human subjectivity in actors involved in network relationships at the communicative sites of publics" (2005: 7). Admittedly, she does not utilize quantitative network analysis. Nevertheless, she inspires us to reflect carefully, and with attention to historical detail, on how the norms, etiquette, and content of interaction within particular networks echo, complement, and/or reinforce the structural arrangements of those networks.

Ann Mische's (2008) research on the changing composition of activist networks in Brazil over a twenty-year period in the late twentieth century offers a similar perspective. Her self-professed goal is "to study not just the structure of relations, but also the way that individuals and groups made sense of these networks and responded to the opportunities and dilemmas that they posed" (2008: 8–9). She pursues this goal via data she collected from questionnaires administered to over 300 activists, in which respondents described their involvements, their cultural activities, their socialization networks, their evaluations of the political scene, and their projects for the future (2008: 30).

Particular cultural schemas grow within particular institutional settings and/or particular social networks. Such schemas make sense of participants' joint history, they imply expectations about their future, they assign value to particular practices, they prioritize particular relations, and they steer participants toward some actions while discouraging others. "In this way institutions give birth to recognizable styles of interaction, which in turn contribute to the sustainability of those institutions" (2008: 39) – essentially, this is White's notion of netdom. However, in a setting where multiple networks exist, multiple styles are in play, and they *intersect* in two ways. First, they intersect in those individuals who have experience from multiple network settings – say, involvement in both student organizing and labor movement mobilization. Such individuals – especially leaders – become the bearers of hybrid styles of communication that are a product of their complex biographies across multiple different kinds of network involvements. Second, they intersect in events in public spaces where people or organizations from different networks interact. So, in short: networks trace out activists' and activist organizations' involvements; the clustering of those involvements produces several distinct cultural orientations within networks (netdoms); individuals are the vessels and publics are the spaces where intersections across netdoms arise; and out of these intersections are melded different styles of communication and leadership to be exercised in interaction (such as at rallies). Experience of multiple involvements tends to bestow upon leaders a certain amount of autonomy (2008: 45) with respect to particular strategies, and a certain capacity for dispassionateness with respect to particular organizations' goals.

Within these interaction settings, or "encounters" (2008: 47), skills of networking are put in play: leaders "often draw on ambiguity and ritual to find points of connection that generate productive relationships and new forms of joint action" (2008: 21). Leaders search each other out tentatively, establishing conversational frames (or "footings") that entail "implicit or explicit norms as to what kind of talk is appropriate" (2008: 47). Footings also convey identities: aspects of the individual or group that can be used to establish connections with others. It is an important matter of strategy not only to express some identities, but to suppress others that would jeopardize ties between groups. Strategic talk in these encounters has a palpable network dimension, because talk frequently invokes the nature of social ties possible between specific groups. Networks are *represented*, and thus constituted, in encounters.

Finally, these encounters can often produce conflict or tension or rupture, but skilled leaders find ways to mediate across networks. Those who bridge between otherwise unconnected parts of a network can be "brokers" (Tarrow and McAdam 2005), and they can reap rewards from such positions (Burt 1992). But Mische stresses that the meaning of bridging is crucially shaped by the intentions, experiences, and rhetorical repertoires of the persons or groups who occupy those positions. Some mediate in order to advance their own agenda; others to bridge between groups and facilitate cross-fertilization. The upshot is that we need to observe cultural content and cultural signaling in interaction to ascertain the meaning of structural patterns.

Network Cultures in Organizations

As I noted above, organization theorists began to pay considerably more attention to network forms of organization starting in the late 1980s (Powell 1990). At first, the network approach was applied principally to relations among economic organizations, stressing the way companies developed recurrent and long-lasting relations with each other, guided by a kind of norm of reciprocity and favor exchange (Uzzi 1996) and utilizing symbolic gestures of cooperation rather than formal contracts as a mechanism for doing business (Macaulay 1963). There remains ample opportunity, though, to study workplace networks (Smith-Doerr and Powell 2005), and workplace styles of interaction (for example, Morrill 1991) conjointly. And networks of both formal and informal relationships across all kinds of organizations, not just economic ones, are spaces in which talk takes place, and where cultural schemas that affect network topologies are activated and negotiated (Hallett 2003).

One recent germane example is Sameer Srivastava and Mahzarin Banaji's (2011) research exploring how culture and cognition impact upon the formation of networks of collaboration among employees at a biotechnology firm. They deploy an idea that has increasing centrality in the sociology of culture and cognitive psychology: that humans exhibit a dual-processing type of cognition. The "dual-process model" holds that while a certain portion of our cognition is "slow, deliberate, and conscious" (Vaisey 2009: 1683), employed whenever we give rational accounts (or rationalizations) of our behavior, much of the way we engage with the world perceptually and cognitively is actually quick, automatic, and unconscious (Kahneman 2011). This automatic cognition is guided by deeply held, essentially unquestioned assumptions.[2] Within organizations that value collaboration, say Srivastava and Banaji, all employees feel compelled to assert their commitment to collaboration. But some employees are more deeply and immediately committed to collaboration than others – something that is apparent from the more automatic, less deliberative type of mental processing they exhibit in certain kinds of cognitive exercises, rather than in their "politically correct" responses to interview questions. These automatic, unconscious commitments to collaboration are better predictors of actual collaboration than people's self-conscious assertions of commitment. Furthermore, these implicit commitments to collaborate are picked up by others as signals to collaborate! Thus, the networking activity of research collaborations within the firm they study grows out of these implicit, cognitive, cultural value commitments and signals.

Some of the most interesting research that studies interaction dynamics within network-like organizations is by David Gibson (2005, 2012). Gibson writes that "networks and interaction lie at the heart of our everyday experiences, but the study of one is, by and large, removed from the study of the other" (2005: 1561). With an eye to closing that gap, he gathered data on turns taken at speaking during seventy-five meetings of small groups of employees (three to twelve per group) at a large financial services corporation. In addition to coding this conversational data, he gathered network data on relations of friendship and degree of co-working among the participants, to detect the effect that these social network ties might have on how the participants related to each other during the meeting. "Whom you speak to, after, and in place of" are relationally relevant gestures (2005: 1564) – thus, they are a locus of social interaction in which network effects could well be evident.

Gibson found that, within the constraints of conversational norms operative in this setting[3] – taking turns, not talking over others, periodically addressing the group, not ignoring completely what has just been said – participants enacted "incremental modifications of conversational norms in light of relational commitments" (2005: 1591). That is to say, networks matter for how conversation unfolds. More specifically, subordinates replied directly to superiors when spoken to and they amplified superiors' remarks. Superiors spoke more than subordinates, but infrequently in response to particular people. Instead, they commonly spoke to initiate threads meant to engage the whole group. Finally, friends and co-workers commonly piggybacked on each other's comments, whether directed to the group as a whole or toward a particular individual.

Gibson set up this study, methodologically speaking, to measure the effects of network positions on conversational turn-taking. However, we need not see the network ties as more primary than the conversational episodes. Indeed, conversation may have a certain primacy. Conversation is structured by its own norms and etiquette that prevent it from simply replicating or expressing network relations (Goffman 1983). Network ties cannot always be activated. Some animosities cannot be expressed no matter how strongly felt. Alternatively, for example, you may wish to support your friend Clarence at a meeting; but if Clarence never ever speaks, the opportunity to support him never arises! Furthermore, although it may be harder to measure, networks are quite likely to be influenced by what happens in conversational settings. In fact, the relation between network structure and interaction dynamic is synergistic. This is why Gibson sees his work as a "first step" toward developing a program for comparative study of netdoms (2005: 1564).

In his recent work (2012) on the discussions among President Kennedy's cabinet during the Cuban Missile Crisis, Gibson stresses again that talk must be examined *in situ* and at length – not on the basis of how it is recalled after the fact. Too often what is said and how it is said is lost in post hoc accounts. This is highly problematic, given that our beliefs about the world and judgments about what to do (such as to impose a naval blockade on Cuba) are "the product of conversational dynamics rather than simply something articulated by means of them" (2012: 11). By the sequence of turns taken in talk, reality is created, not merely reported.[4] Furthermore, given that talk *produces* outcomes, reality will often be a function not simply of conversation and the contingency or "vicissitudes" with which it flows, but, more precisely, it will depend on the "rules, constraints, and procedures" (2012: 10) through which it routinely unfolds. In the case of Kennedy's cabinet in particular, Gibson stresses that participants engaged jointly in the narration of stories, especially hypothetical stories about the future, which rationalized the group's decisions.

Networks appear in at least two distinct ways in Gibson's account. One is that different micro network structures enable different modes of talk. When two people are present, they direct their talk at each other. A group of two can jointly steer themselves toward different views of reality, but almost all of the time, when they talk, they address each other. The presence of a third member of the group, or more, opens up the possibility for people to direct their comments to different individuals than the one who previously spoke, or to multiple individuals, including indirectly to the group as a whole. The other way that networks impinge on the flow of talk, and hence the outcome of decision processes, emerges from Gibson's measurement of the aggregate level of participation of different speakers, how their participation was elicited by previous turn-takers, and their distinctly different substantive roles in steering the conversation in different directions (2012: 53). Not surprisingly, Kennedy occupied the most central position in the network of communication participants during the Crisis, but the significance of his centrality was not simply that he spoke the most (though he did do that). His network centrality made it possible for people to change the topic from what it had been simply by directing their comment to him (2012: 60). In the absence of such a conversational authority and arbiter, the talk would have undoubtedly flowed differently, producing different constructions of the emergency, and conceivably impelling the participants toward a different decision.

Contemporary Global Social Movements and the Public Sphere

Today, global communication technologies permit network forms of social movements that span the globe, and these networks, according to Manuel Castells (2013) and others, nourish particular norms and practices of democratic participation. Political power is supported through "the construction of meaning in people's minds" (2013: 5) – hence its cultural basis – and it can only be combatted via the spread of counterhegemonic images and meanings within the public sphere that stands in opposition to established institutions of power. As Castells states poetically, opponents of the established order "overcome the powerlessness of their solitary despair by networking their desire" (2013: 9). Networks of Twitter feeds, and personal narratives uploaded to Tumblr, diffuse political dissatisfaction like a contagion and reassure others that their dissatisfaction is shared (2013: 172–3).[5] Thus, social networks are conceived "not simply [as] tools, but organizational forms, cultural expressions and specific platforms for political autonomy" (2013: 103). Hence meaning is, for Castells, thoroughly woven into them.

Castells identifies anecdotally the way captivating and succinct protest themes (like chants of "Tunisia is the solution!") spread across locales in 2011, from Iceland, to Tunisia, to Egypt, to New York (2013: 20). The symbolism of political activism spreads via networks (also see, for example, Shifman 2014: 132). Networks also permit, for example, the crowdsourcing of the political process, as in the Icelandic constitution of 2011 (Castells 2013: 39). Networks become a kind of schema for how politics could be done. Technological change precipitates a "deep cultural transformation," and the blogosphere comes to "prefigure what democracy could and should be like in society at large" (2013: 125–6).

Nevertheless, Castells does not link his cultural and theoretical approach with concrete and empirical social network analysis. Some intriguing work by network analysts exists tracing growth in the networks of communication and spread of messages during times of political and social protest, such as the Spanish May 15th movement in 2011 (Borge-Holthoefer et al. 2011), the Arab Spring (Hussain and Howard 2013), and the Occupy movements (Conover et al. 2013; Fábrega and Sajuria 2014; Bastos et al. 2015), but it is generally lacking in attention to cultural content, or theoretical framing regarding how cultural factors impact social media-based mobilization. No doubt dealing with cultural content and form with such massive data poses exceptional challenges. Nevertheless, some of this research exhibits a tendency to treat mobilization processes as entirely akin to natural processes of spontaneous organization, implicitly discounting the importance of cultural factors and communicative processes beyond barebones specification. Analysis sometimes proceeds as if it doesn't matter what messages are tweeted or what photographs are uploaded. Some other research indicates that internet-based network ties don't produce very "active" forms of activism (Lewis et al. 2014). What we need eventually is a combination of the tracing of network pathways with more attention to the content and formal properties of communication in these instances of networked protest.[6] The richer the framings of need, and the more that network-based activism draws on cultural schemas and tropes that are meaningful to recipients, the more likely movements are to succeed in generating effective participation. Scholars with expertise in identifying the formal properties of visual messages may become especially helpful contributors to this research agenda.

Characterizing the "Network Society"

For some contemporary social theorists, the increased capacity to spur political mobilization through social media is just one part of a wholescale transformation of social life brought about by the internet. Deleuze and Guattari (1988), Hardt and Negri (2004), Turkle (1995), and Latour (2005) are among those who, in different ways, have inspired a belief that networks constitute a new social order. Hardt and Negri (2004: 142), for example, claim that "we see networks everywhere we look." Turkle (1995) has argued that to be online is to transform ourselves into fluid and multiple selves, putting on and taking off different selves in different settings, protected by anonymity as we go. The contemporary self "takes on the attributes of a network – a lattice of nodes linked by ties of varying strength and duration, through which identity is practiced" (Barney 2004: 153).

We can easily get carried away viewing the internet through Linux-tinted glasses, and thinking about it too naïvely as a bright new frontier and too simplistically as a singular object. Much of the internet is taken up, of course, with quite traditional forms of capitalist money-making and interpersonal communication. Also, despite the occasional mental association of the internet with a myth of openness and access, it remains a highly unequal space, in which a subset of participating nodes – many of them sites owned by large media conglomerates – controls a disproportionate percentage of communication channels. The issue of inequality is as serious on the "consumer" side as on the "producer" side, as scholars not so long ago were deeply concerned about the existence of a "digital divide": inequality in access to the internet between social classes and between rich and poor countries (DiMaggio et al. 2001; Hargittai and Walejko 2008). So, although in principle we might believe the internet is horizontal, open, free, and participatory, it – like many other networks, social and otherwise – exhibits a tendency toward unequal degree distributions and hugely unequal distributions of influence over the system as a whole (Barabási 2002). Further, as Cavanagh (2007: 50) notes, the excitement surrounding the term "network" turns it into something of a "prenotion": it has become so loaded with positive evaluations, so fashionable, and so encumbered with supposedly universal properties, that we risk discounting the need to explore how social networks really work by means of empirical analysis guided by sociological concepts.[7] Sociologists must try to trace concrete patterns of internet interaction and circulation using social network analytic tools, but alongside interpretive techniques.

Networked Individualism on the Internet

Barry Wellman has been a pioneer in exploring empirically the way social networks, and especially social networks in the age of social media, concretely affect the ways we conduct our lives. In his most comprehensive statement (Rainie and Wellman 2012), Wellman refers to the culture that we operate with in this world of networks as "networked individualism": people connect with each other increasingly as individuals, not by virtue of their membership in social groups. Networked individualism in the age of the internet connotes that people exercise considerable agency in creating ego-networks comprised of alters from many different domains of their lives, such as workplace friends, college friends, childhood neighbors, fellow jazz enthusiasts, fellow soap opera buffs, fellow animal rights supporters, and so on. Undoubtedly some of these relationships can be thin; but Rainie and Wellman argue that they can often be activated to do more for us on specific occasions. This tendency toward individuals forging unique personal networks is a modern phenomenon predating the rise of the internet and mobile communication – certainly it is anticipated by Simmel – but the internet and mobile connectivity have dramatically accelerated our capacity to "network" more expansively, instantaneously, and constantly than ever before. "Networking" can be raised to the level of an "art" (2012: 4–5), but it also signifies a set of practices and habits many of us operationalize routinely every day – hence it is, in certain respects, our culture.

The individualization of social network structures that we pursue, in particular through social media, takes place in a social and cultural environment of increasing fragmentation: families have become more like networks than groups, with less time spent in face-to-face engagements. More non-traditional family structures involve more active cognitive construction of what family means and where its boundaries lie (2012: 27). Work is more often done from home and is more creative, resulting in shifting networks of production and collaboration (2012: 177). And culture is more fragmented, too, as people consume more individualized ensembles of popular (and high) culture in à la carte fashion (2012: 30). Nevertheless, Rainie and Wellman, along with some of Wellman's students like Keith Hampton and Jeffrey Boase (for example, Hampton and Wellman 2003; Boase 2008; Hampton et al. 2010; Hampton 2011) present evidence that mobile technologies and internet-based communication augment and complement traditional face-to-face bases of community rather than replacing them or unraveling them. "Networked" is not better or worse than (nor is it wholly different from) previous forms of social connectedness. Determining where and when the change from pre-internet, pre-mobile modes of communication is greatest is a matter for empirical study.

What are the emergent "norms" (Rainie and Wellman 2012: 125) and routine practices undertaken by ordinary people under networked individualism? Some of these norms and practices may seem trivial, but the extent to which they pervade everyday life renders them rather profound. Is Facebook-friending your students or your professor an acceptable practice? How wary should one be of befriending one's friends' friends? When, according to emerging etiquette concerning mobile technologies – what Rainie and Wellman call "metiquette" (2012: 105) – is it permissible during a face-to-face meeting to take a call or take time out to send a text message? Are we supposed to be "always on?" Along with emergent norms, we can trace out common interaction practices in the world of mobile, internet-based technologies, for these practices too comprise a new culture of social interaction. It is common for people to mix internet communication technologies in certain modal ways: a pre-meeting phone call lowers interaction barriers during face-to-face time; the in-person conversation can make reference to the pre-meeting phone call to get the conversation rolling; a call or text afterwards reassures participants "that the interaction lingers" (2012: 100). These are, so to speak, basic building blocks of the emerging 21st-century "interaction order." We need to think more about how changes in the way cues are given in social interaction in online settings, relative to face-to-face settings, affect the quality of interaction. One might argue that the quality of intimacy declines – or, more positively, that the *character* and achievement of intimacy changes considerably – in online settings.

Finally, in addition to documenting changing norms of interaction, Rainie and Wellman identify changing cognitive practices in the way that people use information technologies today. People read more "horizontally" than "vertically" (2012: 225). That is, rather than reading a story (or a scholarly article, or a book) top to bottom, we are easily distracted by and curious about embedded links to other stories, or other websites. While this technology in principle permits us to develop more expansive horizons and expose ourselves to more disparate cultural material and diverse cultural perspectives, it seems unfortunately to be the case that we often gravitate to internet information sources that confirm our existing prejudices.[8] As Cavanagh (2007: 90) notes, "frame diffusion . . . is unlikely to be effective where the audience is self-selected, homophilous and fragmented" – precisely the way much of the internet is actually organized! Furthermore, different media effectively present us with different story content and framing: for example, bloggers most often gravitate toward ideologically charged stories that elicit emotion, whereas YouTube most commonly provides us with humorous material. Neither overlaps much with mainstream media content. In short, as Rainie and Wellman (2012: 227) conclude, stories in different media "cover different subjects, have a different narrative sensibility, and have different pathways to capture the attention of their audience."

Blogs and Games:
The Future of Network/Culture Intersections?

I close my discussion of different contemporary meldings of networks and culture with a brief and selective treatment of a set of areas of online life which could be lumped under the term "virtual communities." I write this section, not as a confident reviewer and synthesizer of developed literatures, but as someone intrigued by the hints of ways in which the analysis of social networks could be integrated with the study of culture in the coming years to explore vast, new zones of social life.

Community is a complicated term (Cavanagh 2007; Giuffre 2013) in all of sociology, and no less so with respect to communities online.[9] Rainie and Wellman (2012) argue that we effectively form "communities" around ourselves via networked individualism. And, of course, in part Facebook works like this (Lewis et al. 2008, 2012). We can definitely identify the structure of Facebook networks; we can identify those individuals who have an inordinately great number of friends (thus likely enjoying a relatively high degree centrality in the Facebook network as a whole); and we can analyze patterns of triadic closure among Facebook users. In conjunction with such structural analysis, we can observe the etiquette utilized on Facebook to produce (or respond to) messages, and we can analyze the style and content of messages – in general, and within particular components or between particular dyads in the network. Analyses of network structure and culture within Facebook can also be carried out on a smaller scale, at a more local level. For example, one might study the Facebook profile pages of pets, the network connections among these pets, and the network connections between the animals and human users (Giacobbe 2014). Of course, the pets aren't actually posting on Facebook! But the humans writing in their voice utilize idiosyncratic language and imagery (for example, "furiend" and "the rainbow bridge") when posting, and they practice a kind of suspension of disbelief at the supposed human-like sentiments and capacities of the animals. Essentially, this is a Facebook subculture – undoubtedly one among many which can be studied for the styles, norms, and values that energize them. And we have the technology to map out patterns of relationships and interaction dynamics in such subcultural networks more concretely than ever before.

Beyond Facebook, we may tap more fully into the "participatory culture" that has grown substantially on the internet in the last decade or so. Participatory culture refers to a social setting "with relatively low barriers to artistic expression and civic engagement, strong support for creating and sharing one's creations, and some type of informal mentorship," along with a feeling among participants of "some degree of social connection with one another" (Jenkins et al. 2005: 3). Such a setting is conceptually associated with the notion of "Web 2.0" (see, for example, Creeber and Martin 2009). Measurably more and more people are creating and sharing material online: ratings, blogging, advocacy, mash-ups of existing media, and so on. Rainie and Wellman (2012: 199) cite a 2011 Pew study with figures about this participation in the production of information: 65% of internet users write on Facebook and other social media sites; 55% share photos online; 37% rate products; 33% create content tags; 26% supply comments on internet bulletin boards or blog in some way; and 15% remix online content. This is collaborative cultural work. Most or all of these practices (except email) are more commonly practiced by young people than by older people, suggesting the percentages will almost certainly go up in the coming years. As a participatory culture, Web 2.0 allows audiences "to become increasingly involved in the creation and dissemination of meaning" (Creeber and Martin 2009: 5). Because that creation is accomplished digitally and leaves traces of interactions, in principle at least we can follow and analyze the network structures through which such collaborative creation is accomplished. Ideally this would mean studying some bounded group of actors, connected via multiple ties to many of each other, engaging in some common purpose or focus, or sharing some common values or schemas reflected in observable and measurable cultural practices.

YouTube is a notable site of participatory culture (Burgess and Green 2009). Its "related videos" feature permits cultural content as well as participants to be linked to each other within genres and styles, and by means of symbolic content (memes), in network-like ways. Various kinds of cultural tastes and moral values are expressed by users via their consumption patterns, especially by the comments they post (which usually refer to original user-generated content – hence they are instances of interpersonal communication). While some video uploads are undoubtedly meant as simple self-expression or for the consumption of a limited number of people, others are competitions for popularity oriented toward social network formation. Vital internet resources such as Wikipedia are sites of knowledge creation and storage that are inherently produced through networks of participating contributors. Wikipedia itself provides network information concerning its authors and linked sites: knowledge is crowdsourced, but in – at least hypothetically – traceable ways that permit the application of rigorous network analytic techniques to see how (or whether) consensus forms about particular topics. The same goes for crowdsourced philanthropy through organizations such as kiva.org and kickstarter.com, a practice which in principle allows us to trace network ties between donor individuals and recipient individuals (or, at least, types of recipient profiles) and explore how network patterns are linked to cultural representations of the recipients. Is it possible that the "participatory culture" of the internet promotes a new level of altruism – not only in the specific sense of philanthropic donations, but also in the far more widespread practice of providing information and advice for free to fellow netizens on a wide variety of message boards and blogging sites? Do particular network structures support and sustain such altruism? In Renaissance Florence, citizens were highly attentive to their reputations (*fama*), and they offered gifts, favors, and information to each other to enhance those reputations for personal loyalty and commitment to the community. How is that so different from people offering advice on ask.com or recommendations on Angie's list, or seeking karma on Reddit.com (Tong 2013), or pursuing upvotes on Facebook, or maintaining a high ratio of music posted to music downloaded on sites like The Pirate Bay? Who doesn't want to be andrewsmith1986?

Acknowledging the surprising group-oriented generosity of some of these forms of social life is not to deny the importance of unpleasant elements in the social organization and cultural constitution of these spaces. For one thing, Cavanagh (2007: 114) claims that ethnographic accounts of life in online communities "consistently show that power is central to their operation," through techniques of shaming, threats of removal, and the like. Trolling is a common online cultural activity – a kind of deviant norm – distinctly suited to the affordances of virtual communication.[10] Trolling, notes Tepper (1996: 41), involves a "complicated play of cultural capital" and requires considerable verbal dexterity. It is typically based on a system of cultural references that only insiders understand, thereby constantly marking the boundaries of the group through interaction. Trolling can be terribly annoying, of course, but it remains a common practice and style of interaction. It is, in a sense, one of the forms by means of which participants generate stories that the group tells about itself, and it provides chunks of raw material for those stories, thereby reinforcing a sense of the community's identity. Indeed, it rises to become almost a modal form of interaction in some online settings (parts of 4chan.org being a case in point). Where, how, and to whom is trolling behavior most evident? What is the network structure of trolling – that is, who "trolls" whom?[11] And how does the relative anonymity of the internet, along with the nature of the technology, encourage the development of such a "norm?" Clearly, there is no one-size-fits-all formula here. Different internet interaction spaces will develop different institutional practices, or firmly established norms and procedures for dealing with common group tasks.

Finally, and again only briefly, massively multiplayer online gaming provides another frontier at which we can observe interactions between emergent cultures (or idiocultures) and network structures, where those network structures may be amenable to analysis because the flow of interactions has been digitally recorded. The discipline of game studies is growing fast, and it is highly attuned to tracing patterns of interaction and subcultural content within game play (see, for example, Juul 2005; Taylor 2006; Boellstorff 2008; Pearce 2009; Quandt and Wimmer 2009; Ducheneaut 2010; Nardi 2010; Hung 2011). Like any culture, online game play is constructed according to norms and traditions. When to trash-talk, whom to do it with (or against), when to cheat and how much to do so, what degree of difficulty is appropriate to avoid playing the game "cheaply," what kind of avatar to use, understanding the acronyms used by regular participants – these are some of the many ground rules and cultural schemas gamers learn and absorb as they play (Consalvo 2007; Consalvo and Harper 2009; Khanolkar and McLean 2012). Especially in multiplayer settings, a good deal of talk takes place in streaming chat forums, either among players previously eliminated from play (Ducheneaut 2010), or among members of guilds fighting together (Pearce 2009: 45; Nardi 2010: 15). Within-game death (sometimes called "wiping") seems especially catalytic for prompting conversation to take place among participants. Here we have access to transcripts of interaction dynamics more or less of the kind Gibson (2005) has analyzed meticulously to understand office politics! Participation in guilds and raiding parties and such, in games such as *World of Warcraft*, exemplifies small group interaction within online settings. Such participation requires the development of a "shared orientation toward gameplay" (Williams et al. 2014: 136). What are the structural and discursive determinants of guild success and guild durability? How important are leaders, and what kind of persuasive work do they do? From both patterns of interaction and patterns of discourse within the game, we should be able to discern the social organization of leadership in games like *World of Warcraft* or *League of Legends*.

Pearce offers some particularly trenchant comments on the value of the study of online games within a framework that considers culture and social networks jointly. Networks "amplify the scale, progression, and geographical reach of play communities" (2009: 5). Complex interactions such as can be modeled in a network analytic framework provide the raw material to help explain the emergence of culture in particular ways – not unlike the way scholars at the Santa Fe Institute study the emergence of complex life forms. Culturally shaped play produces networks via patterned social interaction, which in turn generate emergent cultural forms and practices. Among these emergent phenomena, which are shaped by *both* the concrete pathways that network structures trace out, *and* the existence of cultural raw materials for ongoing sociation, one could mention online weddings, game-wide protests, the development of guilds, and the emergence of various types of social and fashion trends – not to mention emergent cultural phenomena outside the game itself, such as the sale of avatars and character equipment and the development of currencies. Pearce (2009: 49) summarizes the potential research agenda by saying that "social network theory . . . provides excellent methods for understanding the movement of information and the overall structures of social networks," although in the case of the study of gameplay it needs to be connected to the study of "intersubjective social transactions of meaning-making from which cultures are constructed" (2009: 49) to bear the greatest fruit.

Conclusion

My main goal in previous chapters was to explore how culture could be seen as having causal effect on network structure, or, conversely, how network structure could be seen as having an influence, causally or as an intervening factor, on the creation or diffusion of cultural objects, roles, practices, norms, beliefs, and so on. In this chapter, I focused more on synergistic effects between networks and culture, especially thinking about how particular norms exist and are sustained in social structures that have largely "horizontal" network structural properties. I have described cases from various times and places in which network-based social structures are paired particularly tightly with specific cultural practices and schemas – either cultures of networking, or etiquettes that guide processes of social interaction in small group settings where the connections among group members can be traced out using social network analytic concepts and techniques.

However, especially in the most recent topics of study reviewed in this chapter, we need to work harder to integrate network structural and cultural perspectives and data collection efforts. In the analysis of Twitter feeds in the massively significant political protests of the last few years, techniques for examining network structure have been developed in abundance, but thinking about the content of such ties and the norms that guide and motivate them lags far behind. There is, one might say, "lots of structure, not enough culture." Conversely, in game studies, considerable attention has been paid to the norms and cognitive and emotional frameworks players bring to games, but relatively little to the formal analysis of the social organization of games. There is "lots of culture, not enough structure." We should aim for a more balanced approach, because in fact networks and the schemas and norms of social interaction are always with us, co-shaping social behavior.

Notes

1 Culture and Social Networks: A Conceptual Framework

1 For a treatment of the early years of network analysis, I recommend looking at a general overview book on networks, such as Kadushin (2012) or Scott (2013).

2 A vast percentage of the huge, ongoing accumulation of data in the world is network-type data: phone records, Facebook records, Twitter tweets, hyperlinks, visits to internet sites, GPS tracking of human visits to social locales, and so on. Bail (2014) notes that we currently collect more data every two days than was collected in all of history prior to the dawn of the twenty-first century, and a lot of it is this kind of social network data. Chances are network research will continue to grow exponentially in a corresponding manner.

3 Key exemplars of that turn include Clifford Geertz (1973), Marshall Sahlins (1976), Pierre Bourdieu (1984 and 1990), Lynn Hunt (1984), William Sewell (1992), and Fredric Jameson (1998).

4 By "positivist," I mean a method of doing research that centrally involves hypothesis testing, typically carried out by means of the statistical analysis of quantitative data.

5 Indeed, some exemplary efforts at studying culture quantitatively and/or formally have recently come under scathing attack (Biernacki 2012a).

2 The Nuts and Bolts of Networks, through a Cultural Lens

1 While I define important network concepts here and describe their significance when thinking of networks from a cultural standpoint, I do not discuss how to gather data or how to code and measure data using these concepts. For that, you should consult an excellent overview of the methods of network analysis, such as the still classic and comprehensive work of

Wasserman and Faust (1994), or the recent texts of Kadushin (2012) or Borgatti et al. (2013).

2 As I will discuss later, it is not uncommon for centrality to be quite unevenly distributed in networks, especially as they grow larger.

3 Set aside for the moment that words like "the" and "and" are the most "central" in most texts, but contribute very little to their meaning!

4 We *could* proceed without considering attributes. For example, we can map "likes" in Facebook without any information on who likes and who is liked; we can graph phone calls in geographical space without any sense of who is calling whom, or why; we can find out that some people have many more contacts than others, and observe that distribution across many networks, without caring which particular attributes some possess that others lack. Such research on contemporary social media can be terrific – but it has limited value in terms of understanding the cultural content and cultural drivers of such communications.

5 This idea is linked to the notion of *duality*, a concept which I discuss in chapter 7, where it is most germane.

6 For various pop cultural examples of this kind of connectivity, see http://tvtropes.org/pmwiki/pmwiki.php/Main/KnowsAGuyWhoKnowsAGuy. Saul Goodman from the television program *Breaking Bad* comes to mind as an amusing example.

7 This topic connects the idea of network structure to Robert Merton's classic notion of status set: the bundle of roles we play and the question of their compatibility or incompatibility.

8 Granovetter (1973) largely eschews substantive definitions of strong and weak ties, and instead offers a *structural* account: the stronger the tie between A and B, the more third parties there will be that are tied to both A and B. That structural closure is likely to be more common, he says, when A and B spend a lot of time with each other, and thus have little time to spend with others separately. So the strength of the A – B tie is discerned by means of the embedding of that dyad in larger network structures.

9 I don't mean that we should never get past thinking about that cultural constitution of relations. Interpretation of the nuances can go on *ad nauseam*. We can also get hung up thinking about how the meaning varies from one actor to another, from one pair of actors to another, from one context or time to another, and so on *ad infinitum*. But if we do that, we will never have an adequate justification to cluster or categorize ties at all. Better give up on network analysis if you cling to such a radical viewpoint.

10 Among such properties, I have in mind things we haven't quite got to yet, like a skewed degree distribution and the notion of small worlds.

11 To be more precise, homophily entails the matching up of partners who share some attribute or attributes to a greater extent than is true in the population from which they are drawn.

12 Sometimes those processes of finding another like oneself arise without any institutional support or infrastructure. Discovering a partner who shares one's tastes in food, music, people, and so on, often seems like a spontaneous, serendipitous confluence of tastes and values leading to a desire for a deeper connection. However, frequently those processes of finding each other are facilitated by settings where people with similar tastes and values are likely to congregate: websites, clubs, discussion groups, formal organizations, and the like.

13 The definition, counting, and statistical analysis of directed-tie triads is at the very heart of contemporary social network analysis, and the significance of directed-tie triads for discerning the "meaning" or "character" of larger network structures is immense. While these assumptions are powerful and enlightening, I will argue below that they can be tendentious.

14 I use the term "interaction" here to suggest there is some back-and-forth and communication in these processes, rather than the term "exchange," which connotes less concern over the content of these "transactions," and less commitment to the idea that actors' identities are affected by the process of interaction – rather than only by the resultant distribution of resources and structural positions. Blau (1964) provides an extended treatment of the social order in this light, including both pros and cons of such hierarchies.

15 "Density" refers to the number of ties actually present in a network as a percentage of the total possible ties.

16 Consequently, network analysts have developed concepts that relax the idea of *clique*, such as the *n-clique*, in which each member of the group can reach every other member in at most *n* steps, and the *k-core*, in which each member of a cohesive subgroup is tied directly to at least *k* (though not all) members of the group.

17 Another problem is that some scientists – especially evolutionary anthropologists – do not pay enough attention to the vast variation in patterns of social structure and social interaction – not only in human communities, but also in animal communities (Martin 2015: ch. 5), where one might think (erroneously) that such patterns are more hard-wired. We too frequently jump to explaining too many highly complex and nuanced behaviors on the basis of simple assumptions that are frequently rooted in fallacious functionalist forms of reasoning.

18 Any set of nodes in which each node can reach every other node along a chain of ties, no matter how many steps it takes, is called a component. Components may exhibit more than the minimal cohesiveness when more than one cut is required to break them into separate parts, such as in the *k-component* concept: a structure in which at least k edges would have to be removed to break it apart (Moody and White 2003).

19 Granovetter (1973) himself alluded to this idea: from the standpoint of the individual, weak ties provide mobility opportunities; but because they

knit together otherwise disconnected groups, they do more to create an all-encompassing form of social cohesion than highly local strong ties do.

20 Once in a (long) while, for example, my beloved Toronto Maple Leafs can beat the despised (but superior) Montréal Canadiens.

21 These different conceptualizations of centrality are best understood via a networks textbook like Wasserman and Faust (1994).

22 The term *centrality* is a property of nodes, whereas we use "centralization" with respect to entire networks as a summary measure of the unevenness of the distribution of centrality scores across nodes.

23 The uneven distribution of degrees in some networks follows what is called a *power-law distribution*. These networks are often referred to as *scale-free networks*. Barabási (2002) provides a good overview of such ideas.

3 Basic Culture Concepts, with a Networks Inflection

1 Hermeneutics may be defined simply as the science of interpretation. It originally referred to the interpretation of Biblical scripture. Many characters and stories in the Bible can be interpreted as signs of each other; for example, Old Testament characters such as Moses and David can be interpreted by Christian readers as prefigurations of Jesus, Jesus' parables have symbolic meaning with respect to eternal salvation, and sheep and shepherd imagery appears scattered throughout the books of the Bible, indirectly referencing other instances in a network-like way whenever they occur.

2 For a slightly dated but impressive treatment of different theoretical perspectives on culture, see Griswold (2001).

3 We *could* see primary socialization as a place where these values and beliefs are inculcated, and we can imagine one's connections with one's parents and other family members as a kind of local network. But that was not the exact way in which the pervasiveness of certain beliefs was actually conceived. The emergence of such beliefs was not studied as much as the fact of their difference across cultures (e.g., Almond and Verba 1963).

4 However, such a viewpoint on the importance of value orientations in directing behavior is achieving a renewed currency in the sociology of culture.

5 Actually, things are a little blurry here. I say this in reference to Vaisey's (2009) elaboration of the dual-process theory of culture and cognition. To the extent we emphasize bricolage and agency in the assembly of cultural materials, we veer toward the deliberate processing end of the spectrum. To the extent we emphasize *Gestalts*, we veer more toward the automatic processing side.

6 So defined, there is a lot of resemblance between the notion of schema and the notion of habitus developed by Pierre Bourdieu (1990). However, I delay discussing habitus until the section on Bourdieu below, because his work touches on the networks and culture intersection in many ways.

7 Bourdieu formalizes and measures this correspondence through the technique of Multiple Correspondence Analysis. People esteem objects. This pithy assertion expresses a kind of network tie between people and the objects (or activities) predicated of them. Formally, and conceptually, the set of actor-to-object links is effectively a two-mode network – that is, elements on a list of entities of one kind linked to elements on a list of entities of a different kind (Breiger 1974).

8 Similar ideas can be generated for other artworlds. Paintings require paint and canvas, and museums, and critics; books require paper, and presses, and acquisitions editors; and so on.

9 We can develop a richer approach to communication, as Fuhse (2009, 2015) has done. It is just somewhat premature to do so at this point in the exposition of White's framework.

10 Put this way, what White is talking about sounds not so different from what G. H. Mead (1934) was talking about in his discussion of the emergence of the Generalized Other.

11 We should distinguish between uncertainty and ambiguity. Uncertainty is confounding, whereas ambiguity can be positively strategic, and we may develop some scripts for sustaining ambiguity. Flirtation, for example, is a form of subtle talk based on ambiguity of intentions.

12 In fact, White and his co-authors sometimes seem to use the term "netdom" to signify that networks always have cultural content, rather than signifying the mapping of a particular and coherent cultural content onto a particular network structure. It doesn't really clarify things very much when they say "war" or "art" or "politics" is a netdom (Godart and White 2010: 572).

13 Their discussion of those concepts is really not very rigorous in my judgment.

14 Recall that Mead used baseball as a metaphor for how we learn the rules of social interaction: first at the dyadic level, like a network of dyadic relations between positions on the field and their mutual responsibilities, subsequently generalizing to an understanding of the "rules of the game," when we begin to imagine how all positions relate to each other.

4 Culture through Networks: Diffusion, Contagion, Virality, Memes

1 Strang and Macy (2001) and Aspers and Godart (2013) remind us, though, that sometimes growth does not simply slow as the market is saturated. Frequently products are abandoned as they obsolesce or go out of fashion.

2 That said, in this era of social media and Web 2.0, the boundary between broadcast messages and messages diffused via personal contacts, the latter of which entails the active agency of participants, is increasingly blurry.

3 However, more recently, Watts and Dodds (2007) have questioned the

assumed importance of opinion leaders in all diffusion processes, arguing that the "easily influenced" may be more important engines of diffusion.

4 The work of Noah Friedkin (1998 and 2001; Friedkin and Johnsen 2011) is especially rich here. I will discuss research on influence a bit in chapter 5, insofar as it deals with processes of reciprocal influence within a closed group of co-presenting interacting individuals. Nevertheless, the distinction between diffusion and influence is somewhat imprecise.

5 It also goes back to the work of Durkheim's contemporary and rival, Gabriel Tarde (Sampson 2012), who believed that society is constituted by micro-level emanations or vibrations and processes of imitation that together produced contagions. Tarde's framework is wonderfully suggestive, but it is at odds with the approach of social network analysis, in that he perceived that such action takes place at a distance, not via concrete network channels, and he saw this social radiation as "an insubstantial or inessential relationality" (Sampson 2012: 41, 87) rather than trying to map concrete pathways.

6 Also see Katz and Lazersfeld (1955), Festinger et al. (1950), and Newcomb (1961). The importance of social networks for certain kinds of consumption decisions is explored by DiMaggio and Louch (1998), for example.

7 Note that this part of the diffusion process is distinct from the question of kindling and keeping aflame the emergence of a new idea or new commitment.

8 Centola and Macy (2007), discussed below, agree. If few actors are connected to multiple hubs, and/or hubs are not connected to each other, and/or whatever signal is sent from a peripheral actor to his or her hub is drowned out by the "countervailing influence" (2007: 727) of the hub actor's other ties, then diffusion will be inhibited.

9 Actually, a single contact with an HIV-positive person need not lead to infection (see Kadushin 2012: 150–1). In reality, infection is more likely to spread when exposure to several infected people occurs concurrently. Moreover, the timing of contact affects the likelihood of disease transmission (just like people's colds are more contagious at different times in the trajectory of their illness). So the distinction I am setting up here between epidemiological and cultural diffusion is somewhat overstated.

10 A similar point regarding cultural framing is made by Lee and Strang (2006) with respect to the diffusion of the policy of reducing the size of public-sector bureaucracies. Such policy was more likely to diffuse when it conformed with policy-makers' *beliefs* about what actions would be legitimate from the standpoint of current economic theory.

11 Tepper and Hargittai (2009) make this argument: that, despite the widespread availability of music on the web and in other broadcast media, social networks continue to play a role in people's search processes for songs they like.

12 In a recent article, Brashears and Gladstone (2016) provide evidence that the quality of the cultural equipment used in communication also affects diffu-

sion. Put overly simply, text messages written in plain English can be received and in turn passed on to others with high fidelity; txt msgs full of ☺ and lol abbrevs much < so, imh. In the latter case, "mutations" of the message are likely to occur via the diffusion process.

13 See Traugott (2010) for a treatment of the barricade as a diffusing technique of social protest in the nineteenth century. A more recent example would be the tactic of self-immolation, witnessed during the Arab Spring, first in Tunisia, subsequently in Egypt (Castells 2013: 54), and now again in Tunisia and in India.

14 This wave of political change curiously echoes similar earlier waves of change in Europe in 1848, across Iron Curtain countries after Stalin's death in 1953, and with the decline of the Soviet Union's hegemony in Eastern Europe after 1989.

15 They furthermore tell us that "extensive use was made of rock concerts, street theater, marches, and unusually widespread distribution of posters, stickers, and T-shirts to expand interest in the election and voter registration" (Bunce and Wolchik 2010: 150). Howard (2011) describes a similar transposability of democratization strategies from one country to another in Islamic countries in recent years.

16 Bunce and Wolchik (2010: 152–3) illustrate the point eloquently: "Just as protesters in Lebanon in 2005 made repeated references to the Orange Revolution in Ukraine in 2004 and the opposition in Kenya in 2007 named itself after that very revolution, student leaders of a movement opposing the constitutional amendments proposed by Hugo Chavez in Venezuela in 2007 indicated that they had been influenced by the accomplishments of the student movement in Serbia in 2000."

17 Scott (2012: 244) refers to the similar notion of "buzz," which he defines as "the infectious power of rumours and recommendations circulating through dense cultural intermediary networks."

18 For an empirical application, see Padgett and McLean (2006), who offer a networks-based account of the emergence and diffusion of the Florentine business partnership system in the late 1300s, along with diffusion of the associated practices of double-entry bookkeeping and current accounts.

5 Culture from Networks: The Network Genesis of Culture

1 The classic example of such an aggregation of actors is Marx's treatment of the peasantry as a class-in-itself (his image is a sack of potatoes) in *The Eighteenth Brumaire of Louis Bonaparte*: structurally equivalent with respect to other classes and with respect to Bonaparte as a charismatic authoritarian figure, but lacking in internal connections that would foster their self-identification as a cohesive group with shared interests.

2 Faulkner also touches on the idea of the "duality" of composers and

producers, and of people and projects (Breiger 1974), an idea I discuss in chapter 7. And his understanding of Hollywood networks and networking (i.e., culturally rich interactions within networks) as a "freelance social organization" fits with what I discuss in chapter 8.

3   Among actors, a salient example of the discrepancy between quantity of credits (high) and alleged quantity of talent (low) is Nicholas Cage (Suzanne-Mayer 2014).

4   As one of Faulkner's informants wryly expressed it, "It's better to be a shit in a hit, than a hit in a shit" (1983: 72).

5   Giuffre invites us to think of this relational structure in a radical way. One's own position is constantly a function of where one has been, where others are, and where others have been. Showing your photographs in a gallery that once showed the art of a young Mapplethorpe may be worth more than showing in an equally prestigious gallery without that past association. Showing them in a gallery that has not shown the work of any photographer as well known as Mapplethorpe since that time may not be so good.

6   A more recent article by Giuffre (2009) also uses blockmodels to understand the structure of a population of artists on the Polynesian island of Rarotonga. She suggests that artists may find themselves backed into blocks comprised of structural equivalents, constituted at least in part by virtue of their shared criticism of, or even contempt for, other artists. Structural blocks then express the contending subgenres within a field.

7   Balazs Vedres and David Stark (2010) spin a somewhat similar story using the somewhat similar concept of "structural fold": a point of especially dense overlaps between fairly well-connected groups. Companies that straddle multiple different groups can play a coordinating role across groups and thereby develop a capacity for innovation through recurrent recombination of resources and skills possessed by their neighbors.

8   For example, see King 2004; Torfason and Ingram 2010; Zwingel 2012.

9   Other interesting work on influence processes would include Marsden (1981), Ridgeway and Smith-Lovin (1994), Skvoretz and Fararo (1996), and Yeung and Martin (2003).

10 Centola et al. remind us that it was a naïve boy in Hans Christian Andersen's story who called the Emperor's clothes for what they really were. A similar contemporary example is a boy in a Charles Schwab advertisement who bothers to question why a broker should be paid if his client loses money on an investment – a question that his dad is apparently too timid or too preoccupied to pose.

11 This is not to say that everyone participates equally. As with Hollywood, some have many credits (publications), others few. But those with few pay considerable attention to those with many.

12 A recent collaborative research project on the insularity of academic disciplines with respect to each other (Vilhena et al. 2014) measures such

insularity via an analysis of the language that scholars use in the descriptions of their research, located in the abstracts of their scholarly articles. The distance between disciplines is rooted in the extent of the existence of non-shared terminology across the disciplinary divide. Those of us in the social sciences are made painfully aware of this distance any time we skim the abstract of an article in biochemistry, for example.

13 Hutchins (1995) examined in meticulous detail the way in which the location of a vessel at sea is determined through the coordinated joint action, information collection, and processing of a group of participants. One could easily apply the same framework to the operation of forensics teams – or, to some extent, sports teams.

14 While Collins' mastery of so much philosophical material is impressive, the application of network concepts to such influence at a distance can be problematic. As Richard Biernacki (2012b) points out, identifying influence as network ties only scratches the surface of the cultural mechanisms that produced that tie: how that predecessor came to be read, what was found there that resonated with a contemporary concern, and so on. There is also the problem of sampling by virtue of historical survival: chances are many people were influential who are now lost to posterity. This must be especially true the farther one goes back in time.

15 One could just as readily go back to the English coffee-houses of the eighteenth century celebrated by Habermas (1989 [1962]), or ahead to the internet cafes of current times where the organizers of contemporary democratization movements meet, to find cases worthy of study.

16 See also Faulkner's interesting collaboration with Wayne Baker (Baker and Faulkner 1991). They analyze changes in the composition of the network "triad" of key production roles in film – producer, director, and screenwriter – during the onset of the blockbuster era in Hollywood. Historically these roles were most commonly distributed across three different persons. But with the rise of the blockbuster, Baker and Faulkner observe a growing fusion of the screenwriter and director roles, and greater specialization in the producer role as films required larger capital investments. Furthermore, they find that films with a single writer-director enjoyed a growing appeal among audiences. The fused writer-director role gave its occupant cachet, and so it became prized – rather like the way that a "singer-songwriter" enjoys a certain prestige as an artist who writes his own material. Baker and Faulkner stress not the translation of structural positions into roles, but the agentic adaptation of roles through manipulation of the structural "kernel" of the Hollywood creative production process.

17 They furthermore suggest that, if connection among small worlds grows too much, such that those worlds become mutually indistinct, creativity is likely to peter out and cultural homogeneity will predominate.

18 It is important to note, though, that Crossley sees the development of a

music scene as the joint product of social network structures and dynamics, resources that can be mobilized, and social conventions that legitimize some practices more than others.

19 Accominotti (2009), for example, also makes this kind of argument regarding painters.

20 Another frequently cited study of the network organization of jazz is Paul Lopes' (2002) book, *The Rise of a Jazz Art World*, though he does not utilize formal network analytic tools. Recently Charles Kirschbaum (2007, 2015) has used evolving patterns in networks of co-performing jazz musicians to trace the shift from a commercial logic of jazz production in the 1930s and 1940s to an artistic logic featuring greater concern for producing internally consistent styles in the 1950s and 1960s.

21 Phillips' interest in reception and classification of artistic output in a cultural market hearkens back to research emphasizing the importance of cultural categories, legitimacy, and status claims in economic markets. See, for example, Podolny (1993), Zuckerman (1999), Phillips and Zuckerman (2001), Zuckerman et al. (2003), and Hsu (2006).

22 Farrell (2001), for example, uses network language in a richly metaphorical way in the concluding chapter of his book, but his analyses are not quantitatively formalized. Nevertheless, he does suggest interesting hypotheses, such as the idea that collaborative circles of innovative artists or literati tend to arise in the vicinity of existing, "establishment" concentrations of resources and reputations, but on the margins of those concentrations. So, for example, the Impressionists formed their associations with each other in Paris, but there they remained "cut off from the most respected masters who controlled access to resources and rewards" (2001: 267). He also offers an intriguing account of what he sees as the typical, structural "life-history" of circles – that is, how their structure tends to evolve from first formation to final dissolution.

23 This is rather like the fashion industry and to some extent the Hollywood film industry, in both of which predicting which products will be successful and which ones will flop is highly uncertain.

6 Networks from Culture: How Norms and Tastes Shape Networks

1 See Emirbayer and Goodwin (1994) for an influential, but now somewhat dated, complaint about the lack of culture or the epiphenomenal quality of culture in networks-oriented comparative-historical sociological research.

2 As McFarland et al. (2014) point out, there was also some idea that network structural processes were time- and space-invariant, ignoring the fact that networks can look very different in different ecological (as well as cultural) contexts.

3 At the same time, one should not make light of certain challenges in making these comparisons. For instance, disparities in network size can make comparison difficult. Slight differences in coding and measurement approaches can blur comparison, too, never mind complicated differences in institutional and cultural contexts.

4 Another interesting idea concerns the way that particular social *settings* are laden with meaning, with important consequences for network formation. I discuss this idea in chapter 8.

5 That history is far too complex to summarize effectively here. In the structural-functional sociology of Talcott Parsons, cultural patterns were understood as harmoniously connected to patterns of social structure – even as a reflection of such structure. A long and mammoth history of criticism has challenged that view, exploring the autonomy of culture, critically unpacking the power inherent in hegemonic cultural apparatuses, and seeking to carve out a space for culturally informed agency, both in the reproduction of the social order and in the forms of resistance mounted against that order. Some of the most highly esteemed and influential social theorists of the 1980s and 1990s (for example, Bourdieu 1977 and 1990; Giddens 1979 and 1984; Archer 1988; Sewell 1992; Emirbayer and Mische 1998) wrestled at length with the culture–structure–agency nexus. The counterpoint between networks and culture plays out as a kind of structure–culture relationship, only using a more "precise" and somewhat less abstract (and some might say, pejoratively, a more mechanical) understanding of structure than the leading social theorists adopted.

6 Abstinence from certain goods often constitutes a kind of status claim. For example, priests' abstinence from sex is a claim to spiritual purity, and hiring someone else to clean one's house signifies that one is above such ignoble tasks.

7 It is worth noting that Mark (2003: 320) consciously avoids what he sees as messy issues of cultural meaning. He (1998) also avoids dealing with important complications such as the ongoing, fractal multiplication of music genres over time, and the complex combination of musical tastes that many people exhibit, in the interest of specifying a workable model of how network processes influence the space of tastes.

8 In everyday experience, we may overestimate the importance of culture over networks and other forms of social structure. We find someone on campus who, like us, is a fan of Douglas Adams, or Matisyahu, or the Dave Mathews band (Wimmer and Lewis 2010), and we imagine our shared idiosyncratic cultural tastes are what lead to our mutual friendship. But we tend to underestimate the importance of spatial proximity and population sorting in putting us close enough to someone to get to know that we have tastes in common in the first place.

9 One informant said, "I'd have to pick Blake and Sarah. With his lacrosse and

her squash, they'd really get along ... on the trading floor" (2012: 1009). That statement would be quite puzzling if you didn't know something about the social significance of these particular sports as prep school favorites, and hence strongly associated with affluence. However, not all firms are looking for upper-crust recruits. Firms develop distinct styles, such as "country club," "fratty," "scrappy," or "rough and tumble" (2012: 1008–9).

10 Nick Drake was an English singer and songwriter in the late 1960s and early 1970s. A few recordings of his music exist, but no film footage of him as an adult. His music was not widely appreciated in his lifetime, and he died of a drug overdose in 1974. But many musicians since then have credited him with being a significant influence on their music.

11 See Cardon and Granjon (2005) for an intriguing ethnographic take on this point.

12 They use Eric Leifer's (1988) notion of "prelude to interaction" to characterize lighting up a smoke. Smoking together, especially sharing a cigarette, can establish a tone of intimacy between people which can turn into a relation. Stereotypically, sharing a cigarette after sex could be thought of as a postlude to interaction! In both cases, the smoking marks the beginning and ending of a particular relation. Randall Collins (2004) extends the idea of smoking together into a collective activity, in which the idea of social networks formed through shared cultural practice is made even more concrete.

13 Most broadly, they assert that "contemporary work on culture (commonly instantiated by, e.g., meanings, local practices, discourse, repertoires, and norms) and social networks (often operationalized by dyadic social ties, homophily, actor nodes, dual networks of persons and groups, and social position) can for important purposes be usefully seen as mutually constitutive and coevolving with common roots in relational thinking" (Pachucki and Breiger 2010: 206).

14 In another place, Burt (2001: 46) is quite attuned to the idea and value of sociability as we are discussing it here. He writes: "Identity is at the heart of the broader motive behind gossip. Gossip is not about information. It is about creating and maintaining relationships .... Conversations about social structure are an integral part of building and maintaining relationships."

15 Citing some of Ostrower's earlier work, Lachmann et al. (2014: 63) suggest that donations to cultural institutions provide an opportunity for social climbing and networking – a simpler way in which cultural institutions and networks go together.

16 For example, much of the detail in a novel – the color of a couch, how long it rained, the length of the protagonist's hair – is superfluous from the standpoint of advancing the plot, but essential for painting a detailed and believable, "inhabitable" picture of the novel's world (Radway 1984).

17 To be a little more specific, they gathered network information on sexual contact of various sorts from 832 students in a school of approximately

1,000 students in total, located in a mid-sized Midwestern city. Such contact included intercourse, but also more generally "genital contact . . . resulting in fluid exchange in the past year."

18 The effort to understand the genesis of macro-level network structures out of micro-level interactions and motivations is a guiding idea in much of the recent "school" of so-called "analytical sociology" (for example, see Hedström and Bearman 2009). The idea of understanding the overall structure of networks from an assessment of the frequency with which particular micro-level structures such as stars, triads, and reciprocal dyads are observed is also a distinguishing feature of exponential random graph models. For overviews of such models, see Robins et al. (2005) and (2007). Martin (2009) correctly points out that most micro-level network structures do not (and cannot) actually aggregate into large network structures while preserving the logic of their organization. For example, we tend to befriend our friends' friends; but if we always did that, we'd eventually become friends with absolutely all of our friends' friends – an overwhelming and highly unrealistic prospect.

19 I don't mean that the feelings of indignation, resentment, status anxiety, and so on in the midst of games of honor lack cultural content, for they are symbolically and interactionally extremely rich. But one could hypothetically measure relative status as a factor leading to increased violence without much reference to such cultural content.

20 Homicide in general is anything but random, with a very high percentage of victims being well acquainted with their killers, frequently intimately so.

21 When I examined the etiquette and rhetoric of networking in Florence as a set of cultural skills (McLean 2007), I could only do that illustratively, and mostly at the level of individual dyads. That is, the letters I analyzed illustrate network tie formation in interaction; but the corpus of letters I could gather does not correspond to some complete network of friendship or loyalty ties that one could analyze and represent visually. Conversely, in the case of the interpersonal credit ties described here, we have basically a complete network, and we can hypothesize which norms and schemas were responsible for its shape. But scant documentary evidence exists regarding the content of these actual ties to support our hypotheses.

22 Fuhse (2013) develops a similar line of thought in a somewhat more general way.

23 As we put it (Gondal and McLean 2013a: 132), "borrowers should have no capacity to lend, and lenders should have little predilection to borrow."

24 Next time you head to the bar, remember to ask your bartender how many times she has commiserated with customers about fickle spouses, heartless children, and dying parents.

7 Networks of Culture: Culture as Relational Structures

1 This is just as true for spoken as for written language, where this relational nexus includes not only other words, but also the social context in which words are uttered. Consider the meaning of a spoken word like "dude," which is heavily dependent on the context of other words, sentiments, and situations in which it is uttered. The meaning of "dude" in the sentence "He went to a dude ranch" has little to do with its meaning in the statement "Some dude cut in line in front of me at the movies," which has nothing to do with the meaning of the interjection "Dude!" when your friend makes a great shot in ping pong, which is different yet again from the statement "Duuuude . . ." when you ask someone to quiet down or back off. In each case, the way the word is used signals some social standing of the speaker in relation to others.

2 One can extend this idea to three-mode networks and higher. See, for example, Mische and Pattison (2000) on the three-way relationship between organizations, political projects, and protest events in the 1990s democratization movement in Brazil.

3 Incidentally, this exercise can help to identify which particular figures brokered ties between artistic movements, as well as those forgotten or secondary figures who actually played a significant role at the time in sustaining particular movements.

4 DJs also engage in virtuosic recombinations of music, or ingenious juxtapositions of musical elements in performance. Essentially these performances, too, and playlists for that matter, might be thought of as networks of musical elements.

5 Evans' (2012) study of small literary magazines in the early twentieth century provides a similar perspective. In these ephemeral magazines, iconic symbols – black cats, for example, or purple cows – appear and re-appear in a system of esoteric and/or parodic references to each other and to contemporary literary figures.

6 The converse of this development is that scholars from outside the humanities proper have begun to treat literary texts quantitatively, via the new research area "culturomics." See, for example, Michel et al. (2011).

7 Map analysis implicitly studied these subject and predicate relations, but it still tended to treat all words as having equivalent standing and fulfilling more or less equivalent functions. Franzosi distinguishes much more rigorously between nouns and verbs in his analysis in order to identify events with more precision.

8 Vilhena et al. (2014) develop a similar approach to discern disciplinary boundaries rather than changes over time. McFarland, Ramage et al. (2013) also provide a useful summary of a number of efforts in computer science to achieve increasingly sophisticated natural language processing, speech recognition, and the like.

9 I am paraphrasing considerably from Mohr et al. here (2013: 686) to suggest the way an analyst might extrapolate a smooth statement from the more syntactically jerky output the topic model algorithm actually generates.

10 To be more precise, he coded the specific services of these organizations, such as "provide shelter" or "offer religious education." Part of the rationale for doing so is to get at the patterns of concrete action at a disaggregated level. Of course, organizations might actually offer a multiplicity of diverse services.

11 Rawlings and Bourgeois (2010) do something similar, mapping the cognitive classification of academic programs and disciplines in US higher education, and the status hierarchy that differentiates them, by virtue of a mapping of the schools that offer those programs.

12 Wouter de Nooy (2003) makes a similar theoretical point, that we can map the objective relations among cultural elements on their own (one-mode analysis, or an analysis of the structure of the field in a Bourdieuan framework), and we can map their meaning relative to each other via how they are used by particular actors or social classes (two-mode analysis, or Correspondence Analysis in a Bourdieuan framework). However, beyond those kinds of mappings, social network relations at the dyadic level – local relationships or conversations – can also have an effect, typically reproducing structure, but also potentially altering meanings at the level of the discursive field as a whole (de Nooy 2003: 321).

13 An assertion such as "He writes in a Kafkaesque style" implies some assemblage of elements of narrative and imagery and so on, but one that is associated with a particular practitioner. To say a garment is in the style of a Chanel suit has that same set of resonances: a set of internally related properties, predicated of a particular actor or set of actors.

14 Martin points to Bourdieu's analogous argument in *Distinction*, where the heavy-set jovial man pictured as a butcher seems to be the very quintessence of butcherness. As Martin (2000: 200) puts it, he doesn't just handle and sell meat, "he *is* meat." Bourdieu himself conducted an interesting exercise, reported in Appendix 4 of *Distinction*, in which people were asked to map well-known French politicians onto various objects – hats, animals, cartoon characters, and so on – to get at cognitive processes whereby we associate the meaning of these objects in a shorthand way with particular human characteristics. This is metaphor in operation.

15 It is not the physiological features of the animals that determine their role in the Busytown division of labor. One might expect the pilot to be a bird, but he is a fox, as is consistent with his fairly high-status white-collar position. Some mix of physiological traits and our imagination of the animal's character traits seems to be at work.

8 Networks as Culture, or Networks and Culture Fused

1 Learning how to do social network analysis is a far cry from learning how to "network," although many newcomers to the field don't understand the distinction. Social network analysis uses certain tools – mostly quantitative, but also some qualitative methods (Crossley 2010b) – to describe patterns of social structure. "Networking" is a strategy or set of strategies and/or routine practices people can use to make friends and forge acquaintances – making and maintaining networks rather than analyzing them scientifically. Only in some cases will network structures be the product of networking strategies, but it is cases of that sort that are of interest in this chapter.

2 Such assumptions can concern more or less morally "neutral" judgments, such as whether there is a lamp on my desk, but Vaisey argues across a number of articles that they can have considerable moral content, not unlike the way Bourdieu's concept of habitus entails a moral orientation to things and persons in the world.

3 Some norms of conversational interaction may obtain cross-culturally (Brown and Levinson 1987), but others are more culture-specific, and occasionally quite local in their operation. The tendency not to talk over others at the dinner table may vary considerably by ethnic group, for example, and by family.

4 Consider how decisions at a faculty meeting on which job candidate to hire can be randomly affected by who is able to show up for the meeting, or who among the decision-makers has laryngitis or indigestion that day. Later on, we rationalize the decision as having been based on sound criteria, but such explanations may be quite fanciful.

5 Song (2015) describes a similar situation in Korea, where protesters took turns narrating their personal experiences of frustration with the government. There is ample opportunity to trace out the power of narratives and the diffusion of narratives or narrative elements in contemporary protest.

6 Lietz et al. (2014) move a bit in this direction by trying to harness White's theoretical framework and analyze different kinds of tweets by and between German politicians in a 2013 electoral campaign. But there remains quite a gap between observing tweeting patterns and actually dealing with the cultural content or rhetorical form, say, of tweets, in a detailed way. Wang and Menczer (2015) attempt to assess what makes particular topics popular on Twitter and link popularity to social network structure and a measure of the diversity of the tweets a person posts. This has the merit of paying attention to content, but not yet in a very sophisticated way.

7 The new science of networks has effectively promoted a very strict (con-stricting) agenda of not only looking for, but *expecting* to find, power law distributions, preferential attachment, small worlds, phase transitions, and so on in any network we examine of any size – and big is seen as inherently better and more informative than small (Lazer et al. 2009).

8 Valdis Krebs has depicted, using network methods, the emergence of a polarized reading public in America around the time of the 2008 Presidential election. See Krebs, http://orgnet.com/divided.html. Jeffrey Dowd (2014) documents how participants on right- and left-wing political blogs police the boundaries of what they consider to be valid discourse about racially charged incidents in American civil society, and how they defend and uphold ideologically charged frames for interpreting those incidents.

9 Generally, by "community" we think we are referring to some group with a shared culture, in which there is some density and volume of interaction to support the group's sense of itself as a group. However, Benedict Anderson's (1991) famous discussion of national groups as "imagined communities" belies that definition, as does contemporary usage when we say things like "the Sikh community," "the gay community," or the "African-American community." Such sets of actors rarely feature dense networks of interaction beyond micro-level settings, and they may exhibit a great deal of internal disagreement over norms, conventions, speech practices, and so on.

10 Wikipedia defines an internet troll as someone "who sows discord on the Internet by starting arguments or upsetting people, by posting inflammatory, extraneous, or off-topic messages in an online community."

11 We can say the same about "flaming" (Millard 1996), a transgressive behavior involving vitriolic verbal attack on another which strangely can become a new norm of how to interact in virtual spaces.

References

Abbott, Andrew. 1995. "Things of Boundaries." *Social Research* 62: 857–82.

Accominotti, Fabien. 2009. "Creativity from Interaction: Artistic Movements and the Creativity Careers of Modern Painters." *Poetics* 37: 267–94.

Adams, Julia, Elisabeth S. Clemens, and Ann Shola Orloff, eds. 2005. *Remaking Modernity: Politics, History, and Sociology*. Durham, NC: Duke University Press.

Adut, Ari. 2008. *On Scandal: Moral Disturbances in Society, Politics, and Art*. New York: Cambridge University Press.

Alexander, Jeffrey C. 2003. *The Meanings of Social Life: A Cultural Sociology*. New York: Oxford University Press.

Alexander, Jeffrey C., Ronald N. Jacobs, and Philip Smith, eds. 2012. *The Oxford Handbook of Cultural Sociology*. New York: Oxford University Press.

Alexander, Jeffrey C., and Philip Smith. 1993. "The Discourse of American Civil Society: A New Proposal for Cultural Studies." *Theory and Society* 22: 151–207.

Alexander, Jeffrey C., and Philip Smith. 2001. "The Strong Program in Cultural Theory: Elements of a Structural Hermeneutics." Pp. 135–50 in *Handbook of Sociological Theory*, ed. Jonathan H. Turner. New York: Kluwer.

Allen, Michael P., and Anne E. Lincoln. 2004. "Critical Discourse and the Cultural Consecration of American Films." *Social Forces* 83: 871–93.

Almond, Gabriel A., and Sidney Verba. 1963. *The Civic Culture: Political Attitudes and Democracy in Five Nations*. Princeton: Princeton University Press.

Anderson, Benedict. 1991. *Imagined Communities: Reflections on the Origin and Spread of Nationalism*. New York: Verso.

Anderson, Elijah. 1999. *Code of the Street: Decency, Violence, and the Moral Life of the Inner City*. New York: Norton.

Archer, Margaret Scotford. 1988. *Culture and Agency: The Place of Culture in Social Theory*. New York: Cambridge University Press.

References

Asch, Solomon E. 1951. "Effects of Group Pressure upon the Modification and Distortion of Judgments." Pp. 177–90 in *Groups, Leadership, and Men*, ed. H. Guetzkow. Pittsburgh: Carnegie Mellon University Press.

Aspers, Patrik, and Frédéric Godart. 2013. "Sociology of Fashion: Order and Change." *Annual Review of Sociology* 39: 171–92.

Bail, Christopher A. 2012. "The Fringe Effect: Civil Society Organizations and the Evolution of Media Discourse about Islam since the September 11th Attacks." *American Sociological Review* 77: 855–79.

Bail, Christopher A. 2014. "The Cultural Environment: Measuring Culture with Big Data." *Theory and Society* 43: 465–82.

Baker, Wayne E., and Robert R. Faulkner. 1991. "Role as Resource in the Hollywood Film Industry." *American Journal of Sociology* 97: 279–309.

Bakhtin, M. M. 1986. *Speech Genres and Other Late Essays*, trans. Vern W. McGee, ed. Caryl Emerson and Michael Holquist. Austin: University of Texas Press.

Baldassarri, Delia, and Peter Bearman. 2007. "Dynamics of Political Polarization." *American Sociological Review* 72: 784–811.

Baldassarri, Delia, and Mario Diani. 2007. "The Integrative Power of Civic Networks." *American Journal of Sociology* 113: 735–80.

Barabási, Albert-László. 2002. *Linked: The New Science of Networks*. London: Perseus Books.

Barbalet, Jack. 2014. "The Structure of Guanxi: Resolving Problems of Network Assurance." *Theory and Society* 43: 51–69.

Barney, Darin. 2004. *The Network Society*. Cambridge: Polity.

Bastos, Marco, Dan Mercea, and Arthur Charpentier. 2015. "Tents, Tweets, and Events: The Interplay Between Ongoing Protests and Social Media." *Journal of Communication* 65: 320–50.

Baym, Nancy K. 2010. *Personal Connections in the Digital Age*. Cambridge: Polity.

Bearman, Peter S. 1993. *Relations into Rhetorics: Local Elite Social Structure in Norfolk, England, 1540–1640*. New Brunswick, NJ: Rutgers University Press.

Bearman, Peter S., and Paolo Parigi. 2004. "Cloning Headless Frogs and Other Important Matters: Conversation Topics and Network Structure." *Social Forces* 83: 535–57.

Bearman, Peter S., and Katherine Stovel. 2000. "Becoming a Nazi: A Model for Narrative Networks." *Poetics* 27: 69–90.

Bearman, Peter S., James Moody, and Katherine Stovel. 2004. "Chains of Affection: The Structure of Adolescent Romantic and Sexual Networks." *American Journal of Sociology* 110: 44–91.

Becker, Howard S. 1963. *Outsiders: Studies in the Sociology of Deviance*. London: Free Press of Glencoe.

Becker, Howard S. 1982. *Art Worlds*. Berkeley: University of California Press.

References

Bennett, Andy. 2004. "Consolidating the Music Scenes Perspective." *Poetics* 32: 223–34.

Bennett, Andy, and Richard A. Peterson, eds. 2004. *Music Scenes: Local, Translocal, and Virtual*. Nashville: Vanderbilt University Press.

Bian, Yanjie. 1997. "Bringing Strong Ties Back In: Indirect Ties, Network Bridges, and Job Searches in China." *American Sociological Review* 62: 366–85.

Biernacki, Richard. 2012a. *Reinventing Evidence in Social Inquiry: Decoding Facts and Variables*. New York: Palgrave Macmillan.

Biernacki, Richard. 2012b. "Rationalization Processes inside Cultural Sociology." Pp. 46–69 in *The Oxford Handbook of Cultural Sociology*, ed. J. Alexander, R. Jacobs, and P. Smith. New York: Oxford University Press.

Blau, Peter M. 1986 [1964]. *Exchange and Power in Social Life*. New Brunswick, NJ: Transaction Books.

Boase, Jeffrey. 2008. "Personal Networks and the Personal Communication System." *Information, Communication & Society* 11: 490–508.

Boellstorff, Tom. 2008. *Coming of Age in Second Life: An Anthropologist Explores the Virtually Human*. Princeton: Princeton University Press.

Bonnell, Victoria E., and Lynn Hunt. 1999. *Beyond the Cultural Turn: New Directions in the Study of Society and Culture*. Berkeley: University of California Press.

Boorman, Scott, and Harrison C. White. 1976. "Social Structure from Multiple Networks. II: Role Structures." *American Journal of Sociology* 81: 1384–446.

Borgatti, Stephen P., Martin G. Everett, and Jeffrey C. Johnson. 2013. *Analyzing Social Networks*. Los Angeles: Sage.

Borge-Holthoefer, Javier, Alejandro Rivero, Iñigo García, et al. 2011. "Structural and Dynamical Patterns on Online Social Networks: The Spanish May 15th Movement as a Case Study." *PLoS-ONE* 6.8: e23883. doi 10.1371/journal.pone.0023883.

Bourdieu, Pierre. 1977. *Outline of a Theory of Practice*, trans. Richard Nice. Cambridge: Cambridge University Press.

Bourdieu, Pierre. 1984. *Distinction: A Social Critique of the Judgment of Taste*, trans. Richard Nice. Cambridge, MA: Harvard University Press.

Bourdieu, Pierre. 1986. "The Forms of Capital." Pp. 241–58 in *Handbook of Theory and Research for the Sociology of Education*, ed. J. G. Richardson. New York: Greenwood Press.

Bourdieu, Pierre. 1988. *Homo Academicus*, trans. Peter Collier. Cambridge: Polity.

Bourdieu, Pierre. 1990. *The Logic of Practice*, trans. Richard Nice. Cambridge: Polity.

Bourdieu, Pierre, and Loïc J. D. Wacquant. 1992. *An Invitation to Reflexive Sociology*. Chicago: University of Chicago Press.

References

Brashears, Matthew E., and Eric Gladstone. 2016. "Error Correction Mechanisms in Social Networks Can Reduce Accuracy and Encourage Innovation." *Social Networks* 44: 22–35.

Breiger, Ronald L. 1974. "The Duality of Persons and Groups." *Social Forces* 53: 181–90.

Brooks, Cleanth. 1947. *The Well-Wrought Urn: Studies in the Structure of Poetry.* New York: Harcourt Brace.

Brown, Penelope, and Stephen C. Levinson. 1987. *Politeness: Some Universals in Language Usage.* Cambridge: Cambridge University Press.

Bryson, Bethany. 1996. "'Anything but Heavy Metal': Symbolic Exclusion and Musical Dislikes." *American Sociological Review* 61: 884–99.

Bunce, Valerie, and Sharon Wolchik. 2010. "Transnational Networks, Diffusion Dynamics, and Electoral Change in the Postcommunist World." Pp. 140–62 in *The Diffusion of Social Movements: Actors, Mechanisms, and Political Effects,* ed. R. Givan, K. Roberts, and S. Soule. Cambridge: Cambridge University Press.

Burgess, Jean, and Joshua Green. 2009. *YouTube: Online Video and Participatory Culture.* Cambridge: Polity.

Burris, Val. 2005. "Interlocking Directorates and Political Cohesion Among Corporate Elites." *American Journal of Sociology* 111: 249–83.

Burt, Ronald S. 1987. "Social Contagion and Innovation: Cohesion versus Structural Equivalence." *American Journal of Sociology* 92: 1287–335.

Burt, Ronald S. 1992. *Structural Holes: The Social Structure of Competition.* Cambridge, MA: Harvard University Press.

Burt, Ronald S. 1999. "The Social Capital of Opinion Leaders." *The Annals of the American Academy of Political and Social Science* 566: 37–54.

Burt, Ronald S. 2001. "Bandwidth and Echo: Trust, Information, and Gossip in Social Networks." Pp. 30–74 in *Networks and Markets,* ed. James Rauch and Alessandra Casella. New York: Russell Sage Foundation.

Burt, Ronald S. 2004. "Structural Holes and Good Ideas." *American Journal of Sociology* 110: 349–99.

Cardon, Dominique, and Fabien Granjon. 2005. "Social Networks and Cultural Practices: A Case Study of Young Avid Screen Users in France." *Social Networks* 27: 301–15.

Carley, Kathleen M. 1993. "Coding Choices for Textual Analysis: A Comparison of Content Analysis and Map Analysis." *Sociological Methodology* 23: 75–126.

Cartwright, D., and Frank Harary. 1956. "Structural Balance: A Generalization of Heider's Theory." *Psychological Review* 63: 277–93.

Castells, Manuel. 1996. *The Rise of the Network Society.* Malden, MA: Blackwell.

Castells, Manuel. 2013. *Networks of Outrage and Hope: Social Movements in the Internet Age.* Cambridge: Polity.

Cavanagh, Alison. 2007. *Sociology in the Age of the Internet.* New York: McGraw-Hill.

References

Centola, Damon. 2013. "A Simple Model of Stability in Critical Mass Dynamics." *Journal of Statistical Physics* 151: 238–53.

Centola, Damon, and Michael Macy. 2007. "Complex Contagions and the Weakness of Long Ties." *American Journal of Sociology* 113: 702–34.

Centola, Damon, Robb Willer, and Michael Macy. 2005. "The Emperor's Dilemma: A Computational Model of Self-Enforcing Norms." *American Journal of Sociology* 110: 1009–40.

Chabot, Sean. 2010. "Dialogue Matters: Beyond the Transmission Model of Transnational Diffusion Between Social Movements." Pp. 99–124 in *The Diffusion of Social Movements: Actors, Mechanisms, and Political Effects*, ed. R. Givan, K. Roberts, and S. Soule. Cambridge: Cambridge University Press.

Chang, Kuang-Chi. 2011. "A Path to Understanding Guanxi in China's Transitional Economy: Variations on Network Behavior." *Sociological Theory* 29: 315–39.

Chase, Ivan. 1980. "Social Process and Hierarchy Formation in Small Groups: A Comparative Perspective." *American Sociological Review* 45: 905–24.

Childress, C. Clayton, and Noah E. Friedkin. 2012. "Cultural Reception and Production: The Social Construction of Meaning in Book Clubs." *American Sociological Review* 77: 45–68.

Christakis, Nicholas A., and James H. Fowler. 2007. "The Spread of Obesity in a Large Network." *New England Journal of Medicine* 357: 370–9.

Christakis, Nicholas A., and James H. Fowler. 2009. *Connected: How Your Friends' Friends' Friends Affect Everything You Feel, Think, and Do*. New York: Little, Brown and Company; Back Bay Books.

Císař, Ondřej, and Martin Koubek. 2012. "Include 'em all? Culture, Politics and a Local Hardcore/Punk Scene in the Czech Republic." *Poetics* 40: 1–21.

Cohen, Jere. 1977. "Sources of Peer Group Homogeneity." *Sociology of Education* 50: 227–41.

Coleman, James, Elihu Katz, and Herbert Menzel. 1957. "The Diffusion of an Innovation Among Physicians." *Sociometry* 20: 253–70.

Coleman, James, Elihu Katz, and Herbert Menzel. 1966. *Medical Innovation: A Diffusion Study*. New York: Bobbs-Merrill.

Collins, Randall. 1998. *The Sociology of Philosophies: A Global Theory of Intellectual Change*. Cambridge, MA: Belknap Press.

Collins, Randall. 2004. *Interaction Ritual Chains*. Princeton: Princeton University Press.

Compa, Lance. 2010. "Framing Labor's New Human Rights Movement." Pp. 56–77 in *The Diffusion of Social Movements: Actors, Mechanisms, and Political Effects*, ed. R. Givan, K. Roberts, and S. Soule. Cambridge: Cambridge University Press.

Conover, Michael D., Emilio Ferrara, Filippo Menczer, and Alessandro Flammini. 2013. "The Digital Evolution of Occupy Wall Street." *PLoS ONE* 8.5: e64679. doi:10.1371/journal.pone.0064679.

References

Consalvo, Mia. 2007. *Cheating: Gaining Advantage in Video Games*. Cambridge, MA: MIT Press.

Consalvo, Mia, and Todd Harper. 2009. "The Sexi(e)st of All: Avatars, Gender and Online Games." Pp. 98–113 in *Virtual Social Networks: Mediated, Massive and Multiplayer Sites*, ed. Niki Panteli. Basingstoke: Palgrave Macmillan.

Coulangeon, Philippe, and Yannick Lemel. 2007. "Is 'Distinction' Really Outdated? Questioning the Meaning of the Omnivorization of Musical Taste in Contemporary France." *Poetics* 35: 93–111.

Crane, Diana. 1972. *Invisible Colleges: Diffusion of Knowledge in Scientific Communities*. Chicago: University of Chicago Press.

Crane, Diana. 1976. "Reward Systems in Art, Science, and Religion." Pp. 57–72 in *The Production of Culture*, ed. Richard A. Peterson. Beverly Hills: Sage.

Crane, Diana. 1999. "Diffusion Models and Fashion: A Reassessment." *The Annals of the American Academy of Political and Social Science* 566: 13–24.

Crane, Diana. 2000. *Fashion and Its Social Agendas: Class, Gender, and Identity in Clothing*. Chicago: University of Chicago Press.

Creeber, Glen, and Royston Martin, eds. 2009. *Digital Cultures: Understanding New Media*. New York: McGraw Hill.

Crossley, Nick. 2008. "Pretty Connected: The Social Network of the Early UK Punk Movement." *Theory, Culture and Society* 25: 89–116.

Crossley, Nick. 2010a. "Networks and Complexity: Directions for Interactionist Research?" *Symbolic Interaction* 33: 341–63.

Crossley, Nick. 2010b. "The Social World of the Network: Combining Qualitative and Quantitative Elements in Social Network Analysis." *Sociologica* 1/2010. doi: 10.2383/32049.

Crossley, Nick. 2011. *Towards Relational Sociology*. London and New York: Routledge.

Currid, Elizabeth. 2007. *The Warhol Economy: How Fashion, Art, and Music Drive New York City*. Princeton: Princeton University Press.

Dávid, Beata, Eva Huszti, Ildikó Barna, and Yang-chih Fu. 2016. "Egocentric Contact Networks in Comparison: Taiwan and Hungary." *Social Networks* 44: 253–65.

Davis, Gerald. 1991. "Agents Without Principles: The Spread of the Poison Pill Through the Intercorporate Network." *Administrative Science Quarterly* 36: 583–613.

de Nooy, Wouter. 2003. "Fields and Networks: Correspondence Analysis and Social Network Analysis in the Context of Field Theory." *Poetics* 31: 305–27.

de Nooy, Wouter. 2009. "Formalizing Symbolic Interactionism." *Methodological Innovations Online* 4: 39–52.

Decoteau, Claire Laurier. 2013. "Hybrid Habitus: Toward a Post-Colonial Theory of Practice." *Political Power and Social Theory* 24: 263–93.

Deleuze, Gilles, and Félix Guattari. 1988. *A Thousand Plateaus: Capitalism and Schizophrenia*, trans. Brian Massumi. London: Athlone Press.

References

della Porta, Donatella, ed. 2007. *The Global Justice Movement: Cross-National and Transnational Perspectives*. Boulder and London: Paradigm.

DeNora, T. 1991. "Musical Patronage and Social Change in Beethoven's Vienna." *American Journal of Sociology* 97: 310–46.

Dépelteau, François, and Christopher Powell, eds. 2013. *Applying Relational Sociology: Relations, Networks, and Society*. New York: Palgrave Macmillan.

DiMaggio, Paul. 1987. "Classification in Art." *American Sociological Review* 52: 440–55.

DiMaggio, Paul. 1997. "Culture and Cognition." *Annual Review of Sociology* 23: 263–87.

DiMaggio, Paul. 2011. "Cultural Networks." Pp. 286–300 in *The Sage Handbook of Social Network Analysis*, ed. John Scott and Peter Carrington. Thousand Oaks, CA: Sage.

DiMaggio, Paul, and Filiz Garip. 2011. "How Network Externalities Can Exacerbate Intergroup Inequality." *American Journal of Sociology* 116: 1887–933.

DiMaggio, Paul, Eszter Hargittai, Russell Neuman, and John Robinson. 2001. "Social Implications of the Internet." *Annual Review of Sociology* 27: 307–36.

DiMaggio, Paul, and Paul M. Hirsch. 1976. "Production Organizations in the Arts." Pp. 73–90 in *The Production of Culture*, ed. Richard A. Peterson. Beverly Hills: Sage.

DiMaggio, Paul, and Hugh Louch. 1998. "Socially Embedded Consumer Transactions: For What Kinds of Purchases Do People Most Often Use Networks?" *American Sociological Review* 63: 619–37.

DiMaggio, Paul, Manish Nag, and David Blei. 2013. "Exploiting Affinities Between Topic Modeling and the Sociological Perspective on Culture: Application to Newspaper Coverage of U.S. Government Arts Funding." *Poetics* 41: 570–606.

Dobbin, Frank, Beth Simmons, and Geoffrey Garrett. 2007. "The Global Diffusion of Public Policies: Social Construction, Coercion, Competition, or Learning?" *Annual Review of Sociology* 33: 449–72.

Doerfel, Marya L. 1998. "What Constitutes Semantic Network Analysis? A Comparison of Research and Methodologies." *Connections* 21: 16–26.

Doerfel, Marya L., and George A. Barnett. 1999. "A Semantic Network Analysis of the International Communication Association." *Human Communication Research* 25: 589–603.

Doerfel, Marya L., and Stacey L. Connaughton. 2009. "Semantic Networks and Competition: Election Year Winners and Losers in U.S. Televised Presidential Debates, 1960–2004." *Journal of the American Society for Information Science & Technology* 60: 201–18.

Domhoff, G. William. 2010. *Who Rules America? Power, Politics, & Social Change*. 6th edition. Boston: McGraw-Hill.

References

Doueihi, Milad. 2011. *Digital Cultures*. Cambridge, MA: Harvard University Press.

Dowd, Jeffrey. 2014. "Racial Discourse and Partisanship in Politicized Cyberspace." Ph.D. dissertation, Department of Sociology, Rutgers University.

Ducheneaut, Nicolas. 2010. "The Chorus of the Dead: Roles, Identity Formation, and Ritual Processes Inside an FPS Multiplayer Online Game." Pp. 199–222 in *Utopic Dreams and Apocalyptic Fantasies: Critical Approaches to Researching Video Game Play*, ed. J. Talmadge Wright, David G. Embrick, and András Lukács. Lanham, MD: Rowman & Littlefield.

Durkheim, Emile. 1995 [1912]. *The Elementary Forms of Religious Life*, trans. and intro. Karen E. Fields. New York: Free Press.

Earl, Jennifer, and Katrina Kimport. 2010. "The Diffusion of Different Types of Internet Activism: Suggestive Patterns in Website Adoption of Innovations." Pp. 125–39 in *The Diffusion of Social Movements: Actors, Mechanisms, and Political Effects*, ed. R. Givan, K. Roberts, and S. Soule. Cambridge: Cambridge University Press.

Earl, Jennifer and Katrina Kimport. 2011. *Digitally Enabled Social Change: Activism in the Internet Age*. Cambridge, MA: MIT Press.

Edelmann, Achim, and Stephen Vaisey. 2014. "Cultural Resources and Cultural Distinction in Networks." *Poetics* 46: 22–37.

Eisenstadt, S. N., and Luis Roniger. 1984. *Patrons, Clients and Friends: Interpersonal Relations and the Structure of Trust in Society*. Cambridge: Cambridge University Press.

Elias, Norbert. 1994 [1939]. *The Civilizing Process*, trans. Edmund Jephcott. Oxford: Blackwell.

Eliasoph, Nina, and Paul Lichterman. 2003. "Culture in Interaction." *American Journal of Sociology* 108: 735–94.

Elster, Jon. 2009. "Norms." Pp. 195–217 in *The Oxford Handbook of Analytical Sociology*, ed. Peter Hedström and Peter Bearman. New York: Oxford University Press.

Emirbayer, Mustafa. 1997. "Manifesto for a Relational Sociology." *American Journal of Sociology* 103: 281–317.

Emirbayer, Mustafa, and Jeff Goodwin. 1994. "Network Analysis, Culture and the Problem of Agency." *American Journal of Sociology* 99: 1411–54.

Emirbayer, Mustafa, and Ann Mische. 1998. "What is Agency?" *American Journal of Sociology* 103: 962–1023.

Erickson, Bonnie. 1996. "Culture, Class, and Connections." *American Journal of Sociology* 102: 217–51.

Evans, Brad. 2012. "'Ephemeral Bibelots' in the 1890s." Pp. 132–53 in *The Oxford Critical and Cultural History of Modernist Magazines, Volume 2: North America 1894–1960*, ed. Peter Brooker and Andrew Thacker. Oxford: Oxford University Press.

Fábrega, Jorge, and Javier Sajuria. 2014. "The Formation of Political Discourse

References

Within Online Networks: The Case of the Occupy Movement." *International Journal of Organisational Design and Engineering* 3: 210–22.

Faris, Robert, and Diane Felmlee. 2011. "Status Struggles: Network Centrality and Gender Segregation in Same- and Cross-Gender Aggression." *American Sociological Review* 76: 48–73.

Farrell, Michael P. 2001. *Collaborative Circles: Friendship Dynamics & Creative Work.* Chicago: University of Chicago Press.

Faulkner, Robert R. 1983. *Music on Demand: Composers and Careers in the Hollywood Film Industry.* New Brunswick, NJ: Transaction Books.

Feld, Scott, and Bernard Grofman. 2009. "Homophily and the Focused Organization of Ties." Pp. 521–43 in *The Oxford Handbook of Analytical Sociology,* ed. Peter Hedström and Peter Bearman. New York: Oxford University Press.

Ferguson, Priscilla Parkhurst. 1998. "A Cultural Field in the Making: Gastronomy in 19th-Century France." *American Journal of Sociology* 104: 597–641.

Festinger, Leon, Stanley Schachter, and Kurt W. Back. 1950. *Social Pressures in Informal Groups.* Stanford: Stanford University Press.

Fine, Gary Alan. 1987. *With the Boys.* Chicago: University of Chicago Press.

Fine, Gary Alan. 2012. *Tiny Publics: A Theory of Group Action and Culture.* New York: Russell Sage.

Fine, Gary Alan, and Sherryl Kleinman. 1979. "Rethinking Subculture: An Interactionist Analysis." *American Journal of Sociology* 85: 1–20.

Fine, Gary Alan, and Sherryl Kleinman. 1983. "Network and Meaning: An Interactionist Approach to Structure." *Symbolic Interaction* 6: 97–110.

Fischer, Claude S. 1992. *America Calling: A Social History of the Telephone to 1940.* Berkeley: University of California Press.

Fischer, Claude S., and Yossi Shavit. 1995. "National Differences in Network Density: Israel and the United States." *Social Networks* 17: 129–45.

Fligstein, Neil, and Doug McAdam. 2011. "Toward a General Theory of Strategic Action Fields." *Sociological Theory* 29: 1–26.

Fontdevila, Jorge, and Harrison C. White. 2013. "Relational Power from Switching across Netdoms Through Reflexive and Indexical Language." Pp. 155–79 in *Applying Relational Sociology: Relations, Networks, and Society,* ed. François Dépelteau and Christopher Powell. New York: Palgrave Macmillan.

Foster, Pacey, Stephen P. Borgatti, and Candace Jones. 2011. "Gatekeeper Search and Selection Strategies: Relational and Network Governance in a Cultural Market." *Poetics* 39: 247–65.

Franssen, Thomas, and Giselinde Kuipers. 2013. "Coping with Uncertainty, Abundance and Strife: Decision-Making Processes of Dutch Acquisition Editors in the Global Market for Translations." *Poetics* 41: 48–74.

Franzosi, Roberto. 1997. "Mobilization and Counter-Mobilization Processes:

References

From the 'Red Years' (1919–20) to the 'Black Years' (1921–22) in Italy: A New Methodological Approach to the Study of Narrative Data." *Theory and Society* 26: 275–304.

Franzosi, Roberto. 2004. *From Words to Numbers: Narrative, Data, and Social Science.* Cambridge: Cambridge University Press.

Franzosi, Roberto. 2010. *Quantitative Narrative Analysis.* Thousand Oaks, CA: Sage.

Friedkin, Noah E. 1998. *A Structural Theory of Social Influence.* Cambridge: Cambridge University Press.

Friedkin, Noah E. 2001. "Norm Formation in Social Influence Networks." *Social Networks* 23: 167–89.

Friedkin, Noah E., and Eugene C. Johnsen. 2011. *Social Influence Network Theory: A Sociological Examination of Small Group Dynamics.* Cambridge: Cambridge University Press.

Friedland, Roger, and John Mohr, eds. 2004. *Matters of Culture: Cultural Sociology in Practice.* New York: Cambridge University Press.

Friedman, Sam. 2014. "The Hidden Tastemakers: Comedy Scouts as Cultural Brokers at the Edinburgh Festival Fringe." *Poetics* 44: 22–41.

Frye, Northrop. 1957. *Anatomy of Criticism: Four Essays.* Princeton: Princeton University Press.

Fuhse, Jan A. 2009. "The Meaning Structure of Social Networks." *Sociological Theory* 27: 51–73.

Fuhse, Jan A. 2013. "Social Relationships Between Communication, Network Structure, and Culture." Pp. 181–206 in *Applying Relational Sociology: Relations, Networks, and Society,* ed. François Dépelteau and Christopher Powell. New York: Palgrave Macmillan.

Fuhse, Jan A. 2015. "Networks from Communication." *European Journal of Social Theory* 18: 39–59.

Fuhse, Jan and Sophie Mützel. 2011. "Tackling Connections, Structure, and Meaning in Networks: Quantitative and Qualitative Methods in Sociological Network Research." *Quality and Quantity* 45: 1067–89.

Gambetta, Diego. 2009. *Codes of the Underworld: How Criminals Communicate.* Princeton: Princeton University Press.

Geertz, Clifford. 1973. *The Interpretation of Cultures.* New York: Basic Books.

Gere, Charlie. 2008. *Digital Culture.* 2nd edition. London: Reaktion Books.

Giacobbe, Gina. 2014. "Culture and Friendship in an Online Animal Community." BA thesis, Rutgers University.

Gibson, David R. 2005. "Taking Turns and Talking Ties: Networks and Conversational Interaction." *American Journal of Sociology* 110: 1561–97.

Gibson, David R. 2012. *Talk at the Brink: Deliberation and Decision During the Cuban Missile Crisis.* Princeton: Princeton University Press.

Giddens, Anthony. 1979. *Central Problems in Social Theory: Action, Structure, and Contradiction in Social Analysis.* Berkeley: University of California Press.

References

Giddens, Anthony. 1984. *The Constitution of Society: Outline of the Theory of Structuration*. Berkeley: University of California Press.

Giuffre, Katherine. 1999. "Sandpiles of Opportunity: Success in the Art World." *Social Forces* 77: 815–32.

Giuffre, Katherine. 2009. "The Return of the Natives: Globalization and Negative Ties." *Poetics* 37: 333–47.

Giuffre, Katherine. 2013. *Communities and Networks: Using Social Network Analysis to Rethink Urban and Community Studies*. Cambridge: Polity.

Givan, Rebecca Kolins, Kenneth M. Roberts, and Sarah A. Soule, eds. 2012. *The Diffusion of Social Movements: Actors, Mechanisms, and Political Effects*. Cambridge: Cambridge University Press.

Gladwell, Malcolm. 2000. *The Tipping Point: How Little Things Can Make a Big Difference*. Boston: Little, Brown.

Godart, Frédéric C., and Charles D. Galunic. 2014. "Style Popularity in High Fashion: Resilience, Replication, and Embeddedness of Cultural Elements." *Academy of Management Annual Meetings Proceedings (Meeting Abstract Supplement)*. 15251.

Godart, Frédéric C., and Ashley Mears. 2009. "How Do Cultural Producers Make Creative Decisions? Lessons from the Catwalk." *Social Forces* 88: 671–92.

Godart, Frédéric C., and Harrison C. White. 2010. "Switchings Under Uncertainty: The Coming and Becoming of Meanings." *Poetics* 38: 567–86.

Goffman, Erving. 1967. *Interaction Ritual: Essays on Face-to-Face Behavior*. New York: Pantheon Books.

Goffman, Erving. 1969. *Strategic Interaction*. Philadelphia: University of Pennsylvania Press.

Goffman, Erving. 1974. *Frame Analysis: An Essay on the Organization of Experience*. New York: Harper Colophon Books.

Goffman, Erving. 1981. *Forms of Talk*. Philadelphia: University of Pennsylvania Press.

Goffman, Erving. 1983. "Presidential Address: The Interaction Order." *American Sociological Review* 48: 1–17.

Gold, Thomas, Doug Guthrie, and David Wank. 2002. *Social Connections in China: Institutions, Culture, and the Changing Nature of Guanxi*. Cambridge: Cambridge University Press.

Goldberg, Amir. 2011. "Mapping Shared Understandings Using Relational Class Analysis: The Case of the Cultural Omnivore Reexamined." *American Journal of Sociology* 116: 1397–1436.

Goldenberg, Jacob, Barak Libai, and Eitan Muller. 2001. "Talk of the Network: A Complex Systems Look at the Underlying Process of Word-of-Mouth." *Marketing Letters* 12: 211–23.

Golder, Scott A. and Michael W. Macy. 2014. "Digital Footprints: Opportunities

References

and Challenges for Online Social Research." *Annual Review of Sociology* 40: 129–52.

Gondal, Neha. 2011. "The Local and Global Structure of Knowledge Production in an Emergent Research Field: An Exponential Random Graph Analysis." *Social Networks* 33: 20–30.

Gondal, Neha. 2012. "Who 'Fills in' for Siblings and How? A Multilevel Analysis of Personal Network Composition and Its Relationship to Sibling Size." *Sociological Forum* 27: 732–55.

Gondal, Neha, and Paul D. McLean. 2013a. "Linking Tie-Meaning with Network Structure: Variable Connotations of Personal Lending in a Multiple-Network Ecology." *Poetics* 41: 122–50.

Gondal, Neha, and Paul D. McLean. 2013b. "What Makes a Network Go Round? Exploring the Structure of a Strong Component with Exponential Random Graph Models." *Social Networks* 35: 499–513.

Gould, Roger V. 1996. "Patron–Client Ties, State Centralization, and the Whiskey Rebellion." *American Journal of Sociology* 102: 400–29.

Gould, Roger V. 2003. "Why Do Networks Matter? Rationalist and Structural Interpretations." Pp. 233–57 in *Social Movements and Networks: Relational Approaches to Collective Action*, ed. M. Diani and D. McAdam. Oxford: Oxford University Press.

Grams, Diane. 2010. *Producing Local Color: Art Networks in Ethnic Chicago*. Chicago: University of Chicago Press.

Granovetter, Mark S. 1973. "The Strength of Weak Ties." *American Journal of Sociology* 78: 1360–80.

Granovetter, Mark S. 1978. "Threshold Models of Collective Behavior." *American Journal of Sociology* 83: 1420–43.

Granovetter, Mark S. 1995. *Getting a Job: A Study of Contacts and Careers*. Chicago: University of Chicago Press.

Greif, Avner. 1989. "Reputation and Coalitions in Medieval Trade: Evidence on the Maghribi Traders." *Journal of Economic History* 49: 857–82.

Griswold, Wendy. 2001. "The Sociology of Culture." Pp. 254–66 in *The Sage Handbook of Sociology*, ed. Craig Calhoun, Chris Rojek, and Bryan Turner. Thousand Oaks, CA: Sage.

Griswold, Wendy. 2013. *Cultures and Societies in a Changing World*. 4th edition. Thousand Oaks, CA: Sage.

Gumperz, John J. 1992. "Contextualization and Understanding." Pp. 229–52 in *Rethinking Context: Language as an Interactive Phenomenon*, ed. Alessandro Duranti and Charles Goodwin. Cambridge: Cambridge University Press.

Guthrie, Douglas. 1998. "The Declining Significance of Guanxi in China's Economic Transition." *China Quarterly* 154: 254–82.

Habermas, Jürgen. 1989 [1962]. *The Structural Transformation of the Public Sphere*, trans. Thomas Burger. Cambridge, MA: MIT Press.

Hagstrom, Warren O. 1976. "The Production of Culture in Science." Pp.

References

91–106 in *The Production of Culture*, ed. Richard A. Peterson. Beverly Hills: Sage.

Haidt, Jonathan. 2001. "The Emotional Dog and Its Rational Tail: A Social Intuitionist Approach to Moral Judgment." *Psychological Review* 108: 814–34.

Hallett, Tim. 2003. "Symbolic Power and Organizational Culture." *Sociological Theory* 21: 128–49.

Hampton, Keith N. 2011. "Comparing Bonding and Bridging Ties for Democratic Engagement." *Information, Communication & Society* 14: 510–28.

Hampton, Keith, Oren Livio, and Lauren Sessions Goulet. 2010. "The Social Life of Wireless Urban Spaces: Internet Use, Social Networks, and the Public Realm." *Journal of Communication* 60: 701–22.

Hampton, Keith, and Barry Wellman. 2003. "Neighboring in Netville: How the Internet Supports Community and Social Capital in a Wired Suburb." *City & Community* 2: 277–311.

Han, Shin-Kap. 2003. "Unraveling the Brow: What and How of Choice in Musical Preference." *Sociological Perspectives* 46: 435–59.

Hardt, Michael, and Antonio Negri. 2004. *Multitude: War and Democracy in the Age of Empire*. Cambridge, MA: Harvard University Press.

Hargittai, Eszter, and Gina Walejko. 2008. "The Participation Divide: Content Creation and Sharing in the Digital Age." *Information, Communication & Society* 11: 239–56.

Harkness, Geoff. 2013. "Gangs and Gangsta Rap in Chicago: A Microscenes Perspective." *Poetics* 41: 151–76.

Harsin, Jayson. 2010. "Diffusing the Rumor Bomb: 'John Kerry is French' (i.e., Haughty, Foppish, Elitist, Socialist, Cowardly, and Gay)." Pp. 163–83 in *The Diffusion of Social Movements: Actors, Mechanisms, and Political Effects*, ed. R. Givan, K. Roberts, and S. Soule. Cambridge: Cambridge University Press.

Hebdige, Dick. 1979. *Subculture: The Meaning of Style*. London: Routledge.

Hedström, Peter. 1994. "Contagious Collectivities: On the Spatial Diffusion of Swedish Trade Unions, 1890–1940." *American Journal of Sociology* 99: 1157–79.

Hedström, Peter, and Peter Bearman. 2009. "What is Analytical Sociology All About? An Introductory Essay." Pp. 3–24 in *The Oxford Handbook of Analytical Sociology*, ed. Peter Hedström and Peter Bearman. New York: Oxford University Press.

Heider, Fritz. 1946. "Attitudes and Cognitive Orientation." *Psychological Review* 52: 358–74.

Hill, Vanessa, and Kathleen M. Carley. 1999. "An Approach to Identifying Consensus in a Subfield: The Case of Organizational Culture." *Poetics* 27: 1–30.

Hillman, Henning. 2008. "Mediation in Multiple Networks: Elite Mobilization before the English Civil War." *American Sociological Review* 73: 426–54.

References

Hollands, Robert, and John Vail. 2012. "The Art of Social Movement: Cultural Opportunity, Mobilisation, and Framing in the Early Formation of the Amber Collective." *Poetics* 40: 22–43.

Horne, Christine. 2001. "Sociological Perspectives on the Emergence of Norms." Pp. 3–34 in *Social Norms*, ed. M. Hechter and K. Opp. New York: Russell Sage Foundation.

Howard, Philip N. 2011. *The Digital Origins of Dictatorship and Democracy: Information Technology and Political Islam*. Oxford: Oxford University Press.

Hsu, Greta. 2006. "Jacks of All Trades and Masters of None: Audiences' Reactions to Spanning Genres in Feature Film Production." *Administrative Science Quarterly* 51: 420–50.

Hung, Aaron Chia-Yuan. 2011. *The Work of Play: Meaning-Making in Videogames*. New York: Peter Lang.

Hunt, Lynn. 1984. *Politics, Culture, and Class in the French Revolution*. Berkeley: University of California Press.

Hussain, Muzamil M., and Philip N. Howard. 2013. "What Best Explains Successful Protest Cascades? ICTs and the Fuzzy Causes of the Arab Spring." *International Studies Review* 15: 48–66.

Hutchins, Edwin. 1995. *Cognition in the Wild*. Cambridge, MA: MIT Press.

Ikegami, Eiko. 1995. *The Taming of the Samurai: Honorific Individualism and the Making of Modern Japan*. Cambridge, MA: Harvard University Press.

Ikegami, Eiko. 2005. *Bonds of Civility: Aesthetic Networks and the Political Origins of Japanese Culture*. Cambridge: Cambridge University Press.

Iribarren, Jose Luis, and Esteban Moro. 2011. "Affinity Paths and Information Diffusion in Social Networks." *Social Networks* 33: 134–42.

Jacobs, Mark D., and Lyn Spillman. 2005. "Cultural Sociology at the Crossroads of the Discipline." *Poetics* 33: 1–14.

Jameson, Fredric. 1998. *The Cultural Turn: Selected Writings on the Postmodern, 1983–1998*. London: Verso.

Jasper, James M., and Jane D. Poulsen. 1995. "Recruiting Strangers and Friends: Moral Shocks and Social Networks in Animal Rights and Anti-Nuclear Protests." *Social Problems* 42: 493–512.

Jenkins, Henry. 2008. *Convergence Culture*. New York: New York University Press.

Jenkins, Henry with Ravi Purushotma, Margaret Weigel, Katie Clinton, and Alice Robison. 2005. *Confronting the Challenges of Participatory Culture: Media Education for the 21st Century*. MacArthur Foundation Report on Digital Media and Learning. https://mitpress.mit.edu/books-confronting-chal lenges-participatory-culture.

Jeong, H., B. Tombor, R. Albert, Z. N. Oltvai, and A.-L. Barabási. 2000. "The Large-Scale Organization of Metabolic Networks." *Nature* 407: 651–4.

Jepperson, Ronald L. 1991. "Institutions, Institutional Effects, and Institutionalism." Pp. 143–63 in *The New Institutionalism in Organizational*

References

Analysis, ed. Walter W. Powell and Paul J. DiMaggio. Chicago: University of Chicago Press.

Jockers, Matthew L., and David Mimno. 2013. "Significant Themes in 19th-century Literature." *Poetics* 41: 750–69.

Johnson, Jeffrey C., and M. L. Miller. 1983. "Deviant Social Positions in Small Groups: The Relation Between Role and Individual." *Social Networks* 5: 51–69.

Johnson, Jeffrey C., James S. Boster, and Lawrence A. Palinkas. 2003. "Social Roles and the Evolution of Networks in Extreme and Isolated Environments." *Journal of Mathematical Sociology* 27: 89–121.

Juris, Jeffrey S. 2005. "The New Digital Media and Activist Networking Within Anti-Corporate Globalization Movements." *Annals of the American Academy of Political and Social Science* 597: 189–208.

Juris, Jeffrey S. 2008. *Networking Futures: The Movements Against Corporate Globalization*. Durham, NC: Duke University Press.

Juul, Jesper. 2005. *Half-Real: Video Games Between Real Rules and Fictional Worlds*. Cambridge, MA: MIT Press.

Kadushin, Charles. 1974. *The American Intellectual Elite*. Boston, MA: Little, Brown.

Kadushin, Charles. 1976. "Networks and Circles in the Production of Culture." Pp. 107–22 in *The Production of Culture*, ed. Richard A. Peterson. Beverly Hills: Sage.

Kadushin, Charles. 2012. *Understanding Social Networks: Concepts, Theories, and Findings*. New York: Oxford University Press.

Kahneman, Daniel. 2011. *Thinking Fast and Slow*. New York: Farrar, Straus and Giroux.

Kandel, Denise. 1978. "Homophily, Selection, and Socialization in Adolescent Friendships." *American Journal of Sociology* 84: 427–36.

Kane, Danielle. 2004. "A Network Approach to the Puzzle of Women's Cultural Participation." *Poetics* 32: 105–27.

Kane, Danielle. 2011. "The Gendered Transition to College: The Role of Culture in Ego-Network Evolution." *Poetics* 39: 266–89.

Katz, Elihu. 1999. "Theorizing Diffusion: Tarde and Sorokin Revisited." *The Annals of the American Academy of Political and Social Science* 566: 144–55.

Katz, Elihu, and Paul F. Lazarsfeld. 1955. *Personal Influence*. New York: Free Press.

Kawamura, Yuniya. 2004. *The Japanese Revolution in Paris Fashion*. Oxford: Berg.

Kempe, David, Jon Kleinberg, and Eva Tardos. 2005. "Influential Nodes in a Diffusion Model for Social Networks." Pp. 1127–38 in *Proceedings of the 32nd International Conference on Automata, Languages and Programming*. Berlin: Springer-Verlag.

References

Khanolkar, Preeti R., and Paul D. McLean. 2012. "100 Percenting It: Videogame Play Through the Eyes of Devoted Gamers." *Sociological Forum* 27: 961–85.

Kim, Hyojoung, and Peter S. Bearman. 1997. "The Structure and Dynamics of Movement Participation." *American Sociological Review* 62: 70–93.

King, Marissa. 2004. "Cooptation or Cooperation: The Role of Transnational Advocacy Organizations in the Zapatista Movement." *Sociological Focus* 37: 269–86.

Kipnis, Andrew. 1997. *Producing Guanxi: Sentiment, Self, and Subculture in a North China Village.* Durham, NC: Duke University Press.

Kirchner, Corinne, and John W. Mohr. 2010. "Meanings and Relations: An Introduction to the Study of Language, Discourse and Networks." *Poetics* 38: 555–66.

Kirschbaum, C. 2007. "Careers in the Right Beat: US Jazz Musicians' Typical and Non-Typical Trajectories." *Career Development International* 12: 187–201.

Kirschbaum, Charles. 2015. "Categories and Networks in Jazz Evolution: The Overlap Between Bandleaders' Jazz Sidemen from 1930 to 1969." *Poetics* 52: 154–78.

Kitts, James. 2000. "Mobilizing in Black Boxes: Social Networks and Participation in Social Movement Organizations." *Mobilization: An International Quarterly* 5: 241–57.

Kivinen, Osmo, and Tero Piiroinen. 2013. "Human Transaction Mechanisms in Evolutionary Niches – A Methodological Relationalist Standpoint." Pp. 83–100 in *Applying Relational Sociology: Relations, Networks, and Society*, ed. François Dépelteau and Christopher Powell. New York: Palgrave Macmillan.

Knoke, David. 1993. "Networks of Elite Structure and Decision Making." *Sociological Methods and Research* 22: 23–45.

Knorr-Cetina, Karin. 1999. *Epistemic Cultures: How the Sciences Make Knowledge.* Cambridge, MA: Harvard University Press.

Knorr-Cetina, Karin, and Urs Bruegger. 2002. "Global Microstructures: The Virtual Societies of Financial Markets." *American Journal of Sociology* 107: 905–50.

Krackhardt, David. 1987. "Cognitive Social Structures." *Social Networks* 9: 109–34.

Krackhardt, David, and Martin Kilduff. 2002. "Structure, Culture and Simmelian Ties in Entrepreneurial Firms." *Social Networks* 24: 279–90.

Krinsky, John. 2010. "Dynamics of Hegemony: Mapping Mechanisms of Cultural and Political Power in the Debates over Workfare in New York City, 1993–1999." *Poetics* 38: 625–48.

Kubik, Jan. 1994. *The Power of Symbols Against the Symbols of Power: The Rise of Solidarity and the Fall of State Socialism in Poland.* University Park, PA: Pennsylvania State University Press.

References

Kuehn, Thomas. 1991. *Law, Family & Women: Toward a Legal Anthropology of Renaissance Italy.* Chicago and London: University of Chicago Press.

Kunda, Gideon. 1992. *Engineering Culture: Control and Commitment in a High-tech Corporation.* Philadelphia: Temple University Press.

Lachmann, Richard, Emily Pain, and Anibal Gauna. 2014. "Museums in the New Gilded Age: Collector Exhibits in New York Art Museums, 1945–2010." *Poetics* 43: 60–9.

Lamont, Michèle and Marcel Fournier, eds. 1992. *Cultivating Differences: Symbolic Boundaries and the Making of Inequality.* Chicago: University of Chicago Press.

Lamont, Michèle, and Virag Molnar. 2002. "The Study of Boundaries in the Social Sciences." *Annual Review of Sociology* 28: 167–95.

Landé, Carl H. 1973. "Networks and Groups in Southeast Asia: Some Observations on the Group Theory of Politics." *American Political Science Review* 67: 103–27.

Lane, Christel. 2013. "Taste Makers in the "Fine-Dining" Restaurant Industry: The Attribution of Aesthetic and Economic Value by Gastronomic Guides." *Poetics* 41: 342–65.

Latour, Bruno. 2005. *Reassembling the Social: An Introduction to Actor-Network Theory.* New York; Oxford University Press.

Lazarsfeld, Paul, and Robert Merton. 1954. "Friendship as a Social Process: A Substantive and Methodological Analysis." Pp. 18–66 in *Freedom and Control in Modern Society*, ed. Morroe Berger. New York: Van Nostrand.

Lazer, D., A. Pentland, L. Adamic et al. 2009. "Computational Social Science." *Science* 323: 721–3. doi:10.1126/science.1167742.

Lee, C. K., and David Strang. 2006. "The International Diffusion of Public Sector Downsizing: Network Emulation and Theory-Driven Learning." *International Organization* 60: 883–909.

Leifer, Eric M. 1988. "Interaction Preludes to Role Setting: Exploratory Local Action." *American Sociological Review* 53: 865–78.

Lena, Jennifer C. 2004. "Meaning and Membership: Samples in Rap Music, 1979–1995." *Poetics* 32: 297–310.

Lena, Jennifer C., and Danielle J. Lindemann. 2014. "Who is an Artist? New Data for an Old Question." *Poetics* 43: 70–85.

Lena, Jennifer C., and Mark C. Pachucki. 2013. "The Sincerest Form of Flattery: Innovation, Repetition, and Status in an Art Movement." *Poetics* 41: 236–64.

Lena, Jennifer C., and Richard A. Peterson. 2008. "Classification as Culture: Types and Trajectories of Music Genres." *American Sociological Review* 73: 697–718.

Lévi-Strauss, Claude. 1963. *Structural Anthropology*, trans. Claire Jacobson and Brooke Grundfest Schoepf. New York: Basic Books.

Lewis, Kevin, Marco Gonzalez, and Jason Kaufman. 2012. "Social Selection

References

and Peer Influence in an Online Social Network." *Proceedings of the National Academy of Sciences* 109.1: 68–72.

Lewis, Kevin, Kurt Gray, and Jens Meierhenrich. 2014. "The Structure of Online Activism." *Sociological Science* 1: 1–9. doi:10.15195/v1.a1.

Lewis, Kevin, Jason Kaufman, Marco Gonzalez, Andreas Wimmer, and Nicholas Christakis. 2008. "Tastes, Ties, and Time: A New Social Network Dataset Using Facebook.com." *Social Networks* 30.4: 330–42.

Lietz, Haiko, Claudia Wagner, Arnim Bleier, and Markus Strohmaier. 2014. "When Politicians Talk: Assessing Online Conversational Practices of Political Parties on Twitter." *Proceedings of the Eighth International AAAI Conference on Weblogs and Social Media*, http://arxiv.org/abs/1405.6824.

Lin, Nan. 2001. "Guanxi: A Conceptual Analysis." Pp. 153–66 in *The Chinese Triangle of Mainland–Taiwan–Hong Kong*, ed. A. Y. So, N. Lin, and D. Poston. Westport, CT: Greenwood Press.

Liu, Kay-Yuet, Marissa King, and Peter S. Bearman. 2010. "Social Influence and the Autism Epidemic." *American Journal of Sociology* 115: 1387–434.

Lizardo, Omar. 2006. "How Cultural Tastes Shape Personal Networks." *American Sociological Review* 71: 778–807.

Long, Elizabeth. 2003. *Book Clubs: Women and the Uses of Reading in Everyday Life*. Chicago: University of Chicago Press.

Lopes, Paul. 1999. "Diffusion and Syncretism: The Modern Jazz Tradition." *The Annals of the American Academy of Political and Social Science* 566: 25–36.

Lopes, Paul. 2002. *The Rise of a Jazz Art World*. Cambridge: Cambridge University Press.

Lorenzen, Janet A. 2012. "Going Green: The Process of Lifestyle Change." *Sociological Forum* 27: 94–116.

Lorrain, François, and Harrison C. White. 1971. "Structural Equivalence of Individuals in Social Networks." *Journal of Mathematical Sociology* 1: 49–80

Macaulay, Stuart. 1963. "Non-Contractual Relations in Business: A Preliminary Study." *American Sociological Review* 28: 55–67.

Mann, Michael. 1986. *The Sources of Social Power, Volume I: A History of Power from the Beginning to A.D. 1760*. Cambridge: Cambridge University Press.

Mark, Noah. 1998. "Birds of a Feather Sing Together." *Social Forces* 77: 453–85.

Mark, Noah. 2003. "Culture and Competition: Homophily and Distancing Explanations for Cultural Niches." *American Sociological Review* 68: 319–45.

Marsden, Peter. 1981. "Introducing Influence Processes into a System of Collective Decisions." *American Journal of Sociology* 86: 1203–35.

Marsden, Peter. 1987. "Core Discussion Networks for Americans." *American Sociological Review* 52: 122–31.

Martin, John Levi. 2000. "What Do Animals Do All Day? The Division of Labor,

References

Class Bodies, and Totemic Thinking in the Popular Imagination." *Poetics* 27: 195–231.

Martin, John Levi. 2003. "What is Field Theory?" *American Journal of Sociology* 109: 1–49.

Martin, John Levi. 2009. *Social Structures*. Princeton: Princeton University Press.

Martin, John Levi. 2010. "Life's a Beach but You're an Ant, and Other Unwelcome News for the Sociology of Culture." *Poetics* 38: 228–43.

Martin, John Levi. 2015. *Thinking Through Theory*. New York: W. W. Norton.

McAdam, Doug. 1986. "Recruitment to High-Risk Activism: The Case of Freedom Summer." *American Journal of Sociology* 92: 64–90.

McAdam, Doug. 1988. *Freedom Summer*. New York: Oxford University Press.

McAdam, Doug, and Ronelle Paulsen. 1993. "Specifying the Relationship Between Social Ties and Activism." *American Journal of Sociology* 99: 640–67.

McAdam, Doug, and Dieter Rucht. 1993. "The Cross-National Diffusion of Movement Ideas." *Annals of the American Academy of Political and Social Science* 528: 56–74.

McDonald, Terrence J., ed. 1996. *The Historic Turn in the Social Sciences*. Ann Arbor: University of Michigan Press.

McFarland, Daniel A., Dan Jurafsky, and Craig Rawlings. 2013. "Making the Connection: Social Bonding in Courtship Situations." *American Journal of Sociology* 118: 1596–649.

McFarland, Daniel A., James Moody, David Diehl, Jeffrey A. Smith, and Reuben J. Thomas. 2014. "Network Ecology and Adolescent Social Structure." *American Sociological Review* 79: 1088–121.

McFarland, Daniel A., Daniel Ramage, Jason Chuang, Jeffrey Heer, Christopher D. Manning, and Daniel Jurafsky. 2013. "Differentiating Language Usage Through Topic Models." *Poetics* 41: 607–25.

McLean, Paul D. 1998. "A Frame Analysis of Favor Seeking in the Renaissance: Agency, Networks, and Political Culture." *American Journal of Sociology* 104: 51–91.

McLean, Paul D. 2007. *The Art of the Network: Strategic Interaction and Patronage in Renaissance Florence*. Durham, NC: Duke University Press.

McLean, Paul D. 2011. "Patrimonialism, Elite Networks, and Reform in Late Eighteenth Century Poland." *Annals of the American Association of Political and Social Science* 636: 88–110.

McLean, Paul D., and Neha Gondal. 2014. "The Circulation of Interpersonal Credit in Renaissance Florence." *European Journal of Sociology / Archives Européennes de Sociologie* 55: 135–76.

McPherson, J. Miller, Lynn Smith-Lovin, and Matthew Brashears. 2006. "Social Isolation in America: Changes in Core Discussion Networks over Two Decades." *American Sociological Review* 71: 353–75.

McPherson, J. Miller, Lynn Smith-Lovin, and James Cook. 2001. "Birds of a

References

Feather: Homophily in Social Networks." *Annual Review of Sociology* 27: 415–44.

Mead, George Herbert. 1934. *Mind, Self, and Society from the Standpoint of a Social Behaviorist*, ed. Charles W. Morris. Chicago: University of Chicago Press.

Mears, Ashley. 2010. "Size Zero High-End Ethnic: Cultural Production and the Reproduction of Culture in Fashion Modeling." *Poetics* 38: 21–46.

Mears, Ashley. 2011. *Pricing Beauty: The Making of a Fashion Model*. Berkeley: University of California Press.

Michel, Jean-Baptiste, Yuan Kui Shen, Aviva Presser Aiden, et al. 2011. "Quantitative Analysis of Culture Using Millions of Digitized Books." *Science* 331.6014: 176–82.

Millard, William B. 1996. "I Flamed Freud: A Case Study in Teletextual Incendiarism." Pp. 145–59 in *Internet Culture*, ed. David Porter. New York and London: Routledge.

Mische, Ann. 2003. "Cross-Talk in Movements: Reconceiving the Culture–Network Link." Pp. 258–80 in *Social Movements and Networks: Relational Approaches to Collective Action*, ed. Mario Diani and Doug McAdam. Oxford: Oxford University Press.

Mische, Ann. 2008. *Partisan Publics: Communication and Contention across Brazilian Youth Activist Networks*. Princeton: Princeton University Press.

Mische, Ann. 2011. "Relational Sociology, Culture, and Agency." Pp. 80–98 in *The Sage Handbook of Social Network Analysis*, ed. John Scott and Peter Carrington. Thousand Oaks, CA: Sage.

Mische, Ann, and Philippa Pattison. 2000. "Composing a Civic Arena: Publics, Projects, and Social Settings." *Poetics* 27: 163–94.

Mische, Ann, and Harrison White. 1998. "Between Conversation and Situation: Public Switching Dynamics across Network Domains." *Social Research* 65: 695–724.

Mizruchi, Mark S. 1992. *The Structure of Corporate Political Action: Interfirm Relations and Their Consequences*. Cambridge, MA: Harvard University Press.

mobiThinking. 2014. "Global mobile statistics 2014 Part A: Mobile subscribers; handset market share; mobile operators." MobiForge, May 16. https://mobiforge.com/research-analysis/global-mobile-statistics-2014-part-a-mobile-subscribers-handset-market-share-mobile-operators.

Mohr, John W. 1994. "Soldiers, Mothers, Tramps, and Others: Discourse Roles in the 1907 New York City Charity Directory." *Poetics* 22: 327–57.

Mohr, John W. 1998. "Measuring Meaning Structures." *Annual Review of Sociology* 24: 345–70.

Mohr, John W. 2000. "Introduction: Structures, Institutions, and Cultural Analysis." *Poetics* 27: 57–68.

Mohr, John W. 2013. "Bourdieu's Relational Method in Theory and in Practice: From Fields and Capitals to Networks and Institutions (and Back Again)."

References

Pp. 101–35 in *Applying Relational Sociology: Relations, Networks, and Society*, ed. François Dépelteau and Christopher Powell. New York: Palgrave Macmillan.

Mohr, John W., and Petko Bogdanov. 2013. "Introduction – Topic Models: What They Are and Why They Matter." *Poetics* 41: 545–69.

Mohr, John W., and Vincent Duquenne. 1997. "The Duality of Culture and Practice: Poverty Relief in New York City, 1888–1917." *Theory and Society* 26: 305–56.

Mohr, John W., Robin Wagner-Pacifici, Ronald L. Breiger, and Petko Bogdanov. 2013. "Graphing the Grammar of Motives in National Security Strategies: Cultural Interpretation, Automated Text Analysis and the Drama of Global Politics." *Poetics* 41: 670–700.

Mohr, John, and Harrison C. White. 2008. "How to Model an Institution." *Theory and Society* 37: 485–512.

Monge, Peter R., and Noshir Contractor. 2003. *Theories of Communication Networks*. New York: Oxford University Press.

Moody, James. 2004. "The Structure of a Scientific Collaboration Network: Disciplinary Cohesion from 1963–1999." *American Sociological Review* 69: 213–38.

Moody, James. 2009. "Network Dynamics." Pp. 447–74 in *The Oxford Handbook of Analytical Sociology*, ed. Peter Hedström and Peter Bearman. New York: Oxford University Press.

Moody, James, and Douglas R. White. 2003. "Structural Cohesion and Embeddedness: A Hierarchical Conception of Social Groups." *American Sociological Review* 68: 103–27.

Moretti, Franco. 2007. *Graphs, Maps, Trees: Abstract Models for a Literary History*. London: Verso.

Moretti, Franco. 2013. *Distant Reading*. London: Verso.

Morrill, Calvin. 1991. "Conflict Management, Honor, and Organizational Change." *American Journal of Sociology* 97: 585–621.

Morris, Martina. 1993. "Epidemiology and Social Networks." *Sociological Methods and Research* 22: 99–126.

Mullett, Margaret. 1997. *Theophylact of Ochrid: Reading the Letters of a Byzantine Archbishop*. Birmingham Byzantine and Ottoman Monographs, 2. Aldershot: Variorum/Ashgate.

Nadel, S. F. 1957. *The Theory of Social Structure*. Glencoe, IL: Free Press.

Nardi, Bonnie A. 2010. *My Life as a Night Elf Priest: An Anthropological Account of World of Warcraft*. Ann Arbor: University of Michigan Press.

Neff, G. 2005. "The Changing Place of Cultural Production: The Location of Social Networks in a Digital Media Industry." *Annals of the American Academy of Political and Social Science* 597: 134–52.

Newcomb, Theodore M. 1961. *The Acquaintance Process*. New York: Holt, Rinehart & Winston.

References

Oliver, Pamela E., and Daniel J. Myers. 2003. "Networks, Diffusion, and Cycles of Collective Action." Pp. 173–203 in *Social Movements and Networks: Relational Approaches to Collective Action*, ed. M. Diani and D. McAdam. Oxford: Oxford University Press.

Opp, K. D., and C. Gern. 1993. "Dissident Groups, Personal Networks, and Spontaneous Cooperation: The East German Revolution of 1989." *American Sociological Review* 58: 659–80.

Ostrower, Francie. 1998. "The Arts as Cultural Capital Among Elites: Bourdieu's Theory Reconsidered." *Poetics* 26: 43–53.

Oudshoorn, Nelly, and Trevor Pinch, eds. 2003. *How Users Matter: The Co-construction of Users and Technologies*. Cambridge, MA: MIT Press.

Pachucki, Mark, and R. L. Breiger. 2010. "Cultural Holes: Beyond Relationality in Social Networks and Culture." *Annual Review of Sociology* 36: 205–24.

Pachucki, Mark C. 2012. "Classifying Quality: Cognition, Interaction, and Status Appraisal of Art Museums." *Poetics* 40: 67–90.

Padgett, John F. 2012. "From Chemical to Social Networks." Pp. 92–114 in *The Emergence of Organizations and Markets*, by John F. Padgett and Walter W. Powell. Princeton: Princeton University Press.

Padgett, John F., and Christopher K. Ansell. 1993. "Robust Action and the Rise of the Medici, 1400–1434." *American Journal of Sociology* 98: 1259–319.

Padgett, John F., and Paul D. McLean. 2006. "Elite Transformation and Organizational Invention in Renaissance Florence." *American Journal of Sociology* 111: 1463–568.

Padgett, John F., and Paul D. McLean. 2011. "Economic Credit in Renaissance Florence." *Journal of Modern History* 83: 1–47.

Padgett, John F., and Walter W. Powell. 2012. *The Emergence of Organizations and Markets*. Princeton: Princeton University Press.

Palmer, Donald, P. Devereaux Jennings, and Xueguang Zhou. 1993. "Late Adoption of the Multidivisional Form by Large U.S. Corporations: Institutional, Political and Economic Accounts." *Administrative Science Quarterly* 38: 100–31.

Paluck, Elizabeth L., and Hana Shepherd. 2012. "The Salience of Social Referents: A Field Experiment on Collective Norms and Harassment Behavior in a School Social Network." *Journal of Personality and Social Psychology* 103: 899–915.

Papachristos, Andrew V. 2009. "Murder by Structure: Dominance Relations and the Social Structure of Gang Homicide." *American Journal of Sociology* 115: 74–128.

Pearce, Celia, and Artemisia. 2009. *Communities of Play: Emergent Cultures in Multiplayer Games and Virtual Worlds*. Cambridge, MA: MIT Press.

Pedrona, Marco, and Paolo Volonté. 2014. "Art Seen from Outside: Non-Artistic Legitimation Within the Field of Fashion Design." *Poetics* 43: 102–19.

Peterson, Richard. 1992. "Understanding Audience Segmentation: From Elite and Mass to Omnivore and Univore." *Poetics* 221: 243–58.

References

Peterson, Richard A. 1997. *Creating Country Music: Fabricating Authenticity.* Chicago: University of Chicago Press.

Peterson, Richard A., and N. Anand. 2004. "The Production of Culture Perspective." *Annual Review of Sociology* 30: 311–34.

Peterson, Richard A., and Roger Kern. 1996. "Changing Highbrow Taste: From Snob to Omnivore." *American Sociological Review* 64: 900–7.

Phillips, Damon. 2011. "Jazz and the Disconnected: City Structural Disconnectedness and the Emergence of a Jazz Canon, 1897–1933." *American Journal of Sociology* 117: 420–83.

Phillips, Damon, and Ezra W. Zuckerman. 2001. "Middle-Status Conformity: Theoretical Restatement and Empirical Demonstration in Two Markets." *American Journal of Sociology* 107: 379–429.

Podolny, Joel M. 1993. "A Status-Based Model of Market Competition." *American Journal of Sociology* 98: 829–72.

Podolny, Joel M. 2001. "Networks as the Pipes and Prisms of the Market." *American Journal of Sociology* 107: 33–60.

Porter, David, ed. 1998. *Internet Culture.* New York: Routledge.

Portes, Alejandro, and Julia Sensenbrenner. 1993. "Embeddedness and Immigration: Notes on the Social Determinants of Economic Action." *American Journal of Sociology* 98: 1320–50.

Powell, Walter W. 1990. "Neither Market nor Hierarchy: Network Forms of Organization." *Research in Organizational Behavior* 12: 295–336.

Powell, Walter W., and Paul J. DiMaggio, eds. 1991. *The New Institutionalism in Organizational Analysis.* Chicago: University of Chicago Press.

Powell, Walter W., and Laurel Smith-Doerr. 2005. "Networks and Economic Life." Pp. 379–402 in *The Handbook of Economic Sociology*, ed. Neil J. Smelser and Richard Swedberg. Princeton: Princeton University Press.

Powell, Walter W., Douglas R. White, Kenneth W. Koput, and Jason Owen-Smith. 2005. "Network Dynamics and Field Evolution: The Growth of Inter-organizational Collaboration in the Life Sciences." *American Journal of Sociology* 110: 1132–205.

Price, Derek J. de Solla, and Donald Beaver. 1966. "Collaboration in an Invisible College." *American Psychologist* 21: 1011–18.

Propp, Vladimir. 1968 [1928]. *The Morphology of the Folktale.* 2nd revised edition. Rev. and ed. with preface Louis A. Wagner; intro. Alan Dundes. Austin: University of Texas Press.

Putnam, Robert D. 2000. *Bowling Alone: The Collapse and Revival of American Community.* New York: Simon & Schuster.

Quandt, Thorsten, and Jeffrey Wimmer. 2009. "The Social Impact of Online Games: The Case of Germany." Pp. 75–97 in *Virtual Social Networks: Mediated, Massive and Multiplayer Sites*, ed. Niki Panteli. Basingstoke: Palgrave Macmillan.

References

Radway, Janice A. 1984. *Reading the Romance: Women, Patriarchy, and Popular Literature*. Chapel Hill: University of North Carolina Press.

Rainie, Lee and Barry Wellman. 2012. *Networked: The New Social Operating System*. Cambridge, MA: MIT Press.

Rawlings, Craig M., and Michael D. Bourgeois. 2010. "The Complexity of Institutional Niches: Credentials and Organizational Differentiation in a Field of U.S. Higher Education." *Poetics* 32: 411–46.

Reed, Isaac, and Jeffrey C. Alexander, eds. 2009. *Meaning and Method: The Cultural Approach to Sociology*. Boulder: Paradigm.

Reiter, Herbert (with Massimiliano Andretta, Donatella della Porta, and Lorenzo Mosca). 2007. "The Global Justice Movement in Italy." Pp. 52–78 in *The Global Justice Movement: Cross-National and Transnational Perspectives*, ed. Donatella della Porta. Boulder and London: Paradigm.

Rhue, Lauren, and Arun Sundararajan. 2014. "Digital Access, Political Networks and the Diffusion of Democracy." *Social Networks* 36: 40–53.

Ridgeway, Cecilia, and Lynn Smith-Lovin. 1994. "Structure, Culture, and Interaction: Comparing Two Generative Theories." *Advances in Group Processes* 11: 213–39.

Rivera, Lauren A. 2012. "Hiring as Cultural Matching: The Case of Elite Professional Service Firms." *American Sociological Review* 77: 999–1022.

Rivera, Mark T., Sara B. Soderstrom, and Brian Uzzi. 2010. "Dynamics of Dyads in Social Networks: Assortative, Relational, and Proximity Mechanisms." *Annual Review of Sociology* 36: 91–115.

Robins, Gary, Philippa Pattison, and J. Woolcock. 2005. "Small and Other Worlds: Global Network Structures from Local Processes." *American Journal of Sociology* 110: 894–936.

Robins, Gary, Tom Snijders, Peng Wang, Mark Handcock, and Philippa Pattison. 2007. "Recent Developments in Exponential Random Graph (p*) Models for Social Networks." *Social Networks* 29: 192–215.

Rogers, Everett M. 2003. *Diffusion of Innovations*. 5th edition. New York: Free Press.

Roggeband, Conny. 2010. "Transnational Networks and Institutions: How Diffusion Shaped the Politicization of Sexual Harassment in Europe." Pp. 19–33 in *The Diffusion of Social Movements: Actors, Mechanisms, and Political Effects*, ed. R. Givan, K. Roberts, and S. Soule. Cambridge: Cambridge University Press.

Rootes, Christopher, and Clare Saunders. 2007. "The Global Justice Movement in Great Britain." Pp. 128–56 in *The Global Justice Movement: Cross-National and Transnational Perspectives*, ed. Donatella della Porta. Boulder and London: Paradigm.

Rossman, Gabriel, Nicole Esparza, and Phillip Bonacich. 2010. "I'd Like to Thank the Academy, Team Spillovers, and Network Centrality." *American Sociological Review* 75: 31–51.

References

Sacks, Harvey. 1992. *Lectures on Conversation*, 2 vols., ed. Gail Jefferson. Malden, MA: Blackwell.

Sahlins, Marshall. 1976. *Culture and Practical Reason*. Chicago: University of Chicago Press.

Salganik, Matthew, Peter Sheridan Dodds, and Duncan J. Watts. 2006. "Experimental Study of Inequality and Unpredictability in an Artificial Cultural Market." *Science* 311: 854–6.

Salganik, Matthew, and Duncan J. Watts. 2009. "Web-Based Experiments for the Study of Collective Social Dynamics in Cultural Markets." *Topics in Cognitive Science* 1: 439–68.

Sampson, Tony D. 2012. *Virality: Contagion Theory in the Age of Networks*. Minneapolis: University of Minnesota Press.

Schmidt, Steffen W., James C. Scott, Carl Landé, and Laura Guasti, eds. 1977. *Friends, Followers, and Factions: A Reader in Political Clientelism*. Berkeley: University of California Press.

Schor, Adam M. 2007. "Theodoret on the School of Antioch: A Network Approach." *Journal of Early Christian Studies* 15: 517–62.

Schultz, Jennifer, and Ronald L. Breiger. 2010. "The Strength of Weak Culture." *Poetics* 38: 610–24.

Schussman, Alan, and Sarah A. Soule. 2005. "Process and Protest: Accounting for Individual Protest Participation." *Social Forces* 84: 1083–108.

Scott, John. 2013. *Social Network Analysis: A Handbook*. 3rd edition. Los Angeles: Sage.

Scott, Michael. 2012. "Cultural Entrepreneurs, Cultural Entrepreneurship: Music Producers Mobilising and Converting Bourdieu's Alternative Capitals." *Poetics* 40: 237–55.

Sewell, William H., Jr. 1992. "A Theory of Structure: Duality, Agency, and Transformation." *American Journal of Sociology* 98: 1–29.

Shefter, Martin. 1976. "The Emergence of the Political Machine: An Alternate View." Pp. 14–44 in *Theoretical Perspectives on Urban Politics*, ed. Willis D. Hawley, Michael Lipsky, Stanley B. Greenberg, et al. Englewood Cliffs: Prentice-Hall.

Shen, Cuihua, and Wenhong Chen. 2015. "Gamers' Confidants: Massively Multiplayer Online Game Participation and Core Networks in China." *Social Networks* 40: 207–14.

Shifman, Limor. 2014. *Memes in Digital Culture*. Cambridge, MA: MIT Press.

Simmel, Georg. 1950. "Sociability." Pp. 40–57 in *The Sociology of Georg Simmel*, ed. Kurt H. Wolff. New York: Free Press.

Simmel, Georg. 1955. "The Web of Group Affiliations." Pp. 125–95 in *Conflict and the Web of Group Affiliations*, trans. R. Bendix. New York: Free Press.

Simmel, Georg. 1971a. "Fashion." Pp. 294–323 in *Georg Simmel on Individuality and Social Forms*, ed. D. Levine. Chicago: University of Chicago Press.

References

Simmel, Georg. 1971b. "The Problem of Sociology." Pp. 23–35 in *Georg Simmel on Individuality and Social Forms*, ed. D. Levine. Chicago: University of Chicago Press.

Simmel, Georg. 1971c. "The Stranger." Pp. 143–9 in *Georg Simmel on Individuality and Social Forms*, ed. D. Levine. Chicago: University of Chicago Press.

Simmel, Georg. 1971d. "Subjective Culture." Pp. 227–34 in *Georg Simmel on Individuality and Social Forms*, ed. D. Levine. Chicago: University of Chicago Press.

Singh, Sourabh. forthcoming. "What is Relational Structure? Introducing History to the Debates on the Relation Between Fields and Social Networks." *Sociological Theory*.

Skvoretz, John, and T. J. Fararo. 1996. "Status and Participation in Task Groups: A Dynamic Network Model." *American Journal of Sociology* 101: 1366–414.

Small, Mario. 2009. *Unanticipated Gains: Origins of Network Inequality in Everyday Life*. New York: Oxford University Press.

Smilde, David. 2005. "A Qualitative Comparative Analysis of Conversion to Venezuelan Evangelicalism: How Networks Matter." *American Journal of Sociology* 111: 757–96.

Smith-Doerr, Laurel, and Walter W. Powell. 2005. "Networks and Economic Life." Pp. 379–402 in *The Handbook of Economic Sociology*, Neil J. Smelser and Richard Swedberg. Princeton: Princeton University Press.

Snow, David, E. Burke Rochford Jr., Steven K. Worden, and Robert D. Benford. 1986. "Frame Alignment Processes, Micromobilization and Movement Participation." *American Sociological Review* 51: 464–81.

Snow, David A., Louis A. Zurcher, and Sheldon Ekland-Olson. 1980. "Social Networks and Social Movements: A Microstructural Approach to Differential Recruitment." *American Sociological* Review 45: 787–801.

So, Richard Jean, and Hoyt Long. 2013. "Network Analysis and the Sociology of Modernism." *Boundary* 2: 147–82.

Song, Eunkyung. 2015. "Anonymity and Citizenship in the 2008 Candlelight Protests in Korea." Rutgers University, Department of Sociology working paper.

Sonnett, John. 2004. "Musical Boundaries: Intersections of Form and Content." *Poetics* 32: 247–64.

Srivastava, Sameer B., and Mahzarin R. Banaji. 2011. "Culture, Cognition, and Collaborative Networks in Organizations." *American Sociological Review* 76: 207–33.

Stamatov, Peter. 2010. "Activist Religion, Empire, and the Emergence of Modern Long-Distance Advocacy Networks." *American Sociological Review* 75: 607–28.

Stark, David. 1996. "Recombinant Property in East European Capitalism." *American Journal of Sociology* 101: 993–1027.

References

Stark, Rodney. 1997. *The Rise of Christianity: How the Obscure, Marginal Jesus Movement Became the Dominant Religious Force in the Western World in a Few Centuries.* New York: HarperCollins.

Steinberg, Marc W. 1999. "The Talk and Back Talk of Collective Action: A Dialogic Analysis of Repertoires of Discourse among Nineteenth-Century English Cotton Spinners." *American Journal of Sociology* 105: 736–80.

Strang, David, and Michael W. Macy. 2001. "In Search of Excellence: Fads, Success Stories, and Adaptive Emulation." *American Journal of Sociology* 107: 147–82.

Straw, W. 1991. "Systems of Articulation, Logics of Change: Communities and Scenes in Popular Music." *Cultural Studies* 5: 368–88.

Straw, W. 2002. "Scenes and Sensibilities." *Public* 22/23: 245–57.

Suzanne-Mayer, Dominick. 2014. "In Defense of Nicholas Cage, Internet Mascot and Living Meme." *Washington Post,* August 23, www.washingtonpost.com/news/the-intersect/wp/2014/08/23/in-defense-of-nicholas-cage-internet-mascot-and-living-meme.

Swidler, Ann. 1986. "Culture in Action: Symbols and Strategies." *American Sociological Review* 51: 273–86.

Swidler, Ann. 2001. *Talk of Love.* Chicago: University of Chicago Press.

Tanner, Julian, Mark Asbridge, and Scot Wortley. 2009. "Listening to Rap: Cultures of Crime, Cultures of Resistance." *Social Forces* 88: 693–722.

Tarrow, Sidney. 2010. "Dynamics of Diffusion: Mechanisms, Institutions, and Scale Shift." Pp. 204–19 in *The Diffusion of Social Movements: Actors, Mechanisms, and Political Effects,* ed. R. Givan, K. Roberts, and S. Soule. Cambridge: Cambridge University Press.

Tarrow, Sidney, and Doug McAdam. 2005. "Scale Shift in Transnational Contention." Pp. 121–47 in *Transnational Protest and Global Activism,* ed. D. della Porta and S. Tarrow. Lanham, MD: Rowman & Littlefield.

Tavory, Iddo, and Ann Swidler. 2009. "Condom Semiotics: Meaning and Condom Use in Rural Malawi." *American Sociological Review* 74: 171–89.

Taylor, T. L. 2006. *Play Between Worlds: Exploring Online Game Culture.* Cambridge, MA: MIT Press.

Tepper, Michele. 1996. "Usenet Communities and the Cultural Politics of Information." Pp. 39–54 in *Internet Culture,* ed. David Porter. New York and London: Routledge.

Tepper, Steven J., and Eszter Hargittai. 2009. "Pathways to Music Exploration in a Digital Age." *Poetics* 37: 227–49.

Terranova, Tiziana. 2004. *Network Culture: Politics for the Information Age.* Ann Arbor, MI: Pluto Press.

Thornton, Patricia H., William Ocasio, and Michael Lounsbury. 2012. *The Institutional Logics Perspective: A New Approach to Culture, Structure and Process.* Oxford: Oxford University Press.

References

Tilly, Charles. 1995. *Popular Contention in Great Britain.* Cambridge, MA: Harvard University Press.

Tilly, Charles. 1998. *Durable Inequality.* Berkeley: University of California Press.

Tilly, Charles. 2005. *Identities, Boundaries, and Social Ties.* Boulder: Paradigm.

Timms, Edward. 1986. *Karl Kraus, Apocalyptic Satirist: The Post-War Crisis and the Rise of the Swastika.* New Haven and London: Yale University Press.

Tong, Charles. 2013. "Network Topology, Norms, and Popularity on the Social Networking Site, Reddit." BA thesis, Rutgers University.

Torfason, Magnus Thor, and Paul Ingram. 2010. "The Global Rise of Democracy." *American Sociological Review* 75: 355–77.

Traugott, Mark. 2010. *The Insurgent Barricade.* Berkeley: University of California Press.

Turco, Catherine J. 2010. "Cultural Foundations of Tokenism: Evidence from the Leveraged Buyout Industry." *American Sociological Review* 75: 894–913.

Turkle, Sherry. 1995. *Life on the Screen: Identity in the Age of the Internet.* New York: Simon & Schuster.

Uzzi, Brian. 1996. "The Sources and Consequences of Embeddedness for the Economic Performance of Organizations: The Network Effect." *American Sociological Review* 61: 674–98.

Uzzi, Brian, and Jarrett Spiro. 2005. "Collaboration and Creativity: The Small World Problem." *American Journal of Sociology* 111: 447–504.

Vaisey, Stephen. 2009. "Motivation and Justification: A Dual-Process Model of Culture in Action." *American Journal of Sociology* 114: 1675–715.

Vaisey, Stephen, and Omar Lizardo. 2010. "Can Cultural Worldviews Influence Network Composition?" *Social Forces* 88: 1595–618.

Valente, Thomas W., and Rebecca L. Davis. 1999. "Accelerating the Diffusion of Innovations Using Opinion Leaders." *The Annals of the American Academy of Political and Social Science* 566: 55–67.

van de Rijt, Arnout, Soong Moon Kang, Michael Restivo, and Akshay Patil. 2014. "Field Experiments of Success-Breeds-Success Dynamics." *PNAS* 111: 6934–9.

Van Eijck, Koen. 2001. "Social Differentiation in Musical Taste Patterns." *Social Forces* 79: 1163–85.

Veblen, Thorstein. 1998 [1899]. *The Theory of the Leisure Class.* Amherst, NY: Prometheus Books.

Vedres, Balazs, and David Stark. 2010. "Structural Folds: Generative Disruption in Overlapping Groups." *American Journal of Sociology* 115: 1150–90.

Vilhena, Daril, Jacob Gates Foster, Martin Rosvall, Jevin D. West, James A. Evans, and Carl T. Bergstrom. 2014. "Finding Cultural Holes: How Structure and Culture Diverge in Networks of Scholarly Communication." Paper presented at the 2014 American Sociological Association Meetings, San Francisco, CA.

Villarreal, Andrés. 2002. "Political Competition and Violence in Mexico:

References

Hierarchical Social Control in Local Patronage Structures." *American Sociological Review* 67: 477–98.

Walgrave, Stefaan, and Ruud Wouters. 2014. "The Missing Link in the Diffusion of Protest: Asking Others." *American Journal of Sociology* 119: 1670–709.

Wang, Dan J., and Sarah A. Soule. 2012. "Social Movement Organizational Collaboration: Networks of Learning and the Diffusion of Protest Tactics, 1960–1995." *American Journal of Sociology* 117: 1674–722.

Wang, Lillian, and Filippo Menczer. 2015. "Topicality and Impact in Social Media: Diverse Messages, Focused Messengers." *PLoS ONE* 10: e0118410. doi:10.1371/journal.pone.0118410.

Wang, Yue. 2013. "More People Have Cell Phones Than Toilets, U.N. Study Shows." *Time*, March 25, http://newsfeed.time.com/2013/03/25/more-people-have-cell-phones-than-toilets-u-n-study-shows.

Wasserman, Stanley, and Katherine Faust. 1994. *Social Network Analysis: Methods and Applications*. Cambridge: Cambridge University Press.

Watts, Duncan J. 1999. "Networks, Dynamics, and the Small-World Phenomenon." *American Journal of Sociology* 105: 493–527.

Watts, Duncan J. 2003. *Six Degrees: The Science of a Connected Age*. New York: Norton.

Watts, Duncan J., and Peter Sheridan Dodds. 2007. "Influentials, Networks, and Public Opinion Formation." *Journal of Consumer Research* 34: 441–58.

Weber, Max. 1946. "Class, Status, Party." Pp. 180–95 in *From Max Weber: Essays in Sociology*, trans. and ed. H. H. Gerth and C. Wright Mills. New York: Oxford University Press.

Weissman, Ronald F. E. 1989. "The Importance of Being Ambiguous: Social Relations, Individualism, and Identity in Renaissance Florence." Pp. 269–80 in *Urban Life in the Renaissance*, ed. Susan Zimmerman and Ronald F. E. Weissman. Newark: University of Delaware Press.

Wellman, Barry. 1988. "Structural Analysis: From Method and Metaphor to Theory and Substance." Pp. 19–61 in *Social Structures: A Network Approach*, ed. Barry Wellman and S. D. Berkowitz. Cambridge: Cambridge University Press.

Wellman, Barry, R. Wong, D. Tindall, and N. Nazer. 1997. "A Decade of Network Change: Turnover, Mobility and Stability." *Social Networks* 19: 27–51.

Wellman, Barry, and Scot Wortley. 1990. "Different Strokes from Different Folks: Community Ties and Social Support." *American Journal of Sociology* 96: 558–88.

White, Harrison C. 1993. *Careers and Creativity: Social Forces in the Arts*. Boulder: Westview Press.

White, Harrison C. 1995. "Network Switchings and Bayesian Forks: Reconstructing the Social and Behavioral Sciences." *Social Research* 62: 1035–63.

References

White, Harrison C. 2008. *Identity and Control.* revised 2nd edition. Princeton: Princeton University Press.

White, Harrison C., Scott Boorman, and Ronald Breiger. 1976. "Social Structure from Multiple Networks. I: Blockmodels of Roles and Positions." *American Journal of Sociology* 81: 730–80.

White, Harrison C., Jan Fuhse, Matthias Thiemann, and Larissa Buchholz. 2007. "Networks and Meaning: Styles and Switchings." *Soziale Systeme* 13: 543–55.

White, Harrison C., and Cynthia A. White. 1965. *Canvases and Careers: Institutional Change in the French Painting World.* New York: Wiley.

Whyte, William Foote. 1993 [1943]. *Street Corner Society: The Social Structure of an Italian Slum.* 4th edition. Chicago: University of Chicago Press.

Williams, J. Patrick, David Kirschner, and Zahirah Suhaimi-Broder. 2014. "Structural Roles in Massively Multiplayer Online Games: A Case Study of Guild and Raid Leaders in World of Warcraft." *Studies in Symbolic Interaction* 43: 121–42.

Wimmer, Andreas, and Kevin Lewis. 2010. "Beyond and Below Racial Homophily: ERG Models of a Friendship Network Documented on Facebook." *American Journal of Sociology* 116: 583–642.

Wimsatt, William K., and Monroe C. Beardsley. 1946. "The Intentional Fallacy." *Sewanee Review* 54: 468–88.

Wynn, Jonathan R. 2011. "Guides Through Cultural Work: A Methodological Framework for the Study of Cultural Intermediaries." *Cultural Sociology* 8: 1–15.

Yang, Mayfair Mei-Hui. 1994. *Gifts, Favors & Banquets: The Art of Social Relationships in China.* Ithaca and London: Cornell University Press.

Yeung, King-To. 2005. "What Does Love Mean? Exploring Network Culture in Two Network Settings." *Social Forces* 84: 391–420.

Yeung, King-To, and John L. Martin. 2003. "The Looking-Glass Self: An Empirical Elaboration." *Social Forces* 81: 843–79.

Zerubavel, Eviatar. 1991. *The Fine Line: Making Distinctions in Everyday Life.* Chicago: University of Chicago Press.

Zerubavel, Eviatar. 1997. *Social Mindscapes: An Invitation to Cognitive Sociology.* Cambridge, MA: Harvard University Press.

Zerubavel, Eviatar. 2006. *The Elephant in the Room: Silence and Denial in Everyday Life.* New York: Oxford University Press.

Zuckerman, Ezra W. 1999. "The Categorical Imperative: Securities Analysts and the Illegitimacy Discount." *American Journal of Sociology* 104: 1398–448.

Zuckerman, Ezra W., Tai-Young Kim, Kalinda Ukanwa, and James von Rittmann. 2003. "Robust Identities or Nonentities? Typecasting in the Feature-Film Labor Market." *American Journal of Sociology* 108: 1018–74.

Zwingel, Suzanne. 2012. "How Do Norms Travel? Theorizing International Women's Rights in Transnational Perspective." *International Studies Quarterly* 56: 115–29.

Index

Index

capitalism, 2, 48, 160, 170
Carley, Kathleen, 141–2
Castells, Manuel, 2, 10, 76, 80, 157, 168–9
causality, 5, 20, 36, 102, 108, 116–17, 143, 155, 179
Centola, Damon, 71–2, 96–7, 186 n.8
centrality, 16, 31, 35, 47, 70, 100, 107, 112, 131–2, 142–3, 152, 159, 167, 174
centralization, 32, 61, 170
Chase, Ivan, 25
Childress, Clayton, 97
Christakis, Nicholas, 2, 83, 130
circulation, 10, 31, 37, 48, 54–5, 57, 98–101, 104, 107, 131–2, 159, 171, 187 n.17
citation networks, 100–1, 123, 136, 139, 141
classification schemes, 3, 10, 19, 28, 34, 43, 106, 119, 137, 148–50, 152
clientage systems, 156, 158–60 *see also* patronage systems
clique, 27–8, 70, 94–7, 117
closure, social, 20 n.8, 24, 44, 54, 60, 71, 113, 174
clustering, 4, 23, 27, 29–30, 45–6, 54, 61–2, 70–1, 75–7, 83, 100, 104, 115, 128–9, 131, 136, 143, 145–7, 149, 153, 163
coding, 20, 87, 137, 143, 145, 147, 154, 165, 191 n.3
cognition, 10, 16, 23, 41–2, 44, 51, 76, 82, 101–2, 112, 116, 127, 149, 157, 165, 172–3, 180, 184 n.5, 195 n.11, 195 n.14
distributed, 102
cohesion, 27–30, 60, 100–1, 104, 106, 108, 112, 117, 121, 130, 139, 158, 187 n.1
Coleman, James, 69
collaboration, 21, 49, 78, 89, 93, 99–101, 104, 110, 136, 165, 172, 175, 190 n.22
Collins, Randall, 102
communication, 1–2, 5, 11, 16–17, 20, 28, 34, 50–4, 59, 68, 71, 78, 80–1,

100, 102, 112, 119, 125, 156, 162, 163, 167–72, 177, 183 n.14
communities of play, 157, 177–8
community, 22, 67, 74, 81, 99, 122, 132, 146, 157, 172, 174, 177
competition, 25–6, 70, 114, 160, 176
component, 83, 94, 100, 140, 131, 143–4, 174, 183 n.18
conflict, 11, 164
connectivity, 17, 171, 182 n.6
consumption, 44–6, 49, 72, 74, 99, 113, 151, 160, 175, 186 n.6
contagion, 65, 68, 83, 128, 168
complex, 71, 75, 87
content analysis, 141, 145, 147
context, social and/or cultural, 16, 34, 53, 55, 57, 59, 61, 68, 71, 81, 86, 101, 104, 130, 146, 151, 154, 166, 167, 183 n.12, 190 n.2, 191 n.3, 194 n.1
contextualization cues, 124
control, White's concept of, 52–3
convergence culture, 157
convergence of attitudes, 59, 89, 95, 97–8
conversation, 16–17, 34, 40, 52, 55, 84, 119, 120–1, 126, 165–7, 172, 194 n.1, 195 n.12
convertibility of capital, 44, 47, 120, 159
core discussion networks, 20, 113, 126
corporate interlocks, 2, 82
corporate mergers, 123
cosmopolitanism, 30, 116, 125
Crane, Diana, 83, 100
creativity, 6, 30, 48, 60, 89, 98, 103, 104–6
credit relations, 131–2
critical mass, 66
cross-talk, 122
Crossley, Nick, 58, 104
crowdsourcing, 168, 176
Cuban Missile Crisis, 167
cultural capital, 6, 47, 120, 177
cultural hole, 121
cultural matching, 118
cultural networks, 38–9

Index

Index

Kane, Danielle, 97, 124–5
karma, 176
Katz, Elihu, 68
Kennedy, John F. , 167
Kirschbaum, Charles, 190 n.20
Knorr-Cetina, Karin, 102
knowledge production, 1, 98–100, 102, 146
Krackhardt, David, 58
Krinsky, John, 151

language, 3, 22, 28, 34, 38, 41, 44, 101, 114, 126, 130, 136–7, 140, 142, 145–6, 174, 177
leadership, 78, 80, 132, 156, 159, 163–4, 178 see also opinion leaders
Lena, Jennifer, 139
lifestyles, 55, 113
Lizardo, Omar, 115
Long, Hoyt, 138

Macy, Michael, 71, 96
Maneki cats, 84–5
Mann, Michael, 59–60
map analysis, 141, 147
Mark, Noah, 114–15
marketing, 71
marriage, 17, 22, 42, 159–60, 178
Martin, John Levi, 28, 38, 40, 131, 152
Marx, Karl, 187 n.1
mass media, 79, 83
McFarland, Daniel, 17, 52, 145–6, 190 n.2
Mead, George Herbert, 29, 58, 185 n.10
meaning, 1, 4–5, 7, 17, 25–7, 31, 33–4, 53–4, 58, 76, 87, 111, 121, 131–2, 134–5, 137, 145, 147, 153, 161–2, 168, 179
Mears, Ashley, 107
memes, 6, 74–5, 84–6, 168, 175
metaphor, 144, 154, 195 n.14
micro-macro relations, 8, 30–1, 33, 57, 119, 128, 132–3, 167
Mische, Ann, 122, 156, 162
modes, one versus two, 136–9, 185 n.7, 195 n.12
Mohr, John, 39, 57, 145, 149

Moody, James, 28, 100, 128–9, 183 n.18
Moretti, Franco, 140
multidimensional scaling, 142, 148
multiple correspondence analysis, 185 n.7, 195 n.12
multiple frames, 42, 55, 85
multiple identities, 29, 56, 105, 122, 162, 170
multiple networks, 92, 100, 131, 143, 158, 163, 175
multiplexity, 18, 28, 61, 100, 105, 112, 133 see also overlapping ties
music, 3, 6, 23, 44, 48–9, 67, 72, 89, 95, 98, 103–7, 114, 123
myths, 34, 134, 137

n-clique, 183 n.16
Nadel, S. F., 90
narrative, 36, 52, 56, 136, 140, 142–4, 148, 153, 167, 173, 192 n.16, 195 n.13, 196 n.5
netdom, 54–5, 61, 162–3, 166
network, defined, 16
network society, 157
networked individualism, 157, 171–4
networking, 124, 156–7, 171, 179, 192 n.15 see also actor(s), concept of; strategic action
new science of networks, 2, 4, 196 n.7
New York City, welfare programs in, 149–51
niche, 59
node, definition of, 16
norms, 6, 9, 11, 16, 18, 25, 28, 32, 39–40, 67–8, 75, 83, 95–6, 111–12, 117, 120, 125–30, 133, 156–8, 160, 162, 166, 168, 172, 174, 177, 179–80

occupational structure, 152–3
Occupy movements, 76, 80, 156, 169
omnivore, cultural, 46, 114–15
opinion leaders, 66–7, 96, 99, 108
organizational culture, 61, 98, 141, 156
organizations, 2, 38, 57, 76, 79–82, 95, 98, 117, 122, 129, 136–7, 148–9, 156, 164, 178

Index

Index